8000 YEARS OF ORNAMENT

An illustrated handbook of motifs

EVA WILSON

THE BRITISH MUSEUM PRESS

To the memory of Dicte and Gunnar Sjögren

Frontispiece Mosaic panel from Yorkshire, 2nd cent. AD (see page 46).
Title page Gold plaque showing a coiled predatory animal
from Northern China. 3rd–4th cent. BC (see page 85).

© 1994 , 2001 Eva Wilson
Published by The British Museum Press
A division of The British Museum Company Ltd
46 Bloomsbury Street
London WC1B 3QQ

First published 1994
First published in paperback 2001

British Library Cataloguing in Publication Data
A catalogue record for this book is available from the British Library

ISBN 0-7141-2745-0

Designed and typeset by Roger Davies

Printed in Great Britain by
The Bath Press, Avon

8000 YEARS OF
ORNAMENT

Contents

Preface

At the end of nearly five years' work I look back in gratitude to all those who have helped me in what seems to have been an almost endless exercise. Above all, however, it is an institution that must be acknowledged and praised first. The fascination and beauty of the rich material in the collections, the atmosphere of dedicated scholarship and the unfailing courtesy of the staff of the British Museum have been at once a spur and an inspiration in what would otherwise have been a very lonely task. The people who helped me did so in many ways – they found material, they gave me references, they spent hours in discussion and above all prevented me from making a fool of myself expressing naive and ignorant judgments. This does not mean that they must accept the blame for any of the errors that will undoubtedly appear in the pages of this book, but they must all be thanked.

I must thank those specialists who read parts of this work and saved me from many errors: John Mack, Keeper of the Department of Ethnography, Nigel Barley and Brian Durrans; in the Department of Greek and Roman Antiquities, where nobody escaped my interminable questions and demands, I wish to thank Lucilla Burn and Ian Jenkins and, for her taking trouble in finding relevant references to methods of studying motifs, Louise Schofield. The thoughtful comments by Ellen Macnamara were particularly helpful and I am most grateful to her for taking time and trouble with my text. In the Department of Medieval and Later Antiquities, I am grateful to Judy Rudoe for her assistance. I am grateful to Jessica Rawson, Keeper of the Department of Oriental Antiquities and to Richard Blurton and Jane Portal for reading and correcting my manuscript, and to the Student Room staff for bringing so many objects for me to draw over the years. I want to thank Ian Stead for reading the difficult chapter on Celtic art. I am also thankful for stimulating, wide ranging and enlightening discussions with members of staff of the Department of Prehistoric and Romano-British Antiquities, Jill Cook, Stuart Needham, Timothy Potter and Gillian Varndell. I would like to thank the Keeper, Ian Longworth, for taking time to read relevant portions of the text.

Special thanks must be reserved for Dominique Collon of the Department of Western Asiatic Antiquities, who read the whole work in draft, and who from the beginning encouraged, comforted and corrected me with tact and patience.

I wish to thank Marjorie Blamey for her beautiful botanical drawings and Nigel Hepper of The Herbarium, Royal Botanical Gardens at Kew for discussions about Egyptian flower motifs. I am deeply grateful to my publisher and editor, Celia Clear and Sarah Derry for their patience and continuing help and to Roger Davies for the enormous task of designing the book.

Perhaps my greatest encouragement has been Ann Hecht, who listened to me rabbitting away for hours on patterns in general, patiently taught me about textiles, and has been unstinting in the hospitality of her home. To her go my very best thanks. Finally, I owe this challenge to my husband David Wilson (Director of the British Museum 1977–1992) who took me to live in the Museum and inspired the entire enterprise.

I must apologise for an illogical and not always consistent spelling policy. I aim at a modified European spelling for place names in non-European languages. Unfamiliar letter forms in European languages are, however, also a problem and they may not always be correctly presented. In foreign language publications I am, as a Scandinavian, used to finding an indiscriminate scattering of rings and dots over 'o's and 'a's; I fear I cannot always do better with names in languages with which I am unfamiliar.

Eva Wilson
Castletown, Isle of Man,
May Day 1993.

C·60 MM·II UKRAINE OD·7.-900?

C·62 LATRONICO,LUCANIA, MA·1916,494

C·64 LATRONICO, LUCANIA MA·1916·487

C·66 SEE UJ2 MM·Id KNOSSOS, ABS·1905

C·68 BR·IV MAGLEBY DENMARK NF·I·XXI

C·70 L·M·III TRIPOLYE A. M·S·G·29

C·72 M·M·III MOCHLOS S·M·51

C·74 MONT·V. HANGEBEKENS SWEDEN S·A·K·XII

C·78 -700 PLEVNA BULGARIA TENE MARNE MF6 RV·XIV·LIV

C·80 HITTITE SAE II 60

C·78 TOMSK, AAF.170

C·82 700 IALYSOS PITHOI S·A·A·1926,221

C·84 CYLINDER U.C.

C·86 XII U.C.

C·87 XII MM·I· U.C.

C·88 XII MM·I· U.C.

C·89 XII MM·I· U.C.

C·90 M·M·IIIA KNOSSOS E·P·M·272

C·92 M·M· PHAESTOS M·P·C·122 SEE LC58

C·94 BR·IV· MAGLEBY, DENMARK, NFI·XXI

C·95 -800? GAURA HUNGARY RV·IV, XCIV

C·96 MONT·V· HANGEBEKENS SWEDEN S·A·K·XII

C·98 700? IALYSOS PITHOI. S·A·A·1926,209

C·99 ALEXANDROPOL HUGEL LOW DNEIPER RV·XIII· XXXVI B

D·7 MMI· PLATANOS·X·MXIII

D·35 CRETE M·S·II

D·42 LM·III IALYSOS S·A·A·1926,81

D·63 LM·II KNOSSOS TAP·II 60

D·70 TENE III MURCIA D.F2, 685

D·84 NARCE MA·1894,234.

D·91 ETRUSCAN, LOUVRE, CNG·60

D·14 MMI· PLATANOS·X·MXIII

D·49 HITTITE CYL. H·W 863

D·77 BR AKBUNAR, MACEDONIA, A, 1925,XXVII

D·97 2000-1500? NEW GRANGE M·P·I·86 CNG·59

D·21 MMI·KUMASA·XMIV

D·28 CRETE, M·67·39

D·56 L·H·II KORAKOU B·K·PL·V

Introduction

When I was asked to devise a reference book on ornamental motifs, I had just received as a gift from a friend *Decorative Patterns of the Ancient World*, published in 1930 by Sir Flinders Petrie. Assembled in three short years the book is a remarkable achievement. The drawings, no less than 3064 of them, are arranged on plates, ordered in twenty-seven groups by their motifs with provenance, date and reference being given in simple code underneath each drawing (0:1). The book addresses the specialist and the system does not make for a beautiful layout, but the information provided by the simple outline drawings and the straightforward descriptive terminology and essential data admirably reveal relationships between motifs easily obscured by more detail. It is an impressive testimony to Petrie's wide-ranging knowledge and visual memory. In the introduction, Flinders Petrie wrote:

This collection ... stands as a first outline of an index to all the decorative imaginings of man. The subject is boundless, and to wait for completion would bar any useful result ... I hope that every twenty years or so, supplementary plates will be issued by other workers after me.

I am not aware that anybody has taken up this challenge, at least not in the form he envisaged.

I was instantly enthusiastic about this approach. In this book, therefore, I follow his plan in arranging the material by related motifs. Larger and more explicit drawings will, I hope make it easier to appreciate and evaluate the story as it unfolds. Flinders Petrie's twenty-seven motif groups have been re-arranged in nine chapters, each chapter representing a motif or group of related motifs. It is my intention to show through line illustration the development of the motifs in each group from early to late examples and from different cultures and geographical areas. The British Museum has been my main source of study, and I have chosen subjects for illustration from the Museum's collections where appropriate. In other instances, a measure of chance has determined what has been available to represent my themes. The examples illustrated cannot be the earliest or most typical in all cases nor can they illustrate the wide geographical spread of many of the motifs. The text aims to set the scene and outline sequences of events which have influenced the changing forms of motifs. Readers must supply their own pinch of salt to replace the lack of qualifications for many of my statements. They must add the 'perhaps' and the 'may have been's' which I have omitted to sprinkle throughout the text to cover uncertainties and

0:1 Plate XXXI from Flinders Petrie, *Decorative Patterns of the Ancient World* (1930). It is one of eleven plates which illustrates spiral motifs. Underneath each drawing in a simple code is the provenance, date and reference of the subject.

doubt. To produce my story, it has been necessary to draw with a fine nib and write with a broad brush.

A lifetime of drawing as an archaeological illustrator has filled my visual memory, though by no means as capacious as Petrie's, with images of ancient art of all kinds. In my work many hours of slow and repetitive copying of intricate detail has left me with plenty of time to think about the designs I am drawing. A craftsman myself, I often take great pleasure in a clever solution as when an appropriate design decorates an awkwardly shaped object – and I sometimes admire what the artist is getting away with. I particularly remember a very fine interlaced star decorating a page in a very fine and prestigious copy of the Koran where the twelve points on the outside were reduced to ten in the centre, the lost two and the cover-up being cleverly disguised in the interlace. It has also occurred to me that the same decorative ideas turn up in many guises in different media and styles, and that there is a universal reluctance to go out and find a new leaf or flower in the garden, or even draw a tree seen through a window; instead the old leaf or flower design is amended and altered to suit a new purpose. I have asked myself why that should be and have found a sort of answer in my own experience – asked to decorate something, I turn to a familiar form, one which I can already draw fluently and well – a craftsman's choice, not that of a creative artist.

A craftsman is trained to execute his craft to perfection, not to create new designs – that has always been the preserve of the specially gifted, innovative artist who changes or invents new designs which, if they are successful, in the course of time may be added to the pool of traditional motifs . This can occur at all levels of society. Owen Jones in *The Grammar of Ornament* (1865) tells a story of just such a person. In his notes to plate I, 'Ornament of Savage Tribes' nos. 2 and 9, he writes concerning the stamped design of a bark cloth dress, bought by Mr Oswald Brierly from Tongotabu in the Friendly Islands: 'Nothing … can be more primitive, and yet the arrangement of the pattern shows the most refinement and skill … When Mr Brierly visited the Island one woman was the designer of all patterns in use there, and for every new pattern she created she received as a reward a certain number of yards of cloth.' In other instances the centre of innovation may be a society such as the Minoan civilisation, where artistic creativity was encouraged, or in the court of a king who is a patron of art.

Innovation in decoration does not, however, necessarily (or even usually) mean the creation of completely new motifs. New designs are more likely to derive from the injection of new ideas into traditional styles, or from the conscious revival of motifs from the past. I have indeed been unable to add a single totally new motif to those identified by Flinders Petrie and this realisation has led me to query his view that the subject is 'boundless'. I have come to believe that there are a finite number of motifs which, with variations, account for a large majority of 'man's decorative imaginings'. It is this belief which I have put to the test in this book.

There appears to be no single reason why some patterns have become more popular than others. Some of the motifs found on the earliest Neolithic pottery such as spirals, twists and stripes are among those which, with variations, have continued to please. Motifs which initially served a symbolic or religious purpose – the Indian lotus, for example – have, if they have decorative potential, become purely ornamental. A useful motif like the acanthus leaf, once created, is like a good tool which does not need changing. First developed in Greece in the fourth century BC, it has never been out of use, covering up a join, propping up a major motif, filling an awkward space.

There are a small handful of striking designs, the spiral, circle, cross, swastika, and star, for example, which have from time to time been chosen to symbolise a god, a king, a country or a cause. Among such common motifs are also some animal figures, such as the snake, bull, lion and eagle. There are a number of theories which seek to find reasons for the persistent use of these simple figures with reference to the human body's external symmetry as well as to its disturbing asymmetrical internal organisation. These, together with the views of Freud and Jung and others on the possibilities of the innate or inherited meaning of patterns, lie outside my competence to discuss. I have a simple unsubstantiated belief that 'meaning' is in the eye of the beholder and that there can be no inherent meaning in any pattern. I would very tentatively suggest that motifs which appear to have a kind of energy or property over and above the ordinary, such as spirals and other 'rotating' motifs, and such optical illusions as the mask made up of two confronting animals (2:12,41,97,100), may be perceived as having a touch of magic about them.

Nine groups of motifs have been chosen here to represent the elements which make up a majority of decorative designs. Some groups are broad and general – spirals and scrolls and animal ornament, for example – while others, like the Indian lotus motif, are specific. This division of material has certain drawbacks because motifs from different groups naturally occur together and are subject to the same conditions and circumstances. There is therefore a certain amount of unavoidable repetition when they are discussed separately. This, for example, is the case with animal motifs which are accompanied by spiral and interlacing from the earliest times. There is also a close and confusing relationship between palmettes and acanthus motifs, whilst motifs from all groups, except the Indian lotus, occur in one form or another in Roman mosaic design.

The symbolism of decorative motifs is not my primary concern and symbolic meaning will only be addressed in contexts where there is good evidence for establishing this feature of a design. There is a tendency to deny that a pattern is simply a pattern. Gombrich (1984, p.225) quotes from a catalogue to the World of Islam exhibition in London in 1976 on the arabesque:

It derives from an abstraction of the patterns made by plant forms. It makes possible the creation of partially naturalistic designs with which there is no beginning and no end. Such a visible expression of infinite continuity within an ordered and unified system has religious symbolic connotations. The reference of arabesque to plant forms also touches on two other important aspects of Islamic thought: the very considerable interest in science and the notion of paradise as an enclosed garden of flowers and water.

Gombrich finds this symptomatic of a wish to see in the design more than meets the eye, an initiation into deeper mysteries. 'Being characteristic of Arabic decoration the arabesque must also partake of the essence of "Islamic thought".' In fact many cultures and religions share the same decorative motifs.

There is little evidence and much speculation on what our forefathers and 'primitive' people read into patterns and motifs, although there can be no doubt that art at all times has the potential for a spiritual content. The idea that an image has power is no different from our own knowledge that a work of art is important enough to exhibit, that we benefit from looking at it and are willing to value it at huge sums of money. Symbolism and magic apart, there was surely always a decorative intent, a feeling in the bones that one design was – and still is – so much more satifactory than another.

An attempt is sometimes made to interpret motifs and patterns of the past in the light of the known meaning of similar-looking motifs, collected from recent or modern societies whose lifestyle is assumed to be comparable to those of past cultures. In the study of anthropology and ethnography ornament is regarded as a source of information about beliefs and social custom. Reports concerning primitive peoples often include the explanations given (and sometimes uncertainly translated) concerning the use and significance of commonplace spirals, stripes, squares or general squiggles. There is no reason to doubt that ornament in many instances has a significance over and above its decorative qualities, but I believe that it is futile to attempt to identify meaning by comparing motifs and to transfer meaning from one society to another which is separated in time and space. A well documented example of names and meaning given to simple patterns illustrates some of the reasons why this is such an impossible task.

In 1987 an Indonesian rice barn was built for the British Museum Department of Ethnography. Four builders and carvers, with their materials, were brought to London from the village of Baruppu' in Southern Toraja on the Island of Sulawesi. As the work progressed, the significance of the structure and of the lavish decoration were explained in detail by the builders. It was also an opportunity to learn the names and meaning which they attached to the motifs (Barley and Sandaruppa, 1991). Rice barns are important buildings with a part to play in the practical and ritual life in a modern society where traditional forms are still valued.

The barn was decorated inside and out with carved and painted patterns in which linked spiral scrolls and buffalo heads dominate. Twenty-five motifs were identified and separately named. Of these seven were based on spirals, linked in various ways (0:2). The meaning attached to these patterns ranged from the apparently trivial of a 'fast-growing moss', motif 3, to the decoration on the central load-bearing beam, motif 5, appropriately named 'carry with the load evenly distributed' which refers to a carrying pole, slung over the shoulder. Motif 6 is named 'eight heads'; but its meaning reflects the name of the same pattern elsewhere in the region where it is named after the lid of a basket in which valuables are kept. Motif 11 is charmingly called 'tadpole' and reminds people to live together without harming each other, like tadpoles; whilst motif 20 is known as 'pumpkin vine' and interpreted 'as showing the linking of individuals into groups'. Motif 22 is 'lord' and is said to recall the heavy gold bracelet worn by women of noble rank and therefore a mark of nobility of the owner. Motif 24, 'group', a pattern

0:2 Some of the twenty-five motifs which decorate an Indonesian rice barn. Although all are variations on linked spirals, the names and meaning attached to each one is very different. (From Barley and Sandaruppa 1991, drawing by J.Hudson.)

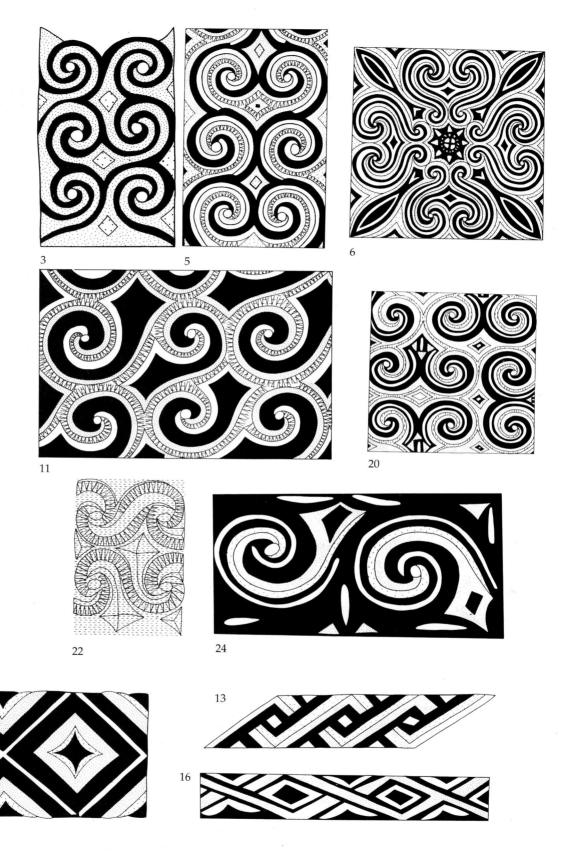

0:3 These commonplace motifs are nonetheless given highly significant names and meaning in the specific context of the decoration on a rice barn in an Indonesian village. (From Barley and Sandaruppa, 1991, drawing by J.Hudson.)

which has also been interpreted as 'boat' (the carvers on this occasion did not have a strong view on this pattern).

Motifs 12, 13 and 16 are common, so common that it is a surprise to find that here they are given very explicit names and meanings (0:3). Nobody could have guessed, for example that motif 12 represents 'movement of body with legs bent' and recalls a ceremonial dance, or that it signifies wealth and nobility. Motif 13, 'swordbelt' recalls bravery and warlike deeds and motif 16, 'bank of ricefield', indicates a display of wealth.

The reason I have gone into such detail is to point out that the different interpretations of such similar patterns are local, and apply to a specific set of circumstances. It is not possible to generalise even beyond the village. There is nothing in the configuration of these patterns that in any way indicates these names and meanings – except perhaps motif 13, the swordbelt (0:3), for the twist is indeed a pattern often used decoratively on clothing.

I have already touched on the reluctance, apparently shared by craftsmen through the ages, to create new designs. The pattern books, which began to be produced in the fifteenth century with the invention of the printing press, bear witness to the practice of providing pattern models for copying which must always have existed in one form or another.

It is a common asssumption that textiles at all times played a major role in the creation and dissemination of patterns. This assumption is based on common-sense arguments and on the experiences of the role textiles play in the decorative arts in primitive as well as highly sophisticated cultures in more recent times. There is, however, not much evidence to support this assumption in the ancient world. Details of dress and cloth depicted in painting and sculpture sometimes indicate patterns realised in woven materials. Patterns in other media, like pottery, are sometimes recognised as those which are most typically produced by weaving. Fragments of surviving cloth support these arguments in a general way.

There is, for example, some written evidence that the Phrygians were famous for their textiles. On a rock relief, the garment worn by Warpalawas, king of Tyana in Central Anatolia, has been identified as the kind of ceremonial garment of Phrygian manufacture distributed as a gift by the kings of the Phrygian kingdom in the eighth century BC (0:4). Excavations at Gordion, the Phrygian capital of king Midas, have revealed elaborately inlaid furniture, tables and stands which have motifs which recall the border of king Warpalawas' garment. Decoration on these and other ornamented Phrygian objects are based on horizontals, verticals, and diagonals which naturally lend themselves, or are indeed suggested by weaving techniques. The repetitions, reversals, inversions and mirror imaging in the inlaid furniture designs from Gordion are indeed the easiest way to vary a simple motif in weaving (0:5). Small fragments of textiles were recovered from the excavations at Gordion which lend support to the suggestion that, in Phrygian art, textile design played a prominent role and that such designs were copied in other media (0:6).

It is with the more abundant preservation of textiles that the role of woven designs can be studied in more detail. Evidence of silk cloth, brocades and embroideries are plentiful from the Tang dynasty in China (618–906 AD) and from the contemporary Sassanian empire. Most of the

0:4 King Warpalawas wearing a Phrygian ceremonial garment on a rock relief at Ivriz, Central Anatolia. Turkey. Second half 8th cent. BC.

0:6 Schematic drawing of the pattern in two colours from a fragment of wool cloth found in a tomb at Gordion. Turkey. End of 8th cent. BC. (After Bellinger in Boehmer 1973 Abb.9c)

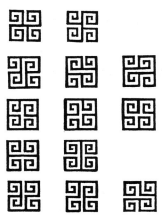

0:5 Reconstructed front face of a serving stand found in a tomb at Gordion. *Below* are details of the variations which occur in the motifs on a screen in another tomb. The same basic design is mirrored, turned and rotated. Turkey. End of 8th cent. BC. (From Simpson, 1988, figs.3, 7).

0:8 In the centre of a Sassanian silver bowl is a closely observed pheasant set within a circle. Iran. 4th–5th cent. AD.

0:7 Birds, set in a plant-scroll medallion as part of a repeat pattern in a Chinese weft-faced silk twill. 7th cent. AD.

0:9 A composite creature, known as a *senmurw* and described as a dog with the wings and tail of a bird, set within a stylised leaf border inside a partly gilt silver dish. Sassanian, Iran. 7th–8th cent. AD.

0:10 A fragment of silk compound twill with a *senmurw* design, found in a reliquary in the Church of St Leu in Paris. ?Iran. 8th–9th cent. AD.

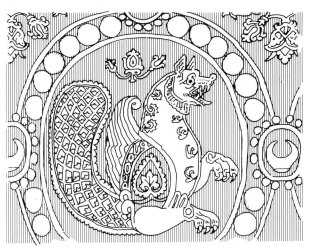

silks were woven on a draw loom (a collective term for various devices for the precise and mechanical repetition of a basic unit of pattern across the width and along the length of a piece of cloth). The use of this loom encouraged well-defined and flexible repeat patterns. Patterns, enclosing animals, organised in staggered repeats, and the interlocking ogival framework, became established as the common textile designs they still are. The motifs which were inserted in the framework were at first taken from the Sassanian repertoire of decorative silverware (0:7–10). A fragment of silk from a reliquary in the Church of St Leu in Paris illustrates the wide distribution of these costly textiles (0:10).

Silk cultivation in the west was introduced in the reign of Justinian (AD 529–565) and Byzantium became one of the main centres for the production and distribution of cloth. The buildings of early Christianity made much use of cloth as curtains, wall-hangings, cushions and carpets. The Sassanian silks with medallion layouts, fantastic beasts and eagle designs were much admired and copied. From the beginning of the ninth century AD inventories from church treasuries detail the large amounts of silk cloth which were used in the great cathedrals of Europe. They came from Syria, Alexandria and Constantinople, and, from c. 800, also from Italy. (It should not, however, be forgotten that silk was probably being woven as far west as Britain in the eighth century AD.) At the same time the influence of the art of Islam is manifest in the increased interest in geometric and palmette designs (0:11).

One of the products of this long process was the 'pomegranate' pattern, a fantastic flower set within an ogee framework. The name was coined by German art historians in the nineteenth century, but the pomegranate motif is a further elaboration by silk weavers of the Italian Renaissance of the designs developed in Islamic art from the Indian lotus motif (0:12; 6:4,21–3). It was an instant and fashionable success, and its many variations are with us today in furnishings and wallpapers (0:13).

From the fifteenth century, the invention of printing radically changed the means by which patterns and motifs became available to craftsmen. Sheets of designs, like the knot patterns of Leonardo da Vinci's Academy (9:26), were at first produced together with samples used in workshops by embroiderers, damask weavers and other specialist crafts. It was the pattern books, however, which brought real changes. One of the earliest was a collection of geometrical and foliate designs for embroidery, published in Augsburg in 1523 by H. Schönperger. The preface to an Italian pattern book, *Esemplario nuovo*, by Giovanni Antonio Tagliente (a version from 1531 of the author's first pattern book *Essempio di Recammi*, Venice 1527 and 1530) sets out the aim of the book (in a free rendering from Peesch, 1983):

To all noble and gentle ladies, also sensitive and devoted readers! … I have made up my mind to put together diligently and with the help of skilled drawing many decorative sketches. These were made by great masters and under their guidance carefully included in my work. I therefore have no doubt that I can teach every able woman and all maidens together with their menfolk and children … My work should give pleasure to all of them while they learn to draw, to sew or embroider … All this I will explain, as is necessary, from the beginning, in drawings and vivid compositions. And there are indeed many kinds of ornaments, that is to say, decorations: splendid medallions, moresques and arabesques, flying birds, animals living on land, flowers of different kinds, beautiful foliage, trees, meadows with fine herbage, vessels, wells and landscapes with figures from history and legend. Following these

0:11 The design on the chasuble of Bishop Willigis (975–1011) is palmettes and stylised leaves set within an ogee framework in a monochrome compound silk twill. Byzantine. 11th cent. AD.

0:12 A detail from Masolino, *The Raising of Tabitha*, in the Brancacci Chapel, Florence, showing two fashionably dressed young men. One has a pomegranate pattern on his cloak, the other on his hat. Italy. Late 14th–early 15th cent. AD.

0:13 Silk velvet with a pomegranate motif. Italian. 16th cent. AD.

pretty things you will find capital letters in roman as well as French type, many other drawings and letters for the sewing of monograms. There too, will be jingles. You will find in my book everything everybody likes in great detail.

In this, as in many other books which followed, the motifs generally came from Italy and included Islamic designs from Venetian metalwork and textiles. Older motifs, such as interlace and Gothic acanthus and other foliage, were also included. Specialist books serving specific crafts gave detailed technical advice on pattern transfer by means of stencils, pin-prick papers or with tables of proportion and scale (2:71). In these books, which were published in large numbers in Italy, Germany, France and the Netherlands, motifs of different origin and style were joined by new motifs and variations at the dictate of fashion. In general, the effect of the pattern books was to disseminate new forms and styles from the artistic centres to the provincial and rural areas. It was through the craft guilds and the requirement of apprentices and journeymen to get work experience away from their own locality that the pattern books (seen and perhaps brought back for use in rural workshops) became influential in the creation of what is known as 'folk art', which can be roughly defined as art practised in rural communities. In a large part of Europe, this art shares motifs and styles based on pattern book models. The vase and flowers motif is a particular favourite. It has a very long history; in this book there are examples from Roman mosaics, Indian temples and Christian churches (5:10,29; 6:13). In the pattern books it is represented in a Renaissance style, characterised by the strict symmetry of the design. In folk art the two-handled vase and the symmetrical arrangement of flowers remain typical features. The flowers are highly stylised – in the late sixteenth and seventeenth centuries, the tulip and the carnation dominate – copied from Italian and French silk brocades, which in turn took the motifs from Turkish Ottoman textiles. Together with these came the fantastic version of the Indian lotus, the so-called pomegranate (6:5). The examples shown here are from the nineteenth century, a painted design on the lid of a wooden chip-box from Austria (0:14), an embroidery from Bohemia/Moravia (0:15), a motif on a painted wall-hanging from southern Sweden (0:16) and a glazed earthenware plate from Pennsylvania (0:17). Early American colonial ornament depended on imported styles and models like the pattern books.

The influence of pattern books gradually declined in the early eighteenth century with the advent of industrial design. The story of the paisley pattern illustrates the coming together of circumstances which together created a fashion, an industry and a popular design which must be the most common decorative textile pattern in the west today.

The fashion in shawls from Kashmir in nineteenth-century Europe introduced new motifs in textile design typified by the Kashmir cone motif, known in England as the paisley pattern. In its stylised, asymmetrical drop form, filled by, and often surrounded with, small leaves and flowers, it represents a general purpose floral design within a flexible framework which could be adapted as a repeat pattern to fill any given space (0:18). Its precise origins are obscure and controversial. The drop-shaped outline of the fully developed Kashmir cone motif has given rise to names like cypress, almond, pine-cone, mango etc., all common semi-naturalistic plant and flower motifs of wide distribution and characteristic of sixteenth and seventeenth century Mogul textile design

0:14 Brightly painted containers in various materials were common throughout Europe, indeed are still produced in many places although more often for the tourist trade than personal use. The symmetrical vase and flower motif is here painted on the lid of a chip-box from Viechtau, Gmunden, Austria, where these boxes were a speciality. 19th cent. (From Wascher 1983, p.47).

0:15 Red cotton embroidery on linen, detail of a border design. The flowers here are clearly the pomegranate motif. Bohemia/Moravia. 19th cent.

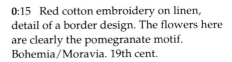

0:16 In Scandinavia from the 17th cent. onwards there was a widespread fashion in painted wall hangings with figural scenes. These were carried out in a variety of local styles by itinerant artists. Dividing one scene from another were formal flower arrangements, often a variety of the vase and flowers motif. Skåne, Sweden. Early 19th cent.

0:17 Glazed earthenware plate with white slip. The design is scratched through the slip to the red body below. The addition of birds is an ancient variety of this motif, sometimes known as the 'tree-of-life' (**5**:28,29). Pennsylvania, USA. *c*.1820.

in Persia. Early examples of shawl designs suggest that the vase and flowers motif contributed to its characteristic form (0:19).

The origins of the shawl industry in Kashmir are not known, although there is some evidence to support a tradition that Turkish weavers were introduced to the country in the fifteenth century to encourage local enterprise. The basic material for this very fine cloth is the fleece of a mountain goat, *Capra hircus*, known in the West as *pashmina* or *cashmere*, imported from Tibet or Central Asia. The weaving was in a technique described as twill-tapestry. There are mentions of a Kashmir shawl industry from the second half of the sixteenth century when the fine shawls were already renowned as prestigious gifts. In the seventeenth century shawls are mentioned in the records of the English East India Company as 'useful articles of bribery'.

Kashmir shawls were first worn in fashionable circles in the West in the third quarter of the eighteenth century, and by 1800, the shawl trade between Kashmir and the West was well established. The popularity of the Kashmir shawl in Europe undoubtedly owed much to romantic associations with the 'mysterious East' and the alleged antiquity and elaborate symbolism of Kashmir motifs and patterns. The Kashmir weavers, however, engaged in a very extensive industry supplying agents from China, Persia, and Turkey, as well as Europe, adapted their designs to the tastes of these different markets. The shawls industry in Kashmir reached its peak in the middle of the nineteenth century but collapsed before its turn.

Attempts to produce imitation Kashmir shawls began in England in the late eighteenth and early nineteenth centuries. The production of shawls became concentrated mainly in Paisley, near Glasgow, a centre for weaving since the second half of the eighteenth century. Jacquard ma-

0:18 The traditional paisley pattern. The design is from a handkerchief bought in 1992, but first produced at Liberty & Co., London *c*.1860. A quarter of the repeating pattern is shown.

0:19 Early Kashmir shawls are plain with decorative borders at the ends. *Left* One of a row of similar flower motifs in the border of a shawl from late 17th cent. *Right* A developed vase and flowers motif in the border of a shawl from 18th cent.

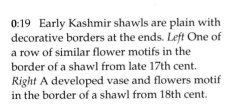

chines were introduced from France, greatly facilitating and cheapening pattern weaving. Shawls from Paisley were so successful that by 1818 they were sold as far afield as Persia, Turkey and even in India. The cheapness of the Jacquard-woven shawl became one of the instruments of its fall from popularity. While the Kashmir shawl had been a luxury fashion, exclusive and exotic, it was abandoned as its cheaper versions increased in popularity among the lower classes. The Kashmir shawl designs deeply influenced the decorative art of Europe. In India, where shawls were produced by weavers from Kashmir, the cone motif was also included in the indigenous repertoire of textile patterns.

In carpet design the Kashmir cone is known as the *boteh* motif. Names of carpet patterns are otherwise not considered here. This is not to deny the great importance of carpet design in introducing 'oriental' patterns in homes throughout the world. These patterns, like those of the paisley shawl, have over the centuries been amended to suit their customers' taste: names given to patterns serve the market and the collector and hold no clue to their origins or meaning.

It may seem that I am denying much of the glamour and magic of many oft-told tales and mysteries with which the motifs of decorative art have been associated. In their place, I have found satisfaction and excitement in tracing the forces which propelled these motifs from east to west and from south to north carried by the practical circumstances of politics, commerce and the universal wish to keep up with the Joneses.

1
Spirals, Scrolls, Meanders and Key Patterns

In the earliest images produced by man, abstract patterns appear alongside more realistic representations of animals and humans. Prominent among these are curving or meandering bands, spirals and scrolls. Such abstract forms have been variously interpreted as casual doodlings or as sexual symbols – anything linear equating to a male principle, anything curved to the female principle. When these motifs occur on tools or personal ornament, however, it may be inferred that their decorative qualities were also recognised, while some of their magic or symbolic meaning was perhaps retained in amuletic form. An exceptionally accomplished example is a twenty-four thousand year old bracelet of mammoth ivory, from Mezin in the Ukraine, decorated with a pattern of linked zigzags and meanders (**1**:1). Elaborate and striking are some Palaeolithic bone or antler points from Isturitz, Lespugue and neighbouring areas of France which date from the thirteenth millennium BC (**1**:2). The deeply carved designs consist of meandering lines which in places form regular spirals, concentric circles or circles with central dots. It is assumed that these objects served a purpose – whether practical or ritual – and that the ornament would be related to that purpose. Some have seen hunting magic or fertility symbols in these designs; but there has also been a suggestion that this could be 'art for art's sake,' an early example of man's joy in pattern-making overcoming the restrictions of symbolic and ritual use (de Saint-Périer, 1929, pp.63–4).

The spiral is a universal element in all decoration, in primitive as well as in the most sophisticated art. The making and linking of simple spirals is discovered, independently and spontaneously, in isolated communities (**1**:3), and may be further developed into very sophisticated decorative systems. The intricate decoration of the Maori in New Zealand, for example, is largely based on spiral elements (**1**:4). Spirals and related figures like the swastika can create the illusion of rotating, an effect often deliberately enhanced and exploited (**1**:49–54). The spiral is a constant element in the depiction of animals, representing hair and marking shoulders and hips (**2**:14,18,41,57,79). It is so widespread that it is possible to speculate that the dynamic 'rotating' character of the spiral suggests the seat of the animal's power of movement.

The spiral occurs in nature in the curving stems and tendrils of many plants. It is a striking image and lends itself to many decorative and symbolic purposes. J. C. Cooper (1978, p.156) summarized some of the symbolic meanings given to the spiral:

It variously represents both solar and lunar powers; the air; the waters; rolling

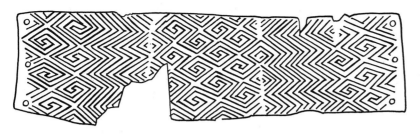

1:1 Bracelet of mammoth ivory. The extended drawing shows skilful linking between zigzag and meander motifs. Mezin, Ukraine. *c.*22 000 BC (After Rudinsky in Golomshtok, 1938.)

1:3 The pattern on a painted mask, modelled on the mummified head of a woman, may imitate tatooing or body painting. From a remote community in Krasnoyarsk Territory, Siberia. Tashtyk culture. 1st cent. BC.

1:2 Bone or antler points of unknown use, from the Palaeolithic in France. *c.*12,000 BC. (From de Saint-Périer 1936.)

1:4 Carved mask as a gable ornament. A Polynesian people, the Maori arrived in New Zealand, probably from Tahiti in the 8th cent. AD. Their art, which developed during centuries of geographical isolation, is still practised today. Poverty Bay, New Zealand. 19th cent. BC.

thunder and lightning; it is also a vortex; the great creative force; emanation. As expanding and contracting it can depict the increase and decrease of the sun, or the waxing and waning of the moon and, by analogy, growth and expansion and death and contraction, winding and unwinding, birth and death ...

The evidence for the symbolic meaning of any particular spiral decoration is often uncertain. Striking figures – the spiral or the swastika, for example – have undoubtedly been used to illustrate or symbolise concepts or beliefs (as meanings listed by Cooper suggest), but there is nothing inherently symbolic in a pattern, and it is the decorative uses of these motifs which are considered in this book. Some of these designs probably had a symbolic significance as well as a decorative function, but generally there is no evidence to suggest what it might be.

The spiral, and the many motifs which can be identified as variations on this basic idea, form a large and varied group. In its most basic form a spiral consists of a single strand beginning at the centre and ending at the outer edge. The single strand of a spiral may travel to the centre and then turn back, leaving both ends of the strand at the outer edge (1:5). One version of linked running spirals is known by a variety of names: running dog, wave scroll or Vitruvian scroll (after the Roman architect Marcus Vitruvius Pollio in the first century BC) (1:6). Spirals made up of several strands can be linked to the same number of other spirals (1:7).

The running spiral and the meander are curved and angular variations of the same motif. Other figures, for example the four-strand spiral and swastika, have similar relationships (1:8). The plain meander consists of a continuous strand which passes from the outside to the centre of each unit and then to the outside again. As with the spiral, the line may be interrupted in the centre (1:9). The meander is simply an angular version of the linked spiral motif (1:8). Key patterns are area-filling versions of meander motifs. A T-shaped element is created and appears dominant (1:10). These patterns are often constructed from strands of equal thickness and contrasting colours.

Less easy to define are related designs constructed of more or less curved or angular lines which approach the perfect spiral and regular meander more or less closely. A confusing variety of names is used to describe them – terms like scrolls, winding bands or meandering motifs – but the application of one rather than another in any particular case cannot be entirely consistent, and when possible, the term most commmonly used is chosen here. There is no single obvious reason why these related motifs take on a curved or angular form, although it can be argued that angular patterns are for technical reasons favoured in textiles and basketry, whilst pottery is more easily painted with curved strokes of a brush; metal wire on the other hand naturally curls into spirals. In practice this division is not helpful. Major forms in this motif group are generally distinct and it is the exception rather than the rule to find a scroll shading into a meander on the same object – it is however seen on a neolithic pot from Cucuteni (1:11).

Spiral and meander motifs, and their intermediate forms, first occur as important sources of decoration in the earliest farming communities in Anatolia in the sixth millennium BC, and become major motifs in pottery decoration throughout neolithic Europe (1:14–18). In the third millennium BC spiral decorations of great sophistication decorate stone monuments in Western Europe and elsewhere (1:12,22). During the sec-

1:5 *Above* Two forms of a single strand spiral. *Below* Linked spirals.

1:8 *Above* The close relationship between the running spiral and the meander. *Below* The four-strand spiral and the swastika can be seen to share a common basic structure.

1:6 Rows of linked spirals are known as running spirals, running dog, wave or Vitruvian scrolls.

1:7 Design of linked three-strand spirals from an Early Hittite stamp cylinder seal impression. Anatolia, Turkey. Mid–2nd millennium BC.

1:9 Meander borders are common in Greek art and architecture. They are also known as 'Greek fret' and 'Greek key' patterns. These borders are often enhanced by inserting motifs between the meander elements. To create a space, elements are turned alternately to right and left. From painted Greek vases of the 6th–5th cent. BC.

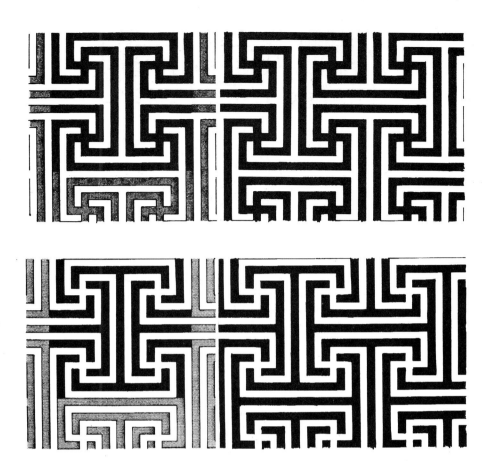

1:10 One of the commonest of the many forms of key pattern is based on a double T-shape linked by swastikas at each corner. The effect of reversing the colours of the strands which make up the design is demonstrated *above* and *below*.

1:11 Spiral scrolls and meander-like motifs are typical of south-east European late Neolithic decoration on painted pottery of high quality. The close relationship between them is well illustrated on this pot from Cucuteni.

ond millennium BC spirals and scrolls were the basic form from which the Minoan potters created a new art in the Mediterranean (1:27,28).

With the emergence of the Mycenaean civilisation on the Greek mainland in the middle of the second millennium BC, objects of metal became common. This new technology generated extensive trade networks along which not only goods, but also ideas, skills and fashions were rapidly disseminated. The great European river systems formed a route to the north and it was in Scandinavia that the most sophisticated ornament on bronze was produced with designs based on spirals, scrolls, concentric circles and meandering bands (1:13,38–39). Meanders and meandering motifs are, however, primarily associated with Greek art and architecture (1:40–43). The figure known as the swastika has a special place among motifs which are invested with symbolic significance. Symbolic meanings attached to the spiral are also thought to have at one time or another been applied to the swastika. There is, however, little evidence to support these claims (1:49–54).

Spiral ornament in the medieval art of the Celts and Anglo-Saxons is discussed in chapter 7, *The Celtic Scroll*.

1:12 Decorated stone from a chambered cairn at Pierowall Orkney, *c*.2500 BC.

1:13 Jewellery worn by Bronze Age women in Scandinavia: arm rings, collar, brooch and a disc worn on the belt. From Bornholm, Denmark. Early 1st millennium BC. (From Müller 1897.)

Spirals, scrolls and meandering motifs in the art of neolithic farming communities

A gradual change from a hunter-gathering society to an economy based on food production by means of farming and animal husbandry marks the beginning of the Neolithic period. This stage was reached at different times in different parts of the world. In the ancient Near East the development took place at some time in the eighth millennium BC, spreading northwards as the climate improved after the end of the last Ice Age to reach Western Europe in the fourth millennium BC.

In association with this basic economic change, pottery then begins to appear in the archaeological record. Pottery is the most common artefact recovered by excavation; fired clay is commonly preserved in the earth when most other materials decay. The sudden wealth of decorative motifs on pottery is not necessarily evidence of increased artistic activity, but may rather be due to the accident of preservation of a new material. Pottery is a straightforward craft and a wide variety of decoration can be produced simply by application in relief, by painting, or by impressing patterns in the soft clay with finger-nails, combs, cord or stamps. Sometimes the ornament on pottery imitates the patterns produced on pre-pottery containers made of other materials – the most important being plant fibres which were woven, twined, knotted and plaited into baskets and nets, hollowed-out wood and bark, and stitched-together skins. While neolithic pottery is often decorated with bands and zigzags typical of basketry (**9**:2), another important group of motifs dominated by meandering bands, spirals and scrolls, is the basis for most pottery decoration during the long Neolithic period.

From time to time, however, a single motif group or arrangement of pattern was favoured and singled out for intense local development.

Most of the motifs of this group which were to remain dominant in decorative art in general occur at Çatal Hüyük in Central Anatolia, one of the earliest known neolithic urban settlements, dating back to the eighth millennium BC. Baked clay stamps from Çatal Hüyük, if impressed on cloth, leather or plaster, would produce decorative repeat patterns. The designs include chevron and meander patterns as well as cross or flower-like designs, spirals and twists (**1**:14; on the possibility that this is a design based on a snake see p. 173 and **9**:4).

The earliest European neolithic settlements are found in the the Balkans, the Danube valley and the surround-

1:14 Patterns on stamps of baked clay. Çatal Hüyük, Anatolia, Turkey, first half of 6th millennium BC.

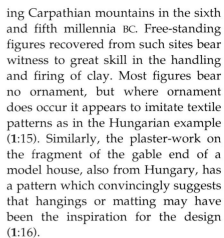

1:15 Figure built like a pot. The pattern which covers the 'body' appears to suggest some form of dress. Szegvár-Tüzköves, Hungary. 4th millennium BC.(From Piggott 1965, fig.18.)

1:16 Fragment of plaster-work on the gable wall of a model house has a design of borders and panels which may imitate hangings and matting. Kökénydomb, Hungary. 4th millennium BC. (From Piggott 1965, fig.47.)

ing Carpathian mountains in the sixth and fifth millennia BC. Free-standing figures recovered from such sites bear witness to great skill in the handling and firing of clay. Most figures bear no ornament, but where ornament does occur it appears to imitate textile patterns as in the Hungarian example (**1:15**). Similarly, the plaster-work on the fragment of the gable end of a model house, also from Hungary, has a pattern which convincingly suggests that hangings or matting may have been the inspiration for the design (**1:16**).

Spirals, scrolls and meandering designs decorate pottery in central and south-east Europe (**1:17**). On Cucuteni-Tripolye pottery, from an area which included south-east Transylvania, Moldavia and part of the Ukraine, these motifs were used with great skill and inventiveness (**1:11**). In the basin of the Danube, in the Balkans, and in south Russia spirals and scrolls recur as major motifs (**1:18**).

In pre-dynastic Egypt the spiral appears sparingly on the pottery of the fourth millennium BC (**1:19**). Early farming communities in the Far East developed variations on very similar basic motifs (**1:20**). In Japan a long period of stable communities of hunters and gatherers, lasting from *c.*10,000 BC to the introduction of rice cultivation in the middle of the first millennium BC, is regarded as the equivalent of the Neolithic elsewhere. Pottery here was decorated with impressed ornament made with cord,

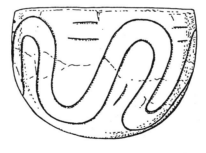

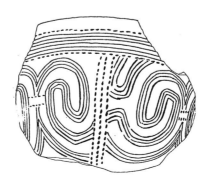

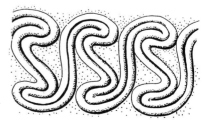

1:17 Pottery known as *Bandkeramik* displays the most common motifs from the earliest Neolithic period in central and south-east Europe in the 5th and 4th millennia BC. *Left* Ludanice, Moravia, *right above* Wettingen, Schweinfurt, Bavaria, *right below* Bödöpester-Höhle, Hungary.

1:18 Winding band motif in low relief on a bowl from Butmir, Bosnia, demonstrates the recurring popularity of this type of ornament in south-east Europe. Late 3rd millennium BC.

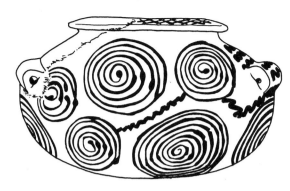

1:19 Clay pots with red painted decoration on a buff ground. Egypt. 4th millennium BC.

1:20 Earthenware urn with painted decoration in black and red on a reddish/buff ground. Gansu, Yangshao culture, China. c.2500 BC.

twists, combs and nails, a common technique in early pottery in many parts of the world (**9**:3). The spiral ornament and the shapes of Jomon pottery (Jomon meaning cord motif), are however far from common elsewhere and, while it is assumed that most was for domestic use, some extreme designs may have had a ritual function (**1**:21).

Under influence from the Mediterranean the farmers of northern and western Europe built large monuments in stone; enclosures, standing stones and tombs for collective burials (the 'megaliths' after which some of these cultures are named). Some stones carry carved or painted decoration. In the different areas where these monuments occur the motifs have certain elements in common, but the differences between them are significant enough to indicate considerable independent development. There is, however, a common repertoire of simple motifs – zigzags, lozenges, straight and meandering bands, spirals, scrolls and circles. The random distribution of such motifs on some of the stones suggests that the importance of the act of marking a stone may have been a feature of the rituals associated with such sites. On other stones, however, the designs are deliberate and carried out with artistic skill (**1**:12,22). The sophisticated use of linked spirals, with lozenges completing an area-filling pattern, is demonstrated, for example, on the kerbstone at the entrance of the New Grange passage grave in Ireland (**1**:22 *above*).

The stone-built monuments of Malta from the third millennium BC, may in some way be related to the contemporary megalithic communities in western Europe. At the so-called 'temple' at Tarxien the dominant spiral design has developed an individual form by the addition of plant-like features (**1**:23). These motifs were, however, not always sacred. In the Mediterranean, at Lerna in Greece for example, large storage vessels were casually decorated with bands of impressed patterns which display many similar features (**1**:24).

1:21 Two large earthenware vessels from the Middle Jomon period *c.*2500–1500 BC. *Left* from Tsunagi, Iwate, *right* from Umataka, Niigata, Japan.

1:22 Kerbstones at the New Grange passage-grave in the Boyne Valley, Ireland. Mid–3rd millennium BC. (Drawing from tracings by Claire O'Kelly.)

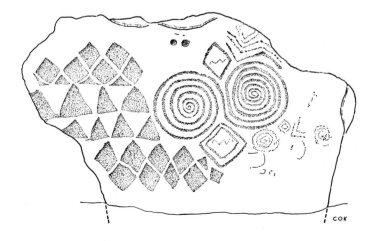

1:23 Distinctive spiral scroll motifs, carved in low relief at the 'temple' of Tarxien in Malta. The addition of plant-like features perhaps provides a clue to the symbolic role played by these decorations in ritual practices. *c.*2700–2300 BC.

1:24 Bands with impressed decoration encircle large storage vessels. Lerna, Greece. Mid–3rd millennium BC. (After reconstructed drawings by Piet de Jong in Wiencke 1970.)

Spirals and scrolls in Mediterranean Bronze Age art

The first use of metals came gradually to the centres of culture around the Mediterranean. Once metal technology was established, however, the search for ore generated a new trade network which brought far-flung regions of Europe and Asia into contact with each other. The spiral and scroll motifs in their varied forms became particularly important and often characterise Bronze Age art styles, not only on metal for which these motifs were especially well suited, but also in all other media.

In the first half of the third millennium BC the Cycladic islands were an important centre in the Aegean from which emanated cultural influences not only to the surrounding islands, but to Crete and to mainland Greece. Spirals and scrolls were already present in the general repertoire of motifs in the area. In the Cyclades, however, spiral motifs were subject to a local development, particularly in the form of linked spirals, which became the dominant decorative motif of the islands (1:25). The curious objects known as 'frying pans', decorated with these motifs, are thought to have fulfilled an unidentified cult purpose (1:26).

The Minoan civilisation of Crete was influenced by the art of the Cyclades with its complicated, but strictly abstract, spiral designs. As the Minoans became the most powerful influence in the Mediterranean at the beginning of the second millennium BC, spiral designs were treated very differently, particularly on pottery. Tendrils and streamers were added to spirals and scrolls creating illusions of movement and changing these ab-

1:25 Design of linked spirals on a Cycladic stone box. Greece. Mid–3rd millennium BC.

1:26 Linked spiral design impressed on the back of a 'frying pan'. Cyclades, Greece. c.2800–2600 BC.

1:28 *Above* The earliest forms of the octopus motif in Crete suggest that it was an adaptation of the ubiquitous spiral scroll. Kamares ware from Phaistos. 18th cent. BC. *Below* The more realistic renderings of this motif are of a much later date. Gournia, Crete. c.1500 BC.

1:27 *Above* The illusion of rotation is greatly enhanced by the addition of streamers to a triple-linked spiral design. *Below* A sense of movement both horizontally and diagonally is created in this design. Note also the cunning positioning of the small white dots in the border at the rim. Kamares ware from Phaistos, Crete. c.1700 BC.

stract motifs to plant- or animal-like forms (**1**:27,28; **4**:13).

The Mycenaean civilisation emerged in mainland Greece in the mid-second millennium BC. Around 1450 there was widespread destruction across Crete. Mycenaean Greeks were perhaps responsible for this catastrophe or, at least, took advantage of it. After that date they may have been in control of the great palace at Knossos, which was less affected by the destruction and continued to be inhabited until the final catastrophe around 1380 BC. The influence of Minoan art was, however, initially still strong; later there was a gradual movement away from the florid versions of spiral designs towards more abstract forms. A wide range of spiral-based motifs, together with rosettes, are the major motifs in decorative Mycenaean art (**1**:29–31).

There was clearly contact between Egypt and the Aegean at this time, but the directions in which the influences flowed are differently interpreted. There were doubtless contacts and exchanges of goods at least from the beginning of the third millennium BC. In the First Intermediate period (*c.*2134–2040 BC) and in the Middle Kingdom (*c.*2134–1797 BC) many scarab designs were based exclusively on linked spirals and scrolls, while others combine such motifs with lucky signs or inscriptions (**1**:32). Painted wall and ceiling patterns from the Middle Kingdom can be inter-

1:29 Gold jewellery from the royal graves (the Shaft Graves) in the citadel of Mycenae shows a wide range of spiral and scroll motifs. *Above* Detail of the complex design on a breast plate, shown here in simple outline. *Below* Designs on a bone button and a mount covered with gold foil. Greece. 1550–1500 BC.

1:31 Detail of the ornament on a carved ceiling in the so-called 'Treasury of Minyas' at Orchomenos, Boeotia, Greece. *c.*15th cent. BC.

1:30 Detail of the design on one of the stones raised over the Shaft Graves at Mycenae. Greece. *c.*1550–1500 BC.

1:32 Linked spiral designs on small scarabs (1–2 cm). Egypt. *c.*2134–1797 BC.

1:33 Wall and ceiling patterns from tombs. Originally brightly painted (shading indicates colour distribution) they may suggest patterned textile hangings. Egypt. *c.*1842–1797 BC.

preted as imitating woven or plaited hangings with angular versions of linked spiral designs (**1:33**). The spiral designs on scarabs and the painted ceiling patterns are indigenous and independent Egyptian variations on simple decorative ideas. Comparisons with similar designs on the Cycladic 'frying pans' (**1:26**), some five centuries earlier, only emphasise that simple designs may arise at any time anywhere.

In the second millennium BC the New Kingdom of Egypt established an empire in the Middle East. Egypt consequently became more influenced by foreign fashions. This was particularly the case in the eighteenth dynasty (*c.*1550-1307 BC). A wall painting in a tomb at Thebes shows a delegation from Crete carrying gifts which include Minoan cult objects and vessels (**1:34**). The influence on Egyptian tastes of such displays of foreign fashions can be seen, for instance, in the painted ceiling pattern in a tomb at Thebes (**1:35**). In this instance, a complicated design may be compared to a broadly contemporary ceiling ornament from a Mycenaean tomb (**1:31**).

After the collapse of the Mycenaean civilisation *c.*1100 BC, Greece gradually became poorer and more isolated. In other parts of the Mediterranean, this was a period of disturbances and migrations caused by the so-called 'Sea Peoples' of whom little is known. In the eighth century there were signs of a gradual renaissance in Greece and, by the second half of the century contacts with the great civilisations of the Near East. Craft skills were re-learned, often under the influence of foreign craftsmen. Pottery produced in Athens was widely exported, mainly as containers for products like oil and perfume. The borders which dominate the decoration on the pottery aim at creating a surface pattern where the light and dark elements achieve a balance. Winding, meandering and castellated forms, which perhaps reflect indigenous ornamental traditions, are particularly suited to these aims (**1:36**).

1:34 *Above* In a tomb wall painting, a delegation from Minoan Crete is shown bringing gifts to the Pharaoh. The vessels, cult figures of bulls, and the designs on their kilts (shown in more detail *below*) are typically Minoan. Egypt. *c.*1504–1450 BC.

1:36 Pottery pitcher (with lid) made in Athens. Meandering motifs, and an even distribution of light and dark elements, are prominent in this style of decoration. Greece. 735–720 BC.

1:35 Painted ceiling pattern from a tomb at Thebes. The dynamic running spiral and the rosettes are typical elements of Aegean decorative styles. (Compare **1:31**). *c.*1504–1348 BC.

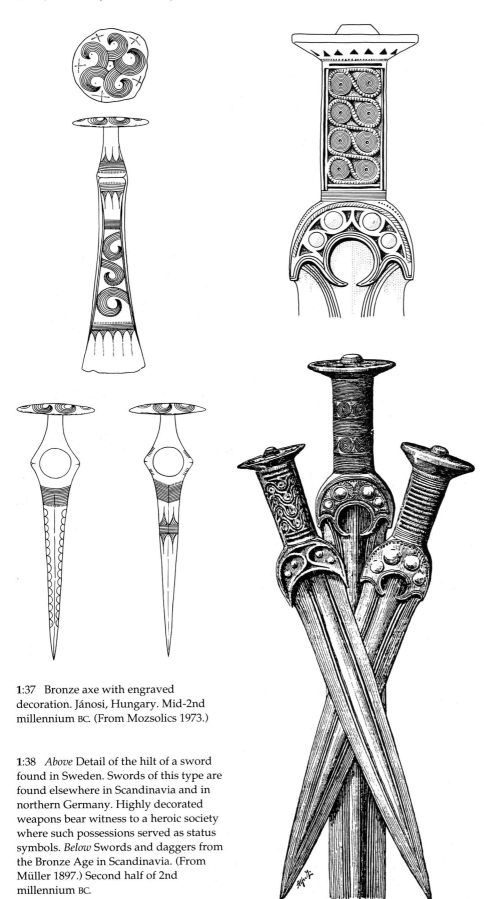

***Spirals and scrolls
in the European and
Scandinavian
Bronze Age***

1:37 Bronze axe with engraved decoration. Jánosi, Hungary. Mid-2nd millennium BC. (From Mozsolics 1973.)

1:38 *Above* Detail of the hilt of a sword found in Sweden. Swords of this type are found elsewhere in Scandinavia and in northern Germany. Highly decorated weapons bear witness to a heroic society where such possessions served as status symbols. *Below* Swords and daggers from the Bronze Age in Scandinavia. (From Müller 1897.) Second half of 2nd millennium BC.

Considerable changes had occurred in Europe in the second half of the third millennium and the early part of the second millennium BC. Some changes were due to a warmer and drier climate, but more important was the introduction of metals, a technological innovation which probably involved the movement of people (although not on the massive scale at one time envisaged).

The social changes brought about by the new technology were considerable. This was due not only to the use of new and superior materials for weapons and tools, but also to the fact that trade brought widely separate areas into closer touch with each other and allowed ideas, skills and fashions to be rapidly disseminated along trade routes. The vital trade routes fanning out from the great and powerful Mycenaean civilisation in Greece must, for example, have exerted a powerful influence.

The important trade in metals generated by the need to supply bronzesmiths in regions where there were no natural deposits, was carried into Europe by way of its great rivers as far as the Baltic. Where the raw material occurred, and where conditions were otherwise favourable, centres of manufacture were established, satisfying local demands as well as producing goods for trade. The knowledge of the new technology thus spread ever further north and west. In these regions individual designs and patterns developed within the overall style, based on the manipulation and variation of the spiral, scroll, concentric circle, and the meandering and winding band motifs. The

1:39 *Above* Section of a linked spiral ornament engraved on a bronze disc. Hverrehus, Viborg, Denmark. Second half of 2nd millennium BC. *Below* Variations on spirals, scrolls and winding band motifs on objects of the Late Scandinavian Bronze Age. (From Müller 1897.) First half of 1st millennium BC.

scroll motif on an axe from Hungary (**1:37**), for instance, is typical of the work of bronze-smiths in the Danube basin, while the swords and daggers illustrated (**1:38**) represent work from centres in northern Europe and Scandinavia.

In northern Europe and in Scandinavia these motifs achieved a very high degree of sophistication in the second half of the second millennium BC, and were to continue in use longer than elsewhere in Europe. Spirals, scrolls, and meandering and winding band motifs were common decorative devices in Mycenaean art (**1:29–31**). It is not necessary, however, to envisage

a direct influence from the art of the Mediterranean to account for the development of the fine and intricate decoration of the Scandinavian bronze-smiths (**1:13,38,39**). Spiral-based ornament was not a new idea in Europe; it had been a recurring motif in south-east and central Europe during the Neolithic period (**1:11,17,18**), and was also known in the art of western Europe (**1:12,22**).

The methods by which these designs were produced are obscure. They have long been assumed to have been punched and perhaps marked out by means of a string compass. A more likely theory suggests that the

spiral ornament – with other ornamental detail – was produced by casting, by means of the lost wax process.

The introduction of the use and working of iron in the eighth century BC by groups of people entering Europe from the east and from Italy, only reached Scandinavia centuries later. Scandinavian ornament therefore continued developing skilful variations on the theme of spirals, concentric circles, arcs and winding bands (**1:39**) longer than elsewhere in Europe. There is some evidence from the Scandinavian Bronze Age that the sun was worshipped at that time, perhaps alongside other deities. Cult objects take the form of discs, decorated with spiral patterns, in association with horses and ships. When, therefore, spiral motifs are ubiquitous on weapons and domestic objects, it is reasonable to suggest that in this context the decorations were perceived as offering protection or good luck.

The art of the Celts in Iron Age Europe and in the British Isles is the subject of Chapter 7, *The Celtic Scroll*. The spiral scroll motifs which played an important role in the art of medieval Britain are discussed in that context.

Meander and key patterns in Greek and Roman decoration

Many names are used to describe this group of motifs – Greek fret, Greek key, labyrinth, maze, key pattern, for example. In an attempt to avoid confusion, the term 'meander' is used here for its basic form (**1**:9) and the term 'key pattern' is reserved for the area-filling design (**1**:10). When the strands of a meander cross at the centre of each element, the term 'swastika meander' is often used, a form which can also be adapted as an area-filling design. Inserted motifs can be accomodated by the alternate turning to the right and left of the swastika units (**1**:41,42). It is generally accepted that the name of the motif refers to the winding River Meander in Anatolia, Turkey. This appears to be an ancient connection as coins of the late fourth century BC from the towns on this river feature the meander motif (**1**:40).

Meander and key patterns developed as important decorative devices in Greek art and architecture. In the eighteenth-century European revival of interest in Greece as a source of

1:40 Coin from Priene, Ionia in Anatolia, Turkey. The trident was the particular symbol of this city on the River Meander. *c.*330–300 BC.

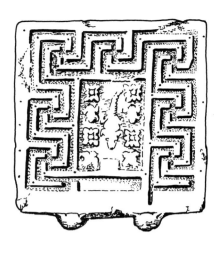

1:41 A libation table carved in limestone from the Mendes region in Egypt. The channels along which liquid flowed, before pouring from one of the heads set at the table's edge, form a continuous swastika meander design. 2nd–3rd cent. AD.

1:42 In the wide border, painted on a sarcophagus from Izmir, Turkey, star motifs are inserted into a swastika meander design. *c.*500 BC.

ornament, it was the meander and key patterns which, above all others, signified Greek style and taste. These patterns have remained constantly popular decorative motifs in the western world since.

With few exceptions, these motifs carry no symbolic message. In Greek vase painting of the fifth century BC, however, the meander became a motif associated with a popular story drawn from the legends concerning King Minos of Crete – that of Theseus slaying the Minotaur and finding his way in and out of the Labyrinth. In these representations Theseus and the

Minotaur – part bull, part man – are shown as realistic figures, while the Labyrinth is often indicated by a simple meander border, attached to a door post or pillar, representing the entrance (**2**:27). In these scenes, therefore, the meander border became the conventional sign or ideogram for the Labyrinth. When the cities of Crete began to issue coins, the link between this story and the island of Crete was so strong that the motifs chosen to represent Knossos – the Minotaur and the Labyrinth – were taken from its legendary history relating to a period some thousand years earlier (**1**:43). At

1:43 Coins from Knossos, Crete. The Minotaur is shown as half man and half bull. On the reverse the swastika meander represents the Labyrinth; the Minotaur is present in the shape of a star – the creature was sometimes described as 'star-like'. *c.*400–350 BC.

1:44 On this coin from Knossos, the Labyrinth is shown in the form of a true maze design. The star represents the Minotaur at its centre. Crete. 4th cent. BC.

1:45 The design of a maze, with the figure of a woman at its centre, is painted on the wall of Sibbo Church, Finland. 15th cent. AD.

first the Labyrinth took the form of a meander; later, in the fourth century BC, the form of the Labyrinth was that of a true maze (**1:44**).

Nobody is sure what the Labyrinth of this story was. In antiquity it was said to have been built by Daedalus in the imitation of the 'Egyptian Labyrinth'. This was the name given to the funerary temple of Amenemhet III (*c.*1844–1797 BC), at a time when it was probably already in ruins. More recently there has been speculation that the Labyrinth referred to ritual dances of intricate pattern. The most commonly held view today is that the Labyrinth is a metaphor of the complex plan of the Minoan palace at Knossos. Sir Arthur Evans, who excavated the Palace at Knossos, and called it King Minos' Palace, gave the name 'the Labyrinth fresco' to a much damaged wall painting from the period *c.*1625–1450 BC (*The Palace of Minos at Knossos*, vol.I, 1921, p.357, fig.256). This reconstruction, possibly uncertain, shows a pattern like that illustrated (**1:10**) – one here termed a key pattern.

The maze design on the coin from Knossos (**1:44**), and the same pattern in circular form, represent a design which can be traced back to at least the second millennium BC in the Mediterranean. In the same form, and apparently in an unbroken tradition, the true maze occurs in the east from the Caucasus to India, in Sumatra and Java and in Europe to the present day. The assumption of a common origin is supported by the complicated design and similarities in the traditions and ideas which are associated with them. In Europe and India alike, mazes or labyrinths are described as 'forts', 'castles', and 'cities'. In Europe they have been associated with the legendary city of Troy, and this name is also inscribed next to a maze design on an Etruscan vase from *c.*600 BC. In early Christian churches, the Theseus legend, with maze and Minotaur, sometimes occurs as a symbol of the tortuous complications of sin, while maze designs laid in the floor of French cathedrals from the thirteenth century were known as *Chemin de Jerusalem* and became an instrument of penance. In England, and in Europe generally, mazes cut in turf or outlined in hedges were places of superstition, pleasure and sport. In northern Europe, many maze designs are set out in stone. Some of these are probably more than a thousand years old, while others were built in more recent times. The maze design painted on the wall of a fifteenth-century church in Finland, has at its centre a figure of a woman emphasizing the likely ingredient of fertility in the ritual or games associated with this ancient design (1:45).

Spirals, scrolls, meanders, key patterns and all possible variations on these motifs were explored by the Romans in their insatiable appetite for decoration in their houses, public buildings and temples as well as for their domestic equipment and personal attire. In the mosaics they left behind throughout their vast empire, these motifs were prominent among many others which were incorporated into the general repertoire of decorative motifs in the western world for many centuries (1:46–48; 9:27,28).

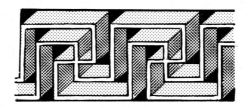

1:46 A swastika meander shaded in an isotropic perspective to imitate the effect of light and shade on carved enrichments in architecture. This and other architectural features are common motifs on Roman mosaics and wall paintings.

1:47 A mosaic panel from Aldborough, Yorkshire, England, has borders of twists and plaits on either side of a broad swastika meander design. 2nd cent. AD. (After Neal 1981).

1:48 *Left* Detail of a mosaic panel from Lullingstone, Kent; swastikas are among other purely decorative motifs set in a geometric framework. Mid-4th cent. AD. (After Neal 1991).

The swastika and other 'rotating' motifs

The swastika is a motif which is easy to recognise but difficult to describe:

A primitive symbol or ornament of the form of a cross with equal arms with a limb of the same length projecting at right angles from the end of each arm, all in the same direction and (usually) clockwise.

This definition in the *Shorter Oxford English Dictionary* illustrates the point. The swastika and the four-strand spiral are angular and curved variants of the same motif (**1**:8 *below*) and both share the property of seeming to 'rotate', which may be the reason why they have sometimes been given a magical or symbolic significance. (On other rotating motifs, p.13, **1**:27; **9**:31.) The name swastika is derived from a Sanskrit word meaning 'well-being', 'fortune' and 'luck'. The Greek word *gammadion*, is sometimes used where the motif appears to have been made up of four *gamma* letters. In English medieval architecture it is known as a

fylfot and in heraldry as a *cross cramponnée*.

The swastika is known from very ancient times. Seals from the Indus Civilisation in the third millennium BC show both clockwise and anticlockwise rotating swastikas (**1**:49). It is one of the eight auspicious signs of the Buddha. In India this sign has maintained the meaning suggested by its Sanskrit name (particularly in its clockwise form), as a generally lucky sign.

In the early Bronze Age in Anatolia the swastika was one of the designs which resulted from the manipulations of horizontals, verticals and diagonals which formed the basis for most of the decorative patterns in pre-Hittite art. In the context of other patterns produced from similar elements, the frequent use of the swastika does not necessarily indicate that it held a special position among these motifs (**1**:50; see also **0**:5).

The swastika is a common motif in Greek and Roman decorative art, where it is used singly and as an element in meander and key patterns (**1**:46–48). There is little evidence to suggest that in this art the swastika had any significance other than decorative and the motif is used in contexts where any meaning is secondary to its decorative character. In Greece, for instance, in the period

1:49 *Above* Seals from Mohenjo Daro, Pakistan, have swastika designs rotating in both directions. Second half of the 3rd millennium BC.

known as the Geometric, designs of meandering bands and other geometric forms on large amphorae also depict complex figural scenes of funeral processions. The swastika appears here as a geometric figure among others and as one of several small motifs which crowd, apparently at random, the empty spaces in the important scenes. When, however, small swastikas are placed between the spokes of the wheels of a catafalque, they may have served a secondary function as an ideogram for motion (1:51). Together with many other motifs from the Roman repertoire the swastika became a part of the stock of patterns generally in Europe.

When secular Roman motifs were used in a pagan culture it is possible that they were reinterpreted in some symbolic way. On the Island of Gotland in the Baltic, stones were raised between AD 400 and 1100, initially with motifs which came from the Roman world. It is assumed that both the technique and the idea of carved and painted memorial stones were introduced to the island, together with the motifs, by some as yet undiscovered route. Gotland was, however, an important trading centre in close contact with the outside world both to the east and the south. The use made of the motifs in the pagan society of Gotland was, however, far removed from the Roman world. There is no evidence to suggest that the sun cult in Scandinavia continued beyond the Bronze Age (p.43). Nonetheless, the whirling disc and spiral ornament on the early Gotland stones may reasonably be associated with some form of sun worship (1:52), although little is known about the people's beliefs at this period. Similarly, the swastikas which decorate pagan Anglo-Saxon funerary urns may have been endowed with a symbolic significance related to beliefs of which now nothing can be known (1:53).

With the increasingly popular taste for Indian ornament and the romantic fascination with the Orient in the nineteenth century, the swastika was reintroduced into western conscious-

1:50 *Left* Bronze stamp seal. *Above* Openwork, bronze 'ceremonial standards' of unknown purpose, from Alaça Hüyük. *Below* Hammered design encircling the body of a gold ewer from Mahmatlar. Anatolia, Turkey, second half of the 3rd millennium BC.

1:51 *Left* Detail of one of the wheels of a catafalque in a painted representation of a funeral procession. Greece, second half of the 8th cent. BC

ness, together with its original Sanskrit meaning of well-being and fortune. (Early editions of Rudyard Kipling's work, for instance, carried the swastika prominently on the covers).

The choice of the swastika as the emblem of the National Socialist Worker's ('Nazi') Party of Germany, has drastically changed our perception of the motif (**1:54**). In combination with the eagle, traditionally the national emblem of Germany, the swastika became the official emblem of the Third Reich. Sinister associations now attach to a sign originally chosen as a symbol of the revival of life, in this instance the life of the German nation.

In time the swastika will perhaps recover its former image as a striking and useful motif, allowing it to be chosen again to symbolise positive ideas and to have its many decorative possibilities exploited.

1:52 Design on a raised memorial stone with motifs which can be interpreted as relating to sun worship. The stone would originally have been brightly painted. Bro Church, Gotland, Sweden. *c.*AD 400–600. (After a reconstructed drawing in Nylén 1978.)

1:53 A row of swastikas, which are further decorated with small stamped motifs, on a funerary urn which held the cremated bones and ashes from a pagan burial. Lackford, Suffolk. Anglo-Saxon, 7th cent. AD.

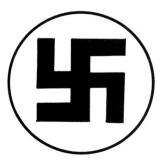

1:54 In Hitler's Germany, the black swastika symbolised a revival of national life and pride.

2

Animals and mythological and imaginary creatures as motifs in ornament

Representations of animals and humans are the most striking of the earliest known images produced by modern man. They have been found as paintings and sculptures in caves and rockshelters in Europe, Asia, Australia and in the Americas. Some are now believed to date back 40,000 years, although this estimate of age may well be revised as dates calculated from such distant periods are at present being refined by new technology. Since they are thought to have served a ritual function, perhaps as some form of hunting magic, such representations do not fall within the remit of a book concerned with motifs used primarily as decoration. It is not, however, always possible to distinguish between cult figures and decoration. A cult figure may be reserved for very specific uses and be regarded with awe, but the same motif can in another context be used as a pleasing design, with the additional advantage of being regarded as a good omen or as a sign to ward off evil in an atmosphere of vague superstition. Repeated copying of a motif sometimes leads to continuing stylisation, until the original motif is no longer recognisable and its significance totally, or almost, forgotten (2:1). A once sacred and potent image can also become a feature of style and fashion; a lion may be the symbol of majesty, or of Christ, but can also embellish an eighteenth-century English chair leg or serve as the logo of a film company. It is necessary, therefore, in view of their development into more or less purely decorative patterns, to consider here certain animal motifs which clearly at one time served as cult figures.

A gradual change from a hunter-gathering economy to one based on food production through farming and animal husbandry began in the ancient Near East in the eighth millennium BC and marks the beginning of the Neolithic period. Çatal Hüyük in Central Anatolia is one of the earliest known Neolithic urban settlements. The walls of shrines and houses are decorated with bulls' heads and leopards in relief; painted motifs include figural scenes of goddesses, birds and hand prints as well as abstract patterns (2:2; 1:14). The animals which are represented at Çatal Hüyük are assumed to have been the subjects of cults. Hunted, herded (and later domesticated) horned animals, predatory animals, birds and snakes remain constant motifs associated with religious practices in the powerful cultures of the ancient Near East for several thousand years (2:3,13,14; 9:4,5). Depictions of the human form usually represent gods, godesses and other superhuman beings (2:3,4,17).

Motifs created in the ancient Near East became central to the development of art further to the east, as well as in the Mediterranean and in

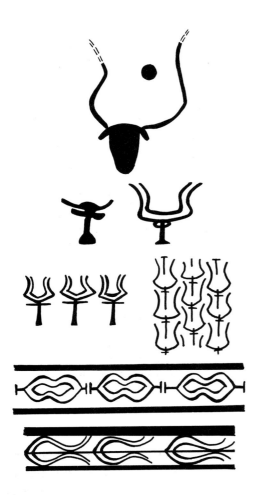

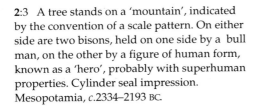

2:1 A series of painted patterns on pottery illustrates through a sequence of motifs how the realistic head of a bull is reduced, by a gradual process of stylisation to increasingly abstract patterns. Tell Arpachiyah, northern Iraq. *c.* 5th millennium BC.

2:2 Detail from a wall painting in a room at Çatal Hüyük. Headless men, together with what looks like a vulture, suggest a burial ritual. The internal organs of the bird are indicated, a feature which sometimes occurs in the art of societies which rely on hunting (cf. **2**:99). Anatolia, Turkey. First half of 6th millennium BC.

2:3 A tree stands on a 'mountain', indicated by the convention of a scale pattern. On either side are two bisons, held on one side by a bull man, on the other by a figure of human form, known as a 'hero', probably with superhuman properties. Cylinder seal impression. Mesopotamia, *c.*2334–2193 BC.

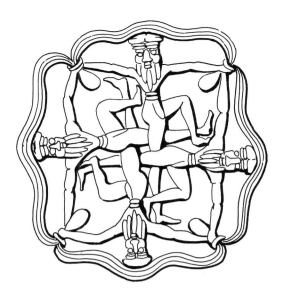

2:4 Four intertwined 'hero' figures holding vessels from which water flows. Interlacing or overlapping are common features of cylinder seal designs (2:15,17). Northern Syria. c.1800–1720 BC.

2:5 A composite creature with the body of a winged stag and the head of a lion with horns and the ears of a mule. Embossed gold plaque from a large hoard found on the banks of the River Oxus in Bactria, Central Asia. 6th–5th cent. BC.

Europe. At the crossroads of the most important trade routes of the ancient world, the eastern Mediterranean seaboard and its hinterland served as a clearing house for ideas of all kinds. As a part of this process, knowledge of patterns and designs were disseminated by a variety of means – as high status gifts between rulers in the cause of political power games, for example, but also by means of seals, painted containers and patterned cloth which accompanied humbler trade goods (1:34 and p.16). Patterns and designs would, however, also develop independently along similar lines in communities which shared similar conditions and preoccupations. The dominance of animal figures over large areas and long periods of time are a measure of their importance in people's lives.

Thousands of seals, or clay impressions of seals, subsequently baked hard in fire, dating from the fifth to the first millennia BC have been found. Their designs, and particularly those of cylinder seals from the middle of the fourth century onwards, can be regarded as representative of motifs in other, now lost, media. The range of motifs is large, the essence of a seal being that its design is distinct. Some of the motifs and compositions first encountered on seals remained in fashion for thousands of years; the combat between hunter and hunted, or between domestic animal and wild predators are prominent among them. Many fantastic creatures are arranged in symmetrical compositions of opposed and sometimes interlocking figures (2:3,4,15,17). Any serious symbolism which may have been expressed in such designs did not prevent these motifs from becoming popular as decorative devices in the art of many subsequent cultures.

With the emergence of Greek civilisation, composite creatures were incorporated into mythology and legend and given names and characters (**2**:24–35). Further distorted they appear as fantastic animals in the decoration of the people of the Eurasian steppes (**2**:5,77–85). Other animals became associated with recognised cycles – the signs of the zodiac, for example – or the compilations of animal tales in bestiaries, which provided models for much Christian iconography. Some developed into the heraldic beasts which in the Middle Ages introduced the animals and composite creatures of the ancient Near East into the common pool of motifs in European decorative art (**2**:64–71).

The hunt is one aspect of the combat motif; it celebrates an activity, more a pastime than a matter of life and death, which can be given a romantic or heroic interpretation and which only occasionally needs to be regarded as symbolic. The hunt was, for example, a favourite motif of the Persians. The scene depicted on a fourth-century AD silver dish of a Sassanian king killing a leopard (**2**:6) is a version of a motif of long standing in western Asia. A very similar motif decorates a painted bowl from twelfth-century AD Iran (**2**:7). In the Muslim world figural representations are not allowed in religious contexts, but in secular art there are no such restrictions. Motifs of the hunt became very popular, reflecting the known obsession with this activity in court circles. Hunting was universally a major preoccupation and favoured leisure activity of the mighty as well as of the common man. The hunt is a common motif on Roman mosaics and on the decoration of domestic ware, produced in the provinces to serve the Roman soldiers and administrators (**2**:8–10). The private houses of the Romans, as well as their official buildings and temples – at home and throughout the Empire – were richly decorated with wall-paintings and patterned mosaic floors. Long after the collapse of the Roman Empire, many of the motifs they introduced into the provinces remained part of the common stock of European decorative art. The popularity of hunting as a pastime and sport accounts for its widespread use, and also for some of the more exotic animals which sometimes occur far from their natural habitat. Although some representations may reveal a huntsman's close observation of his prey, conventional forms are nonetheless the norm (**2**:11).

In China symbolic animal motifs were assigned to the cardinal points as part of a philosophical system. In time these were reduced to decorative motifs, applied to silver and ceramic ware and used as patterns on silk brocades and embroideries. As a result of the extensive trade of Chinese porcelain and textiles throughout Asia and the Western world the dragon and the fantastic bird, for example, are now among the stock of decorative animal motifs universally available (**2**:88–95, pp. 16ff, 91).

In widely separated cultures distortion and even fragmentation of animal bodies were employed as a means of achieving spectacular and varied effects. These techniques were used, for example, in China in the 2nd millennium BC (**2**:12,72–76), among the nomads of Southern Russia and Central Asia in the first millennium BC (**2**:77–85) and by the Germanic peoples of Europe in the middle of the first millennium AD (**2**:36–63). The design of the 'Chilcat Blanket' of the Haida on the North-West coast of North America employs a similar method (**2**:99–101). On Borneo, a dragon motif receives the same treatment (**2**:96–98).

One of the motifs resulting from such manipulations of body parts is a

2:6   A Sassanian king, probably Shapur III (AD 383–388), is killing a leopard in a scene depicted on a silver dish. The motif recalls the Assyrian lion hunt portrayed on the walls of the palace at Nineveh *c*. 645 BC. Iran. 4th cent. AD.

2:7   A bowl with a painted lustre design from Iran is a direct continuation of the traditional form of the motif which sees the hunt as a heroic confrontation between man and beast. 12th cent. AD.

2:8   Detail of the moulded decoration on pottery produced in Central Gaul. The motif of the hunt was one of the most common, reflecting a popular pastime. Pottery with such motifs had a wide distribution in central and western Europe in the 2nd cent. AD.

2:9   The stag and hound motif on a mosaic pavement from a Roman villa at Hinton St Mary, Dorset. First half of the 4th cent. AD.

2:10   Hunting scene from a mosaic from Carthage, a city which fell to the Vandals in 439. The horseman can be identified as of the Vandal ruling class by the style of his dress, showing the continuity of the production of mosaics. Tunis. 5th–6th cent. AD.

2:11   A tile from Chertsey Abbey has a motif which combines combat and hunt motifs using long-established conventions (cf.**2**:24,29,32). Surrey, England. Mid-13th century AD.

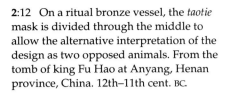

2:12 On a ritual bronze vessel, the *taotie* mask is divided through the middle to allow the alternative interpretation of the design as two opposed animals. From the tomb of king Fu Hao at Anyang, Henan province, China. 12th–11th cent. BC.

frontal mask made up of two profiles. Wherever this motif occurs, the effect is unsettling as the two interpretations, the mask and the profiles, replace each other before the eyes of the observer (**2**:12,41,72–76,97,100,101). Gombrich, discussing the possible meanings which have attached to this phenomenon, can only at the end of a long consideration remark that it appears to express a state of unconscious anxiety (1984, 264ff). The widespread use of this device seems to exclude any single 'meaning' or interpretation; the mask cannot be isolated from the context of the ornament of which it is an integral part and which in each case has a different background and purpose.

The teasing similarities between some expressions of Germanic ornament and the art of Luristan (**2**:23 and **2**:37, for example) have led to speculation about possible connections. The millennium which separates the two art forms alone makes this unlikely. More relevant are the fundamental differences between, on the one hand, an eccentric art developed in a geographically isolated community and, on the other, a highly dynamic art where new motifs are encountered during a period of expansion and transformed in a rapid sequence of different forms. The Luristan pin and the Norwegian brooch are independent responses to the same ancient idea, a figure, tree or other motifs between opposed animals (**2**:3,33). It is this dynamic quality which also sets the Germanic art fundamentally apart from the 'animal style' of the Eurasian steppes with which it has also been compared. Apart from a significant difference in age, the 'animal style' has a very different character, it is an art in which a motif can remain unchanged for centuries (**2**:80,81).

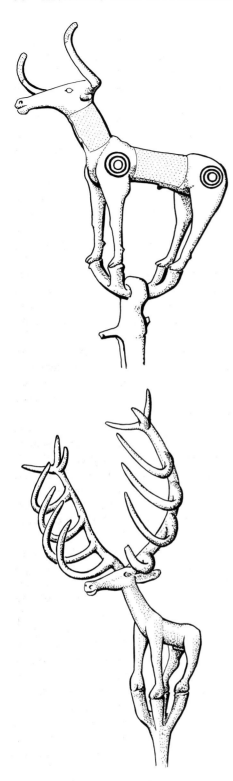

The bull, the lion, and other real or imaginary creatures in the art of the ancient Near East and the Mediterranean

The bull of any herbivore species is an important cult animal in many hunting and herding societies. He can symbolise fertility, strength and domination in his role as head of the herd. Equally obvious symbolism attaches to the cow and calf.

In the ancient Near East there are good grounds for believing that the bull was regarded as such a cult figure. Already present in houses and shrines of the early Neolithic site at Çatal Hüyük in the sixth millennium BC, bulls and stags are prominent motifs in Bronze Age graves of the third millennium BC in Anatolia as well as in Mesopotamia (**2:13,14**). The powerful bull is, however, sometimes depicted being attacked by a feline predator, or a predatory bird. The lion, leopard and eagle were therefore also invested with majesty and power. Such characteristics are assumed to have contributed to the natures assigned to the composite creatures which share some of their features.

In Mesopotamia (present-day Iraq and eastern Syria) texts and designs on clay tablets and engraved cylinder seals (which produced a design when rolled on soft clay) provide information concerning the motifs available in the art of the ancient Near East between the fourth and first millennia BC. The scenes depicted on the seals, with their strange composite creatures and situations, no doubt reflected a rich oral tradition of tales. Clay tablets tell many stories involving gods and superhuman creatures. Certainty that a particular scene on a seal represents a specific story is, however, rarely possible.

Lions are among the principal mo-

2:14 In the rich grave of Queen Pu-abi many objects are decorated with ornament showing animals, the ram and the bull prominent among them. The bull's head, attached to a lyre, is of sheet gold, hammered over a wooden core. The eyes, fringe and beard are carved from lapis lazuli. The Royal Cemetery at Ur, Iraq. *c.*2500 BC.

2:13 *Above* Bronze bull, with silver inlay on shoulders, hips, saddle, horn tips and blaze. *Below* Bronze stag. Found in graves at Alaca Hüyük, Anatolia, Turkey. Second half of 3rd millennium BC.

2:15 Design of long-necked composite creatures with goats' bodies and the heads and tails of a lion. The lion-headed eagle above represents the storm cloud *Anzu*. Cylinder seal impression. Mesopotamia. Late 4th millennium BC.

2:16 Long-necked lionesses, with their attendants. Detail from the central design on one side of a large slate palette, named after Narmer, the King portrayed on the reverse side. Hierakonpolis, Egypt. *c*.3168 BC.

2:17 Two overlapping lions each attack a deer; the deer are supported by 'heroes'. Cylinder seal impression. Mesopotamia. First half of the 2nd millennium BC.

tifs, and lion features form part of many composite creatures, in this art. A cylinder seal from southern Iraq, for example, has a design of two beasts with goats' bodies, lions' heads and tails and long, entwined necks (2:15). Above the crossed tails are lion-headed eagles, which are known to have represented the storm cloud *Anzu*. The name of the long-necked, lion-headed goat is not known, but a similar design occurs on a large slate palette in Egypt, where they are clearly lionesses, albeit with very long necks (2:16). While in this instance the similarities are close enough to suggest a direct link between the two designs, composite creatures also developed independently in Egypt. Many gods and goddesses in the Egyptian pantheon are portrayed as composite creatures with animal features. Indeed, this is a universal device, found in many cultures throughout the world.

On cylinder seal designs the lion is often part of a larger composition, attacking a prey – usually a hunted, herded or domestic animal like a deer, goat or bull. In later versions of the motif, a 'hero', a superhuman figure, intervenes (2:3, 17). When the lion is depicted in the role of an attacker, it often acquires wings and talons and sometimes becomes more like a predatory bird. The lion, and composite creatures with lion-like features also commonly serve as guardians of doors and gates (2:18). Equally persistent is the use of the lion as representing a king, or the power of the king – the Egyptian sphinx is an obvious example where the head of the pharaoh is attached to a lion's body. In Egypt this was essentially a sacred image. (The name *sphinx* is the Greek pronunciation of two Egyptian words meaning 'living image', perhaps in the sense of a god or of the divine king.) In the lion hunt, powerfully portrayed on the panels in Ashurbanipal's palace at Nineveh in 645 BC, the lion is seen as a worthy opponent of the king. The eagle is shown as a predatory animal in its own right, and the double-headed eagle is an im-

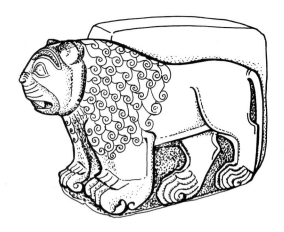

2:18 Guardian lion and composite creature at the gates and walls of Anatolian city-states. *Above* at Aslantepe, near Malatya. *Left* at Carchemish. The winged lion with a human head and snake's tail may be described as a 'chimera' in the sense of a 'hybrid monster'. The chimera in Greek mythology is a similar creature (2:29,32). 10th–9th cent. BC.

age which occurs repeatedly in world art (2:19,68–71).

Heavy symbolism did not, however, always accompany the use of animal motifs. Together with floral ornament such motifs decorate the secular and trivial objects of everyday life. A group of small ivory sculptures or plaques from Anatolia (all less than 10 cm high), for example, are believed to have been attached as decoration to furniture (2:20–22).

In the early part of the first millennium BC a highly advanced bronze casting technique developed in Luristan to the east of the Zagros mountains which today separate Iraq and Iran. Large numbers of richly decorated weapons, tools, horse trappings, and harness mounts, have been recovered from burials. The ornament is based on animal and human figures in compositions which have led to the rather fanciful name of 'master of animals' being applied to a figure standing between opposed animals, usually identified as lions (2:23). This motif, and the other real or composite animals, have, however, a long history in the art of the civilizations of the ancient Near East, with which this area had longstanding contact. The distinctive ornament on the Luristan bronzes represents these same motifs developed to serve the highly individual needs of a geographically rather isolated community (p.57).

2:19 Impressions from seals. *Above* an eagle attacking a goat suckling a kid. *Below* a double-headed eagle. Early Hittite, Anatolia, Turkey. 2nd millennium BC.

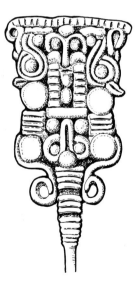

2:23 Two highly stylised animals crouch on either side of a mask-like face on the silver head of an iron pin. Luristan, Iran. 10th–7th cent. BC.

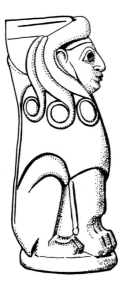

2:20 Ivory figure with lion's body and human head. Acemhöyük, Anatolia, Turkey. 18th cent. BC.

2:21 Openwork ivory plaques: tribute or loot collected from a wide area and found in the Assyrian palace at Nimrud. *Above* Composite creature with a lion's body and the wings and head of an eagle. *Below* A cow suckling a calf. The cow and calf are associated with the Egyptian cult of Isis and her son Horus. The design on the seal illustrated **2:19** *above*, shows, however, that the motif was not new in the Near East. 8th cent. BC.

2:22 Openwork ivory mount depicts a backward-looking stag in front of a symmetrical tree. Altintepe, Anatolia, Turkey. Second half 8th cent. BC.

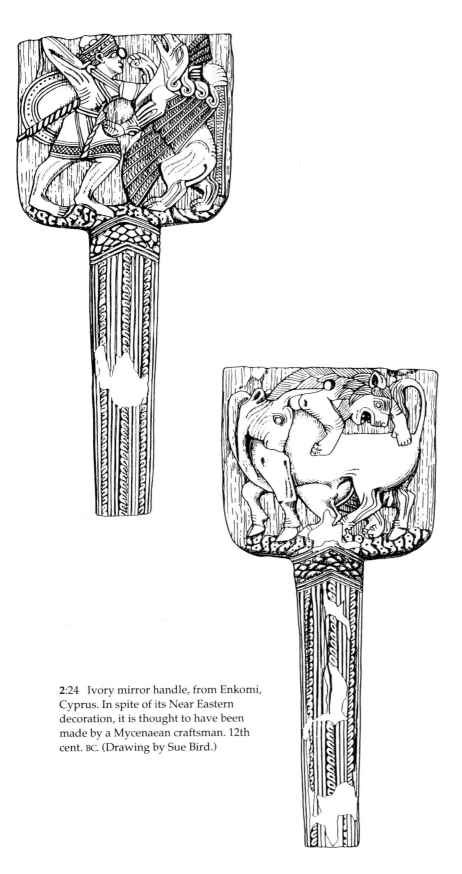

2:24 Ivory mirror handle, from Enkomi, Cyprus. In spite of its Near Eastern decoration, it is thought to have been made by a Mycenaean craftsman. 12th cent. BC. (Drawing by Sue Bird.)

Motifs from mythology and legend in Greek and Roman decorative art

The long road which led to classical Greek civilisation, with its crucial effect on the art and architecture of the western world, began in the eighth century BC under substantial influences from the Near East, already strongly represented in the Eastern Mediterranean (2:24). Friezes of animals, composite creatures, and combat scenes with lions, became part of the Greek repertoire, along with floral and palmette motifs of Near Eastern form (2:25; 3:23; 4:17). The primary motifs in Greek vase painting, however, were descriptive scenes from the life of the gods and popular stories of their dealings with humanity. Other scenes depict hybrid creatures, many of which were given the form of the fantastic monsters of the Near Eastern tradition (2:26).

The number of motifs is very great and only a few can be mentioned here. The story of the hero Theseus, who killed the Cretan Minotaur, was a particularly popular theme; the Minotaur was often represented as a man with a bull's head (2:27, p.44ff). Herakles (Roman: Hercules) was the most popular of the Greek heroes. His complicated story involved the completion of twelve tasks or 'labours', all of which became popular subjects for illustration. The first, for example, involved the killing of the Nemean lion. After completing this deed, Herakles is shown wearing its hide, usually tied by its paws in a reef knot (2:28; 9:14–16). Another hero, Bellerophon, killed the 'chimera', a fire-breathing, lion-headed creature with a goat's body and snake's tail. In representations of this story the chimera can be seen to be modelled on similar fantastic animals of ancient Near Eastern tradition

2:25 A jug, made in the Cyclades, has a griffin-shaped spout. The painted motifs also recall the art of western Asia. A detail shows a predator and its prey. Aegina, Greece. *c*.675–650 BC.

2:26 The head of the gorgon Medusa, surrounded by a frieze of lions, deer, sphinxes and a siren. Painted design inside a bowl, Corinth, Greece. *c*.625–600 BC.

2:27 A painted scene inside a bowl made in Athens shows Theseus pulling the Minotaur, in the shape of a bull-man, from the Labyrinth, which is here indicated by a panel with a meander design. Vulci, Etruria. Italy. 440–430 BC.

2:28 An Etruscan bronze mirror has a design inspired by Greek vase paintings. It shows Herakles abducting a woman named Mlakuch. Italy, c.500–475 BC. (Drawing by Sue Bird.)

(2:18, *left*, 29). Such compositions became the basis in Christian art for representations of St George and the Dragon, St Michael or other similar themes of good fighting evil.

The sphinx in Greek mythology owes little to its Egyptian namesake. An enigmatic monster it has a woman's head and breasts, wings and a lion's body. She posed a riddle, and, when Oedipus solved it, killed herself. Sphinx-like creatures could also signify other mythological monsters, but more commonly the motif was used simply for decorative purposes (2:30).

This repertoire of scenes and motifs and their decorative attributes pervaded all aspects of Greek art and decoration. It was adopted by the Romans, who were deeply interested in Greek art, legend and literature. In the hands of the Roman artist the motifs changed character and were adapted to serve new purposes. On a roof finial, for example, the winged figure of Victory is shown standing on a globe and bearing a captured trophy of weapons and armour. On either side are the zodiac sign of the Capricorn, the Roman emperor Augustus' birth sign (2:31). Private houses as well as official buildings and temples in the Roman provinces were decorated with wall-paintings and floor mosaics with motifs which were common throughout the empire. The design of Bellerophon slaying the chimera is from a Roman villa in Kent (2:32).

The need for equipment for the Roman army was satisfied in the provinces by workshops which produced weapons, brooches, belt and harness mounts to Roman patterns and tastes. Together with spiral scrolls and stylised palmette designs, the faces of Neptune or Oceanus with their dolphin attributes are popular motifs on these trappings, as are composite creatures with fishtails (2:33,34). On a mosaic panel from Carthage, a trident takes the place of a face as a reminder of an association with the sea-god (2:35). With the collapse of the empire these motifs were absorbed and transformed into the art styles of the Germanic peoples.

2:29 The story of the Greek hero Bellerophon who, when riding the winged horse Pegasus, killed the chimera, is illustrated on a terracotta plaque. In this version the horse appears to have no wings; part of these mythological creatures may vary and can be put together in different configurations. Melos, Greece. 460-430 BC.

2:30 On a decorative terracotta frieze opposed sphinxes support a palmette with their tails. Greek, made in Capua, Italy. *c.*350-300 BC.

2:31 Victory, holding trophies of armour and weapons, is the subject of a moulded terracotta roof finial. The zodiac sign of the Capricorn represents here the Roman emperor Augustus. Italy. *c.*AD 40-70.

2:33 Bronze buckle, part of a Roman soldier's outfit, decorated with the head of Neptune – or perhaps Oceanus – with attendant dolphins. Hontheim-an-der-Mosel, Rheinland-Pfalz. Late 4th–early 5th cent. AD.

2:32 The unconvincing chimera and lumpy dolphins suggest that the craftsman who laid the mosaic in a Roman villa at Lullingstone, Kent, England, was a local man, not entirely familiar with the motif. 4th cent. AD.

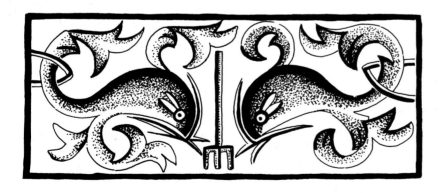

2:34 The central panel of a belt mount in bronze is decorated with a deeply facetted scroll design. At the top are opposed sea monsters. Enns (Roman Lauriacum), Austria. Late 4th–early 5th cent. AD.

2:35 On a mosaic panel, highly decorative dolphins are set in a formal composition on either side of a trident, attribute of the sea-god Neptune. Carthage, Tunis. 4th cent. AD.

A new style of ornament with animal motifs in northern Europe

As, towards the end of the fourth century AD, the Roman Empire weakened and began to collapse, Europe north of the Alps was further weakened by invasions from the east by peoples who had themselves been displaced from their territories. These events give the Migration Period its name.

Two groups of people of Germanic origins (the collective name for the indigenous peoples of Europe beyond the Roman frontiers), the Ostrogoths and the Visigoths, who at this time lived on the Volga by the Black Sea, were defeated by the Asiatic Huns and impelled to move. They in turn invaded Roman territory and, joined by other Germanic groups, brought down the western Roman Empire. In AD 493 the last Roman emperor in the west was replaced by Theodoric, king of the Ostrogothic kingdom. A number of new kingdoms took the place of the western empire. This was, however, not a sudden collapse in the face of large invading hordes; the invading forces were probably not very large, but they provided a ruling class for the defeated populations – both Roman and native. The Christian Church took over much of the civil administration and the new rulers patronised Roman culture and art. In pagan northern Europe, however, (in areas which had never been occupied by the Romans) a new art style arose which, although based on motifs drawn from the classical tradition, developed rapidly and with startling originality.

Throughout the four centuries of Roman occupation in Europe north of the Alps and in southern Britain, the art of the pagan peoples who lived beyond the borders of the empire was surprisingly unaffected by the close proximity of this powerful, but alien, presence. Influences appear to have been almost entirely limited to imported Roman luxury items of glass and precious metal found in burials of obviously rich and important personalities.

It is with the great upheavals of the late fourth and fifth centuries AD, when the Germanic peoples of the north raided and invaded the collapsing empire, that signs of a new artistic movement are reflected in the archaeological material. It is first identified on brooches from the Saxon homeland on the German North Sea coast and in southern Scandinavia (**2**:36,37). The brooches are produced in a technique (chip-carving) developed by the Romans for the purpose of decorating the weapons, brooches, belt and harness mounts of the Roman army. On these metal mounts, geometric patterns, spiral scrolls and palmette motifs are deeply facetted in a manner which recalls chip-carving techniques in wood, while animals and masks in relief decorate the edges (**2**:34). It is not always possible to distinguish with certainty between early Germanic attempts to use Roman designs and their prototypes (**2**:38). It was not long, however, before Germanic taste asserted itself. The motif of a mask between two animals on a Roman buckle (**2**:33) and the same motif on a brooch from Norway (**2**:37), not separated greatly in time and space, represent very different artistic aspirations and perceptions.

This ornamental style, which developed during the fifth century AD, survives mostly in metal – polished bronze, silver, gold or gilt – facetted in the manner of chip-carving, producing a glittering surface and a gaudy effect. In Germanic art, the coming together of this technique (adopted from Roman metalwork) and certain animal motifs (also present in Roman metalwork) resulted in a new and original style of decoration. The eagle motif, and inlay with coloured stone or glass, brought by the migrating Germanic peoples from the Black Sea area (the Pontic region), had a long history

2:36 Motifs from the classical tradition have found a different expression in this detail from a Danish gilt silver brooch. A central field of irregular scrolls is outlined by rows of composite creatures with fishtails and further decorated with animal masks. Skerne, Falster, Denmark. 5th cent. AD.

2:37 Detail from a Norwegian silver gilt brooch. A mask between animals appears in the central field, along the edges are pairs of opposed beaked animals. Lunde, Lista, Norway. 5th cent. AD.

2:38 Detail from a bronze buckle, inlaid with silver. The buckle is of a provincial Roman type and was found in an Anglo-Saxon cemetery. It could have belonged to a German soldier serving in the Roman army, but it may equally well have been produced by the first settlers in England from the Germanic east. Mucking, Essex, England. Early 5th cent. AD.

2:39 Silver gilt brooch found in the grave of a Kentish woman of the 6th cent. AD. The brooch may have been half a century old when it was placed in the grave. It was probably made in Jutland, Denmark. Bifrons, grave 41, Kent, England. Late 5th cent. AD.

in Western and Central Asia (2:19 *below*, 40,45,46; 9:18,31).

In the absence of written evidence, it is not possible to enter into the thoughts and beliefs of the past; consequently we cannot tell whether any symbolism attached itself to the animal elements in these designs. (On the meaning of motifs see also p.13.) In comparing the motifs 2:33 and 2:37 a link appears obvious. The design of symmetrical opposed animals flanking a central feature is, however, very common and has been adapted for centuries to illustrate a multitude of stories and beliefs. By the time the motif appears on brooches like 2:39 (centre of the top panel), it had no doubt found a new identity. In this case the motif is on a brooch found in a woman's burial in Kent. The worn condition suggests that it may have been an heirloom and that it had arrived with settlers from the Danish homeland of the Angles or Jutes. The animals have been translated into a Germanic idiom far removed from their original Roman forms. A motif of a man standing between two beasts in early medieval jewellery has been described as 'Daniel in the lions' den', an interpretation of the ancient motif which is no longer felt to be credible.

There was a gradual change and development of this style of decoration in Scandinavia as the motifs became ever more fragmented. Parts of animals – their heads, trunks and limbs – were treated as separate units, often surrounded by their individual contours and reassembled in a non-organic and increasingly abstract manner. The resulting designs are at once sophisticated and bizarre (2:41,42). Ambivalent designs may be interpreted as two opposed animals or as a mask *en face*, a disturbing effect which is a feature of animal ornament elsewhere, often in association with the fragmentation of an animal motif (2:12,72–76,97,100,101).

Metalwork in this vigorous style, produced in Scandinavia, was exported to Europe where the style which embellished it became fashionable. In many parts it was not only adopted but continued to develop. It has been suggested that the arrival in south-west Germany of a new fashion from Italy of plaited and interlacing ribbon designs provided the impetus for a major change in the style. Intricate plaiting and interlacing ornament was a major motif in early Christian art (p.189 and **9**:34–36). A merger between this and the Germanic animal style initially favoured the regular interlace which was rather uncomfortably provided with animal heads and limbs (**2**:43). This development may have acted as a trigger for a new phase in Germanic animal ornament, which appears almost at the same time in England, Scandinavia and south Germany, as interlacing of ribbon-like animal bodies provided new possibilities of variation and abstraction. It is, however, not necessary to look for foreign prototypes for every design change in the art of the Scandinavians who were original and innovative in their art.

2:41 Sword pommel in gold and filigree decorated with two crouching animals. They each have a rounded head with an eye and long jaws, a drop-shaped shoulder and a front leg with a paw, a round hip and a back leg which crosses behind the body. The design can also be interpreted as a mask. Skurup, Skåne, Sweden. 6th cent. AD.

2:40 Eagle brooch in gold inlaid with garnets. From Domagnano in northern Italy, an area occupied by the Germanic Ostrogoths in AD 488. c.AD 500.

2:42 Two animals, back to back, fill a panel on a silver gilt brooch. The head, neck, body and limbs are treated as separate units inside double contours. With the filling pattern of parallel lines, a near abstract design is produced. Vedstrup, Sjælland, Denmark. 6th cent. AD.

2:43 Detail from the design on a gilt bronze brooch. A plaited knot forms the conjoined jaws of two animals; their ribbon-like, beaded bodies being threaded through the knot. At the top are two simple heads and eyes, at the bottom rudimentary legs. Mülhofen, Koblenz, Germany. c.AD 600.

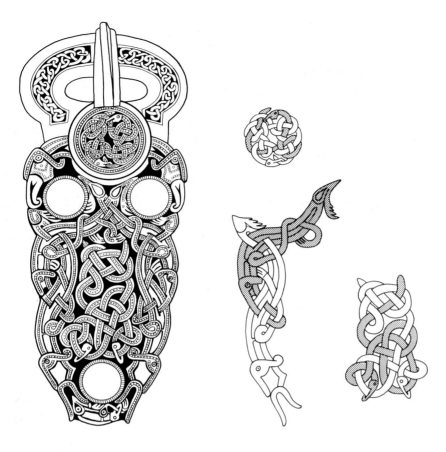

2:44 A gold buckle of local manufacture from the royal burial at Sutton Hoo. Details, shown separately, illustrate the free and asymmetrical use of the animated ribbon interlace. Suffolk, England. First quarter 7th cent. AD.

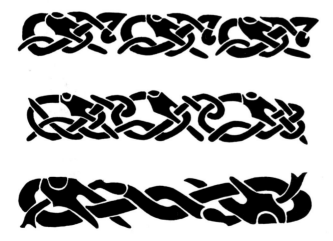

2:45 Animals typical of this style were inlaid in garnet on shoulder clasps in gold which were among the rich finds in the Sutton Hoo burial. Suffolk, England. First quarter of the 7th cent. AD.

Rich burials in Britain and Central Sweden bear witness to the far-reaching contacts and wealth of the Germanic kings or chieftains. In an early seventh-century royal burial at Sutton Hoo in Suffolk a ship contained weapons, jewellery and royal regalia as well as many domestic utensils. A number of articles of gold, some inlaid with garnet, of outstanding quality were produced locally (2:44–46, 9:32). Other objects were imported – bronze and silver vessels of Mediterranean, Byzantine and Egyptian origins as well as weapons from Germany and central Sweden.

The Christian conversion of Anglo-Saxon England was completed in the mid-seventh century, as a result of missions from Rome, Gaul and Ireland. Motifs used in the decoration and service of the Church, with its long tradition in the Mediterranean and the ancient Near East were thus introduced into Anglo-Saxon art. The new religion provided new opportunities for decoration: churches were built and decorated with painting and sculpture and furnished with textile hangings and altar vessels; bibles and service books were copied and illuminated. It is apparent that these contacts with Christian art and decoration served as a great stimulus to the artistic imagination in Anglo-Saxon England. Although little is preserved of the rich furnishings of the churches, a number of books written and illuminated in the religious centres survive and show a remarkable fusion of the vigorous Germanic animal art with the spiral scrolls and interlace of the British and Byzantine traditions (2:47–49; 7:3,20,22; 9:20,37, 38,40). The popular Christian motif of the vine scroll, or tree, which sometimes has birds and animals in its branches, contributed further animal species to the northern menagerie (2:50,51; 5:25–30).

In central Sweden, burials almost as rich as Sutton Hoo have yielded weapons and jewellery decorated with ornament where the ubiquitous animal motifs reflect something of the art   of   contemporary   Europe

2:46   Gold plaque inlaid with garnet and glass from the royal burial at Sutton Hoo, Suffolk, England. First quarter 7th cent. AD.

2:47   Animal designs from the Book of Durrow, a Northumbrian illuminated manuscript of the third quarter of the 7th century AD. The animal ornament can be compared to the style of the jewellery in the burial at Sutton Hoo (**2**:45). England.

2:48   Two details from a carpet page in the Lindisfarne Gospels. The interlaced dog-like animals and birds are enmeshed in their own tails, ears and crests in a design where the over-under weaving of parts is rigorously observed. Lindisfarne, Northumberland, England. *c*.AD 698.

2:49   A decorated letter from the Lindisfarne Gospels illustrates the different elements which came together in this art: the interlacing animals, the ribbon interlace and the spiral scrolls. Lindisfarne, Northumberland, England. *c*.AD 698.

2:51 In trees which decorate plaques from a casket, carved from walrus ivory, animals have become a part of the scrolling branches. England. Mid- or late 7th cent. AD.

2:50 A detail from the inhabited plant scrolls on the Ruthwell Cross, Dumfries, Scotland. Anglo-Saxon, second half of 7th–first half of 8th cent. AD.

2:52 A deeply facetted backward-looking animal is interlacing with itself on a gilt-bronze belt buckle. Grave XII, Vendel, Uppland, Sweden. 7th cent. AD.

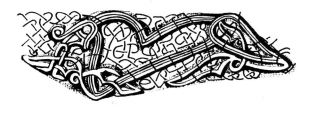

2:53 A more substantial animal form, albeit executed in outline, is enmeshed in the fine background interlace which decorates a gilt-bronze single-edged sword scabbard. Grave 5, Valsgärde, Uppland, Sweden. 7th cent. AD.

2:54 The drawing of a sword guard in openwork gilt silver with niello inlay has been shaded to illustrate the symmetrical nature of this intricate design. Böda, Öland, Sweden. 8th cent. AD.

transposed to the Scandinavian idiom (2:52–54). Applied to the trappings of everyday life and personal jewellery at a time of great wealth in the north, this adaptable animal ornament was further developed throughout north-western Europe and the British Isles. From it developed the art of the Viking Age.

A royal burial of the Early Viking Age, from Oseberg in southern Norway, contained a large number of wooden objects and other organic material which had been preserved owing to unusual soil conditions. The woman buried here c.835 was accompanied by a large ship, in which a chamber was raised. A cart, several sledges, beds and other furniture, chests containing textiles and domestic equipment of all kinds, as well as a young woman, horses, oxen and dogs were also buried with her. The grave was plundered in antiquity of much of its jewellery or precious metal. Nonetheless, this find gives a unique insight into the objects which surrounded the lives of those at the highest level of pagan Scandinavian society at the turn of the ninth century. The impression is of elaborate splendour – many surfaces are richly carved and decorated in a range of motifs, all of which feature animals. Much would originally also have been brightly painted. These motifs are developed in the grand manner and in wood – the medium for which this ornament was surely created (2:55,56). Elsewhere in Scandinavia wood has not generally survived and the early Viking Age styles occur on small objects of metal.

Throughout the ninth and tenth centuries a series of changes to the animal motif of Scandinavia produce new stylistic designs which are translated into new materials and influence the art of the Viking colonies in the west (2:57–59).

A monument at Jelling in Denmark marks the introduction of Christianity into that country in the late tenth century. A stone was raised by king Harald Bluetooth to commemorate his parents and record his claim to have

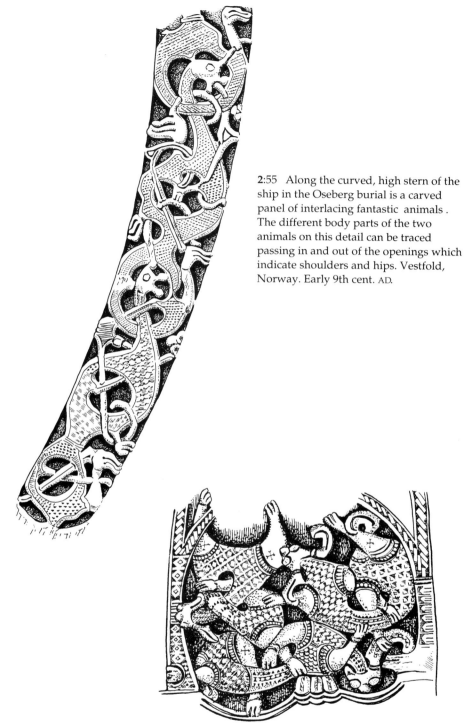

2:55 Along the curved, high stern of the ship in the Oseberg burial is a carved panel of interlacing fantastic animals. The different body parts of the two animals on this detail can be traced passing in and out of the openings which indicate shoulders and hips. Vestfold, Norway. Early 9th cent. AD.

2:56 A different kind of animal fills a panel on the stem of a post terminating in an animal head. Carved in very high relief, are creatures known as 'gripping beasts', clinging to the frame and to each other with tiny paws. Oseberg, Vestfold, Norway. Early 9th cent. AD.

2:57 A small gilt bronze mount from Norway has the design of a backward-looking interlacing animal in a form which suggests a lion. Borre, Vestfold, Norway. *c.*AD 900.

2:58 The 'gripping beast' in a typical stance on a small pendant. It was part of a hoard which was deposited *c.*AD 940. Vårby, Södermanland, Sweden.

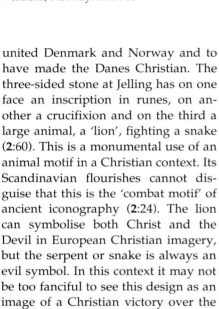

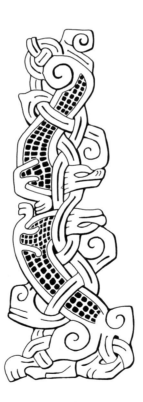

united Denmark and Norway and to have made the Danes Christian. The three-sided stone at Jelling has on one face an inscription in runes, on another a crucifixion and on the third a large animal, a 'lion', fighting a snake (**2**:60). This is a monumental use of an animal motif in a Christian context. Its Scandinavian flourishes cannot disguise that this is the 'combat motif' of ancient iconography (**2**:24). The lion can symbolise both Christ and the Devil in European Christian imagery, but the serpent or snake is always an evil symbol. In this context it may not be too fanciful to see this design as an image of a Christian victory over the evil pagans. The design is in a style with trailing fronds and scrolls which allows, for the first time in Scandinavian art, a role for plant-like motifs.

Plant-like motifs, in the form of tendrils and scrolls as well as acanthus leaves, continued to gain in importance in Viking art of the eleventh and twelfth centuries with increased influence from Christian art (**2**:61–63; **5**:11,12,35–37). In the course of the late eleventh century, Scandinavian art developed most of the ornamental features of the European Romanesque which gradually replaced the Scandinavian animals as Christianity took hold throughout the region.

2:59 The Vikings who settled in the Isle of Man in the Irish Sea in the ninth century soon started to raise carved stones decorated in the Scandinavian styles. The designs are taken from two stone crosses from Braddan, Isle of Man. Second half of the 10th cent. AD.

2:61   On an openwork gilt bronze weathervane is a version of the Jelling stone motif (**2**:60), although the great beast is ensnared not just by snakes but in a thicket of tendrils. Söderala, Hälsingland, Sweden. 11th cent. AD.

2:60   The design on one of the three sides of the Christian monument raised by King Harald at Jelling. It is likely that this imposing stone quite literally influenced other monuments both in Scandinavia and in Britain. Jelling, Jutland, Denmark. *c.*AD 965.

2:63   There is no doubt that this design was made in Ireland – it is carved on a bone, one of many 'motif-pieces' found in Viking Dublin. Such pieces were used by craftsmen to try out patterns. Early 11th cent. AD.

2:62   In a design on a gilt bronze panel from Winchester, the animal motif is no longer apparent beyond the spirals which originally marked the animal's hip and the suggestion of a head and eye about three quarters along from the left. This object could have been made either in Scandinavia or in England. Early 11th cent. AD.

The signs of the
zodiac, bestiaries, fables
and heraldry

Animal motifs used in ornament are rarely taken directly from nature. In the repertoire of the most common motifs, no difference is drawn between real and imaginary animals or between familiar native animals and those which live in other lands. Within the sphere of influence of Greek and Roman art, motifs from mythology, painted on walls and vases or laid in mosaic, provided animal images which were used decoratively (2:24–35). There were, however, other sources of animal motifs in conventionalised forms. The twelve signs of the zodiac are probably the oldest and among the most important of these. The astronomical observations on which this system is based were first carried out in Mesopotamia. Cuneiform documents concerning omens based on observations of the sky are known from the first half of the second millennium BC onwards, and the twelve names of the signs are listed in the order in which they are still known on a cuneiform tablet of about 500 BC.

The signs of the zodiac symbolise groups of stars which lie in the region of the ecliptic, or the band of sky through which the sun, moon and planets, appear to move. The constellations of stars are represented by twelve images which, with the exception of Libra, are all in animal or human form: Aries (the Ram), Taurus (the Bull), Gemini (the Twins), Leo (the Lion), Virgo (the Virgin), Libra (the Balance), Scorpio (the Scorpion), Saggitarius (the Archer), Capricorn (the Goat), Aquarius (the Water-bearer), Pisces (the Fish).

The zodiac, in the modern astrological sense, was defined in the fourth century BC when a catalogue of the stars was drawn up by Greek astronomers and the name 'zodiac' was first used. In c.270 BC, on the basis of this work, Aratos of Soli wrote *Phainomena*, a poetical description of the heavens. Other poets further elaborated the mythology of the constellations which were then also illustrated on globes. The form given to the constellations on the globes was transferred to books which combined astronomy and mythology, (known as *Aratea* after Aratos.) These books became popular, and their illustrations (with their long pedigree of classical motifs and styles) were widely copied. Their influence can be seen in the Middle Ages both in the art of Islam and of Christian Europe.

Since many of the animals of the zodiac are in any case popular motifs – lion, bull, and fish, for example – it is not always possible to establish in individual cases whether or not a design is a reference to a zodiac sign. In the case of creatures with goats' heads and fish tails (2:31), the association with emperor Augustus makes the attribution to Capricorn likely because he is known to have regarded this as his special sign. In other contexts a composite creature with a goat's head may not allow this interpretation. The signs of the zodiac are, however, still potent symbolic motifs; the importance of birth-signs is taken seriously by many people and the animals of the zodiac may be worn as helpful as well as decorative charms.

A different system evolved in China whereby twelve animals, mouse, ox, tiger, rabbit, dragon, snake, horse, goat, monkey, cockerel, dog and boar, combined with ten other elements in a sixty-year cycle. Within this cycle, each animal recurs every twelve years. Since the animal of the year in which a person is born is deemed important the twelve animals have become popular motifs in the art of China, as well as in Japan, where the same system applies.

Christianity became the sole official religion of the Roman Empire in AD 380 after a period during which it co-existed with other beliefs. Throughout most of the fourth century artists were working for patrons of many faiths and the existing conventions of Classical art were used to illustrate Christian as well as non-Christian themes. Christian symbols as, for example, the creatures described in Revelation (derived from Ezekiel) and later assigned to the four Apostles, therefore took the familiar contemporary forms. The Apostles were symbolised by the Eagle (St John), the Lion (St Mark), the Bull (St Luke) and Man (St Matthew). All were at times treated as composite creatures by the addition of wings.

The 'book of beasts' or bestiary was another most important source of animal motifs in Christian Medieval Europe. Its origins lay in the classical world in a collection of stories and descriptions of animals and birds, both real and imaginary. A text known as the *Physiologus* – the Naturalist or Natural Philosopher – was compiled from writings of authors such as Aristotle, Herodotus and Pliny in a Christian community in Alexandria in the second century AD, or soon after. This was a book with a philosophical and Christian doctrinal purpose. The compiler analysed the nature of animals in order to explain the ways of God, and described their habits in terms of their relevance to Christian thinking and morality. In the form of the *Bestiarium*, the illustrated Latin version of the *Physiologus*, enlarged and translated, sometimes in rhyme or verse, became a popular Christian picture book for secular use. The beasts and the stories influenced not only popular thought and literature but all the decorative arts.

It is not possible, nor appropriate, to look at all the many animal scenes which are found in the bestiaries; three animal motifs, which have already figured many times in these pages, will serve as examples of the importance of these illustrations for the development of animal motifs in European Christian decoration. The lion was given priority in the bestiaries, but it was not simply the majesty

2:64   The lion cowering in fear before the white cockerel. From an illustration in an English bestiary. *c.*AD 1230.

2:65   The great strength of the griffin is illustrated as it carries a horse in its claws. From an illustration in an English bestiary. *c.*AD 1230–1240.

or power which were its principal characteristics. Three other attributes were assigned to it, each explained as an allegory. First, if the lion catches the scent of hunters, he wipes away his track with his tail. In the same way, Christ, the spiritual lion, covered his tracks against the Devil. Second, the lion sleeps with his eyes open. Similarly when Christ's body was put to sleep on the cross, his divine nature remained vigilant. Third, the lioness gives birth to dead cubs, but she guards them for three days until their father comes to breathe in their faces and bring them to life. This was interpreted as Christ's restoration to life after three days by the breath of God the Father. Other minor attributes of the lion were also illustrated in bestiaries, examples of courage and compassion and even the objects of its fears – fire, the sound of creaking wheels and of only one other creature, the white cockerel (**2**:64).

The griffin, half lion, half eagle was described as 'awesome' and variously symbolised power, strength, magnanimity and knowledge. But it had no moral significance. Its great strength is often illustrated as it carries off a horse or other prey to its nest (**2**:65). The main story attached to the eagle concerns the failing eyesight and strength of the aging eagle who can no longer see a fish from a great height. The eagle flies towards the sun, where the heat burns the mist from his eyes; he then dives into a spring to regain his strength and sharpens his worn beak on a rock. The story sumbolizes spiritual renewal. A curious sub-plot involves an eaglet whose eyes are put to the test by unblinkingly staring into the sun. If the test fails, he is rejected (**2**:66). (On the phoenix see p.87ff).

Animal fables in illustrated editions also greatly influenced decoration of all kinds in medieval Europe. Some motifs taken from Aesop's fables are, for example, shown in the border of the Bayeux tapestry, demonstrating that the stories were well enough known for an illustration to be instantly recognisable by the eleventh

2:66 A young eagle is thrown from the nest as it fails the test of staring into the sun without blinking. From an illustration in an English bestiary. *c.*AD 1230.

2:67 An embroidered motif in the border of the Bayeux Tapestry has been identified as the story from Aesop's fables which tells of the Fox, who wants a piece of cheese held in the beak of a Crow. Praising her beauty he suggests that if her voice were as sweet as her looks were fair, she would be Queen of the Birds. When the flattered Crow opens her beak to give a loud caw, the piece of cheese falls to the Fox below. *c.*AD 1070.

century (2:67).

The use of emblems to establish ownership and indicate family or other affiliations occurs in many societies. Heraldry in medieval Europe arose not only in response to the specific needs of a feudal society where family relationships were of paramount importance, but also to the urgent needs of easy identification of participants in the complex ritual and fashion of tournaments. Many of the motifs used for arms and badges are beasts, apparently taken from bestiaries which reached a peak of popularity in the late twelfth and early thirteenth centuries and which clearly had a considerable influence on the heraldic imagination. These motifs were, however, strictly disciplined and made to conform to rigid rules. In this form they will not be described here. Heraldic devices, in their turn, influenced pure decoration (2:68).

Ceramic, usually glazed, floor-tiles became a general feature of Gothic building from the late twelfth century onwards. Their designs are representative of the fashionable motifs and styles of the period and include foliage, geometrical patterns, scenes from popular romances, animals of the hunt and animals in heraldic postures. They are a suitable class of objects to illustrate the further fortunes of the three animal motifs, the lion, griffin and eagle. An important and popular series of motifs used in this medium included designs with names and heraldic devices which became a part of the general stock of patterns and were much used in various non-heraldic contexts (2:69–70). The spread of these motifs was not much affected by the growing power of the heralds in the Middle Ages as they had by this time departed from their original strictly heraldic form.

The eagle, like the lion, has an obvious symbolic appeal, and predatory birds were important motifs in the ancient world (2:15,19). The Roman legions carried the eagle as a special emblem and the eagle motif figures prominently in the art of the

2:68 Painted in gold lustre, mock-heraldic animals decorate the underside of tin-glazed earthenware dishes from Valencia, Spain. Mid-15th cent.

2:70 Double-headed eagle on an earthenware floor tile. White slip was applied to the red clay tile; when covered with a lead glaze, the design stood out in yellow against a dark brown or green ground. Hailes Abbey, Gloucestershire, England. *c*.1525–40.

2:69 Patterned floor tiles were an important architectural feature of buildings in the 13th–16th cent. in England. Heraldic devices were among many motifs in general use, as were animals of the hunt. 13th cent.

IONICA   IIII

Folio.   *15.*

Zu lehrnen, wie man bhend in gmein,
Das klein in groß, das groß in klein,
Kan reißen nach dem augenmäß,
Wie die figur anzeiget das.

Germanic peoples (2:40,46). Charlemagne adopted it as a symbol of his Christian empire in AD 800. With the use of the double-headed eagle as a heraldic symbol of the Holy Roman Empire the eagle became popular in all kinds of decorative art in Central Europe. The imperial double-headed eagle appeared on coinage, on city coats of arms and on guild insignia. Guild craftsmen carved eagles on chair backs, cast them in iron on stoves and kitchen utensils and painted them on pottery. The eagle became a most popular motif in European folk art (2:71).

2:71 Decorative designs on a page of a pattern book from 1611 include a double-headed eagle. Half the design is shown, together with a simple method for enlarging or reducing. (From Gabriel Kramer, *Schweiff-Büchlein*.)

The taotie *mask and the dragon-like* kui *motifs in Bronze Age China*

Neolithic cultures in China from *c*.7000 BC have their own particular characteristics but, as was the case elsewhere, the neolithic settlements centred on the rich river valleys. More complex societies, however, evolved rather later in the east than in, for example Egypt and Mesopotamia. The central plain of the Yellow River valley, however, sustained neolithic farming communities of increasing complexity throughout the first half of the second millennium BC, leading to the emergence in *c*.1500 BC of the Shang dynasty, the first Bronze Age civilization in China. Rich in material culture, wheel-made pottery, developed architecture and sophisticated craftsmanship, and skilled in writing, the Shang culture presupposes a long period of development. There is, however, at present considerable uncertainty about the background to the rise of this civilisation. Remains of cities and luxury artefacts recovered from rich burials bear witness to a society ruled by powerful kings, supported by a successful army and an educated group of divines. Here began a tradition of fine bronze casting which continued through the dynasties of Shang and Zhou and lasted until the beginning of the Han dynasty in the third century BC.

While bronze weapons would have been essential to military success, the ritual vessels appear to have played an equally important role in the survival of the state. The vessels were used in ritual sacrifices of food and wine to ancestors. They were produced in sets of different and distinctive shapes, and late Shang examples carry inscriptions which identify their owners. A few provide other information which makes them important as historical records and helps to place them in chronological sequence. The inscriptions do not, however, provide any clues to the meaning of the the real or imaginary creatures with which they are lavishly decorated. Because of the ritual nature of the vessels, it has been assumed that the ornaments had some specific significance. The principal motifs, the monster mask of the *taotie* and the associated dragon-like *kui* motif, have been the subject of much speculation (2:12,73–75). Simple masks on jade objects dating back to the Neolithic period suggest beliefs in spirits inhabiting animal forms, perhaps in a context of shamanistic ritual (2:72). Whether or not such beliefs also influenced the sophisticated decoration on the ritual bronze vessels cannot be established.

The name *taotie*, meaning 'the glutton', was attached to this popular motif in the third century BC; a story accompanied the name. It tells of a monster which, trying to swallow a man and not succeeding, was left with only a head and no body. The moral to the story was a reminder that all excess brings retribution. On the ritual bronzes of the second millennium BC the motif appears more sinister than this slight moral tale suggests (2:74). One can only speculate that this art, created by requirements of ritual and sacrifice, at least initially symbolised spiritual forces. In later developments matters of taste and fashion perhaps took precedence over such considerations.

The bronze ritual vessels were cast by the piece mould technique; masks with eyes, nose, ears and horns are arranged about a vertical line at the centre of each mould section. The *taotie* mask is expressed in its most basic form as a pair of eyes on either side of a vertical line, with scrolls suggesting the rest of the face and extending laterally into a meaningless pattern (2:73). In a further development, areas behind the masks are filled with scrolls (2:12,74). This form of background pattern of tightly wound,

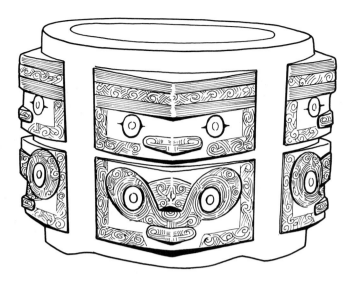

2:72   Ritual object carved in jade with incised decoration of masks and scrolls. Sidun, Wujin, Jiangsu province, China. *c*.2000 BC.

2:73   Early example of the *taotie* mask: the eyes are surrounded by scrolls which complete the mask and make abstract patterns on either side. Detail from a bronze vessel, Panlongchen, Hubei province, China. Shang dynasty, mid-2nd millennium BC.

2:74   *Taotie* masks against a background of *lei-wen* spiral pattern from bronze vesels of the Shang dynasty. China 12th–11th cent. BC.

more or less angular, spirals is known as *lei-wen* ('thunder pattern') so named from the resemblance of the figure to the corresponding Shang ideograph. Scrolls also decorate the mask and body parts (2:75).

Taotie masks are sometimes separated by a median line to produce the effect of two animals nose to nose (2:12,74). This form of the motif is known as the *kui* dragon (not to be confused with the *long*, the true Chinese dragon motif (2:88–91). The single *kui* dragons also developed around 'eyes' to fill subordinate borders. The ambiguity created by the uncertainty as to whether the mask divides to become two animals or whether two animals combine to become one has produced arguments associated with the possible meaning of this feature. William Watson (1974 p.29) addresses the question thus:

Whichever of these two explanations is correct, no symbolic meaning can be read into the process. On the other hand, two important principles of design are involved. It is impossible to see the *taotie* simultaneously as a single mask and as two dragons nose to nose. An awareness of the two possible readings of the shapes disturbs the viewer as soon as they are pointed out to him …

This device is not unique to the Chinese *taotie* mask, it occurs in other contexts where it invariably has the same unsettling effect on the viewer (p.13 and 2:41,97,100,101). In another form of the motif, the mask disintegrates with its constituent parts scattered over a larger field against a background of *lei-wen* or other scrolling patterns (2:75).

The Zhou defeated the Shang in battle *c*.1050 BC and remained in power until 770 BC. In the art of the Zhou diverse styles from various parts of China were assimilated to form new styles in which, however, many of the motifs from Shang art survived. The *taotie*, *kui* and other animal motifs became increasingly abstract. In some designs, interlacing area-filling patterns suggest limbs and masks (2:76). Some motifs and designs in the art of the Shang and Zhou dynasties have been compared to similar motifs in the animal art of the nomads who inhabited the vast steppes of central Asia (**2**:80,82). The question of the extent of external influences on the art of China is, however, subject to great and unresolved controversy. While clearly distinct and independently developed, the animal ornament of the steppes and that of the Chinese Bronze Age dynasties may have arrived at sufficiently similar forms to allow the easy assimilation of motifs from one style to another.

2:75 Detail from a bronze vessel with a design of scattered parts of the *taotie* and *kui* dragon motifs against a background of *lei-wen* spiral designs. Shang dynasty, China 12th–11th cent. BC.

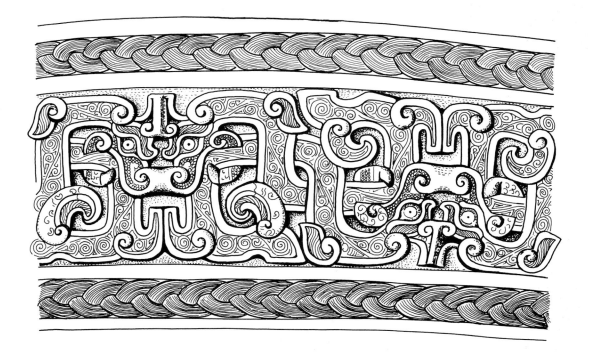

2:76 Masks facing in opposite directions in regular sequence, are linked by interlace which superficially suggests limbs. Above and below are borders representing plaited cord. Border from a bronze bowl. Shanxi province, Eastern Zhou, China. Early 5th cent. BC.

The 'animal style' in the art of the nomadic cattle herders on the Eurasian steppes

In the second and first millennia BC groups of nomads lived by hunting and herding on the grasslands which occupy a vast zone from the Crimea in southern Russia across central Asia to Gansu province in China. Warlike people, frequently attacking (and sometimes conquering) their settled and civilised neighbours, they raided and disrupted the important trade-routes to the south of their large territory and powerfully influenced the course of events in Asia and Europe. No written accounts of the nomads' exploits survive, but their activities brought some groups within the range of recorded history. In writing of the kingdom of the Medes, for instance, Herodotus describes the nomadic Scythians, who held political power in western Iran sometime between 653–625 BC. The names and destiny of other, perhaps equally powerful, groups are, however, lost.

The nomads buried their chieftains with their treasures under imposing barrows. Archaeological evidence, in the absence of written records, gives some indication of their material culture. Exceptional finds from the High Altai mountains in southern Siberia provide rare insights into their art through the wealth of organic material – wood, leather and textiles – which otherwise has perished in the ground. This organic material, found in graves of chieftains and warlords, was preserved in this area because the contents of graves were accidentally sealed in a permanently frozen state beneath cairns of stone. The graves were richly furnished with food and drink, horse trappings of carved wood and leather, together with textiles – wool, silk, and felt. The people of the

2:77 A lotus and palmette motif decorates a bone plaque from a bridle in the burial in Pazyryk. Eastern Altai, Siberia. 5th cent. BC.

2:78 Open-work leather cut-out of two cocks which formed part of the decoration on a coffin in a burial at Pazyryk, Eastern Altai, Siberia. 5th cent. BC.

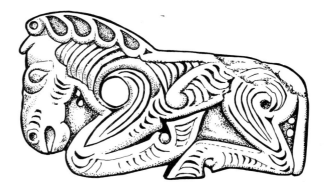

2:79 Reclining horse carved in bone. The incised ornament, which emphasizes its muscular body, was probably filled with a coloured material. From a burial at Tuva, Siberia. 5th–3rd cent. BC.

Altai decorated everything they used, clothes, utensils, weapons, bridles, saddles, and furniture, even themselves – the skin of one embalmed chieftain showed that he had been tattooed over a large part of his body.

The art was decorative and colourful. Some designs and motifs demonstrate that the nomads of the steppes were in close contact with the civilised world of their day. Lotus and palmette motifs, common in Mediterranean art, played a part in the rich medley of decorative motifs in their repertoire (**2**:77), and imported textiles from the Middle East were indeed found in these burials.

Ornament based on animal motifs, however, dominates the art of the nomadic peoples. Known as the 'animal style' it represents a surprisingly uniform group of motifs used by nomads from about the eighth century BC. Horses, predators, elks, stags and mountain goats figure prominently, but composite creatures made up of parts of different animals are equally important. All animals were subject to stylisation and distortion to achieve highly decorative results; a blend of fantasy and closely observed realism. Spirals and scrolls contribute greatly to the style, to the flowing outlines of the designs and to the treatment of surfaces, often emphasizing the shoulders and hips of animals with spirals (**2**:78,79 p.27).

Some forms remain in use over long periods. One of the earliest of these is a coiled, stylised predatory animal making up a circular design (**2**:80). Examples of this motif in very similar form are known from a wide range of dates; the plaques illustrated date from the eighth and the fourth to third centuries BC respectively. Another popular motif shows a reclining stag with exaggerated antlers. The consistency of this motif is illustrated by two examples, one from the Caucasus of the early sixth century BC, the other from Hungary some two hundred years later (**2**:81).

A goat-like creature has the tail and horns in the form of birds' heads, which in turn have big ears (**2**:82).

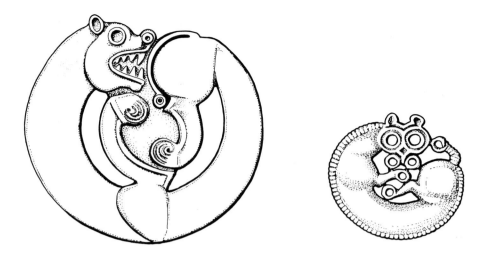

2:80 A coiled predatory animal, identified as a panther, remained a motif in the animal style for several hundred years. *Left* Bronze plaque from a horse harness from a burial at Tuva, Siberia. 8th cent. BC. *Right* A small gold plaque shows the motif in the Ordos style of Northern China. 4th–3rd cent. BC.

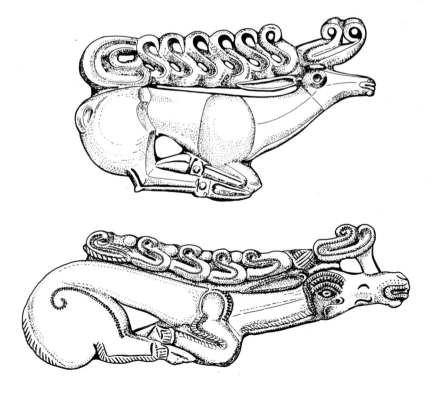

2:81 The stance of the reclining stag has been interpreted as an animal poised for a jump. *Above* Gold plaque of unknown use from a burial in north Caucasus. Early 6th cent. BC. *Below* The same motif occurs on a shield ornament in electrum from Hungary. 4th cent. BC.

2:82 *Right* The goat-like composite creature is part of a design tattooed on the arm of the embalmed chieftain in a burial at Pazyryk, Eastern Altai, Siberia. 5th cent. BC. *Left* In gold, this imposing creature from Shaanxi province in northern China demonstrates the widespread use of this motif. 4th–3rd cent. BC.

2:83 Design in coloured felt applied to a red saddle cloth shows a mountain goat attacked by a griffin-like composite creature. Pazyryk, Eastern Altai, Siberia. 5th cent. BC.

Many designs feature two animals in combat (**2**:83,84). Composite creatures generally include elements of predatory birds (**2**:85). Designs in the 'animal style' often feature a distortion of an animal's hind quarters; they are, as it were, twisted round (**2**:82 *right*, 83,84). There has been much fruitless speculation concerning the reasons for this distortion – for example, that it indicates violent motion. It would, however, seem simply to be a successful decorative device, allowing a figure to be fitted into a compact space.

The Altai burials give a particular insight into the nomads' appearance and accoutrements: bridles decorated with brightly painted, fantastic animals carved in wood, sometimes three-dimensional with leather ears and antlers; saddle-cloths in felt with designs in appliqué; glittering bronze or gold plaques stitched to garments and trappings, all illustrate their love of colour. The wide distribution of the style and its motifs suggests that it was not a jealously guarded individual art of specific tribes or groups, rather that it was held in common by those who shared the nomadic lifestyle. It was an art which made an impression on the people who were harried and conquered by the nomads. And at the same time it played a part in the exchange of ideas across the Eurasian land-mass.

2:84 On a gold belt buckle from Siberia, a horse is attacked by a composite creature; both have distorted hind quarters. This design perhaps illustrates the decorative convenience of the device. Siberia 4th–3rd cent. BC.

2:85 The creatures on a horse harness frontal, carved in wood and originally brightly painted, are predatory birds with antlers, ears and mane. From a burial at Tuekta, Central Altai, Siberia. 6th cent. BC.

The Chinese dragon, 'phoenix' and Dog of Fo

After the unification of China in the third century BC, there was a change towards realism in painting in the art of the Han dynasty. The expansion of the Empire westwards to the borders of Persia in the late second and early first centuries BC brought the art of that region to the attention of high society in China and further encouraged the trend towards realism. Philosophical systems associated in particular with Confucian ideology came to dominate not only government, but all life in Imperial China.

Associated with these beliefs were symbolic animal motifs often based on concepts with a long history in China. Adapted to serve new purposes, they became powerful motifs of great status and importance. Four animals represented the cardinal points of the compass: the Green Dragon of the East, the White Tiger of the West, the Red bird of the South and the Black Warrior of the North (a tortoise entwined with a snake) (**2:86**).

Another constellation of symbols were set out by the philosophical school known as *yin yang wu xing*. *Yin* and *yang* were regarded as the principal forces in the universe; *yin* being associated with the moon (darkness, water, and the feminine principle), while *yang* was linked with the sun (light and the masculine principle). Harmony was achieved when *yin* and *yang* were in balance (**2:87**). *Wu xing* refers to the five elements – earth, wood, metal, fire and water. Colours were assigned to these elements – yellow, green, white, red and black. These concepts – elements, colours and beasts – became symbolic systems from which, for example, a dynasty adopted as its special characteristic an

2:86   The Red Bird of the South, the Green Dragon of the East, The White Tiger of the West, and the Black Warrior of the North. Carved decorations in cave tombs in western China. AD 221.

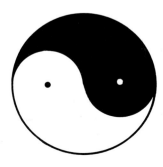

2:87   The perfect harmony between *yin* and *yang* is expressed in the *taiji* figure where two asymmetrical but identical halves form a circle.

element with its attendant colour and animal.

The dragon has a long history in China. In its earliest form, it is a curled-up creature with a pig-like face (**2**:88). Later its body becomes longer and the large head develops blunt horns (**2**:89). These features are reproduced in the character *long*, the Chinese word for dragon. This creature is distinct from the dragon-like *kui* motif on the ritual bronze vessels of the Shang dynasty (p.81ff.). The dragon developed into an increasingly composite creature with legs and wings, while the horns became crests and plumes (**2**:86,90,91).

Animal designs, combined with flower scrolls, developed following the introduction of Buddhism in China in the early centuries AD, and were initially associated with architecture and used to decorate palaces and tombs (see p.149ff.). The use of symbolic animal motifs to decorate metal and ceramic vessels for domestic use was only introduced in the Tang dynasty (618–902 AD). By this time the Tiger of the West – which often took a form similar to the dragon (**2**:86) – and the Black Warrior of the North had become less important. Additional symbolic significance, however, now attached to the dragon, indeed it may have symbolised the Emperor himself. Together with the Bird of the South, the dragon occurs as an important motif on buildings and furnishings, as well as on the silks in which the Emperor and his high officials were dressed.

The Bird of the South, the *zhu niao*, and a similar mythical bird in the Chinese repertoire, the *fenghuang*, are known in the West as *phoenixes*. This is something of a misnomer; in Greek mythology, the phoenix was a mythical bird from India, which lived for many hundreds of years, finally burning itself to death in Egypt and rising from its ashes. In the bestiaries the phoenix is a symbol of immortality and the resurrection of Christ (p.76f.). The name 'phoenix' was applied to the bird motif on imported Chinese porcelain. The Red Bird of the

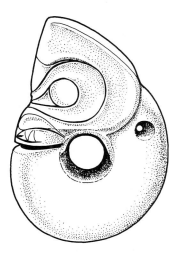

2:88 The earliest kind of dragon has been named the 'pig-dragon'. Carved in jade, it comes from Liaoning in north-east China. 3500–2500 BC.

2:89 A small jade figure showing the characteristic features of the early Chinese dragon. Anyang, Henan Province. Shang dynasty, c.1300–1030 BC.

2:90 Dragon, impressed on a brick from the Maoling tomb of the Emperor Wudi, in a characteristic pose with its head turned back. China, Han dynasty, 1st cent. BC. (Drawing from a rubbing.)

2:91 The fully developed Chinese dragon, painted on porcelain in blue and white. The dragon is set among cloud pattern scrolls. Yan Dynasty, China. 14th cent. AD.

2:92 Two birds, impressed on a brick from the Maoling tomb of the Emperor Wudi, have the long, flowing crest and tail typical of the mythical bird of the South. Han dynasty, China. 1st cent. BC. (Drawing from a rubbing.)

2:93 Detail from a decorated stone slab. Mythical, deer-like creatures are set against a thicket of what is known as 'magical fungus', a variant of the traditional filling patterns based on spirals and scrolls. Dadu, Peking, Yuan dynasty, AD 1280–1368.

2:94 Drawing of a lion, found in a Buddhist cave temple at Dunhuang, Gansu province in China. It is an exuberant, but not a frightening animal. Tang dynasty, late 9th cent. AD.

South and the *fenghuang* were, however, composite creatures made up of parts which could represent several bird species; characteristic features are lavish plumage and long tails (**2**:86,92). As a popular motif in porcelain and lacquer decoration, silk brocades and embroidery, birds take on many forms, always fantastic, sometimes suggesting one species of bird, sometimes another (**0**:7).

The art of the Sassanian empire, which was from the third to the seventh centuries AD a leading world power, is a strong influence in some of these designs. At its greatest extent this empire stretched from Syria to northern India and its influence was felt far beyond these political boundaries. This was a period of high culture and artistic achievement, particularly in the art of the silversmith and the silk weaver (**0**:8–10). Sassanian silverware, being highly prized as gifts and luxury items, was widely distributed outside the Sassanian empire. Chinese cloud and mushroom patterns (**2**:91,93), however, were derived not from the Sassanians but from the indigenous *lei-wen* filling patterns which accompanied animal motifs in the art of the Shang and Zhou dynasties (**2**:72–76).

The lion was associated with Buddhism in India and was regarded as a representative of the Buddha and the Law. Together with other motifs associated with the faith, the lion was introduced into Chinese art. Live lions were not known in China and as a decorative motif it became ever more fantastic. Whilst lions were treated with due respect in funeral monuments, they became extravagant and playful in other contexts (**2**:94). A creature, half dog, half lion is known as the Dog of Fo (Fo is another name for the Buddha). It is claimed that the Pekinese dog was bred to look like these fantasy creatures – a case of nature imitating art (**2**:95).

The influence of Chinese motifs on the decorative art of Europe was profound. The land route between China and Europe (named the silk route after its most spectacular and valuable

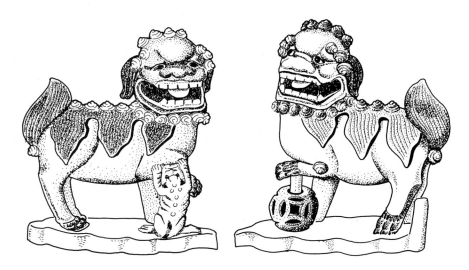

2:95 Pair of painted porcelain lions or Fo dogs. A cub bites the female's leg while the male plays with a ball. Jingdezhen, China. AD 1662–1722.

products – Chinese brocades and silk embroideries) spread Chinese goods and motifs westwards. The dragon and the fantastic birds were prominent among the motifs which, for example, became assimilated into the work of Italian silk weavers in the mid-fourteenth century. With the establishment of a sea route in the fifteenth century, Chinese porcelain (of a quality unparalleled in Europe) and fine laquer – hitherto virtually unknown in the west – were imported and greatly influenced fashion and art. In the second half of the seventeenth century, and in the eighteenth century, this influence culminated in European *chinoiserie* in architecture, furnishing, art and crafts. Chinese motifs in Europe were considerably modified and changed, reflecting notions of the Far East current at the time. In China itself, designs were produced for export in response to European preferences. The bird, for example, went through many changes; sometimes known as the *ho ho bird*, it is described as having 'a long beak, crest, claws, flowing tail and curving neck … often rendered as an amalgam of pheasant, phoenix, bird of paradise, stork and heron' (Lewis and Darley p.160). Although the fashion for *chinoiserie* is long past, many designs based on Chinese motifs are still an integral part of the

decorative vocabulary of the western world.

Chinese expansion and influence was also directed southwards. Indonesia lay in the path of repeated migrations of people who from the earliest times moved south and west out of Asia. The heritage of this chequered history is clearly visible in the lively art of the different groups of people who now inhabit the area. In Borneo, for example, a dragon, together with other Chinese motifs, had already arrived in the first millennium BC. A female creature, it represents the underworld and fertility, and is portrayed locally in different ways, but all tend to have spiralling horns, claws and tails (**2**:96–8). This is not altogether a Chinese animal any more; the local giant lizard, the monitor or 'Komodo dragon' has made its mark somewhere along the way and can sometimes be recognised in the stance of the tiny front legs (**2**:98). Independent elaboration as well has led to the same results as elsewhere in fantastic animal ornament – an emphasis on eyes in many designs, creates a mask, produced from two animals in profile, and the spiralling tails of two opposed dragons penetrate each others' bodies, in much the same way as do the animals in Germanic ornament in a different time and place (**2**:41, **2**:55).

2:96   Dragon design, known as *aso* (dog).
Sarawak, Borneo. 19th cent.

2:97   Painted in black and red on the
wooden boards of a contemporary
meeting hall are designs of dragons. An
emphasis on the eyes is expressed by
various means and the mask made up of
the animals in profile is particularly
powerful. Upper Mahakam, Kalimantan,
Borneo.

2:98   On the boards of a house, two
dragons are interlacing, each penetrating
the other's body with their tails. One
dragon is blue, the other green. Sarawak,
Borneo. Late 19th cent.

The animal art of the 'Chilkat dancing blanket'

In North America, in a narrow strip of land along the Pacific Ocean on the north-west coast, reaching from Yakutat Bay in Alaska to Washington State, native Americans created a style of ornament of great complexity. In this isolated and well-favoured environment was developed a highly structured and organised society in which art played an important part. The social system, based on clans and the importance of family lineages, was expressed in the use of animal crests which form the main motifs in the art.

Apart from brief visits by Russian and Spanish explorers, the first Europeans to examine this region were led by Captain James Cook in 1778. His expedition brought back a collection of artefacts. These, together with other objects collected later in the eighteenth and nineteenth centuries, show that the art was fully developed when Cook arrived.

Certain basic principles of animal representation can be distinguished. The outline of the animal is recognisable, but internal vital organs are also shown (2:99). (This is known as the x-ray style of representation and is not unique to native American art. It is, for example, a feature of the early Neolithic period in Anatolia of the sixth millennium BC (2:2) and of Scandinavian Stone Age rock carvings. It is practised today by some aboriginal peoples in Arnhem Land, Australia.) In other designs, the anatomical relationship between body parts is to some extent retained, but detached parts may be inserted to fill a space. The design on one tunic illustrates some of the complexities involved (2:100). The bear, which is the main motif, has a body in the form of a ceremonial shield made of sheet copper.

2:99 *Above* The Eagle crest, painted in black and red on a wooden drum. Haida. 19th cent. *Below* The Killer Whale crest in appliqué and pearl buttons on a 20th-century blanket. Both animals feature internal organs. North-west Coast, North America.

2:100 The family crest which forms the basis for this design, painted in red and black on a ceremonial skin tunic, is the Bear. It makes up the main outline and is repeated in the centre as the design on a copper shield. This relationship is illustrated in the details below. Tlingit, North-west Coast, North America. *c.*1890.

Such shields were decorated with a painted or etched design of the owner's crest, in this case the Bear. The design emphasizes the division into two symmetrical halves, but the ambivalence between the interpretation of the design as two confronted halves or as one splayed frontal view is incapable of resolution (pp. 13,54ff.).

One of the results of Captain Cook's visit to the area was the rapid development of an extensive fur trade which brought the area into contact with the outside world. The decorated objects produced there became desirable collector's items. Among the objects collected by Captain Cook in 1778 are cloaks of cedar bark fibre in twined weaving. Soon a more elaborate cloak, known as the 'Chilkat dancing blanket' was produced in a technique of tapestry twining, closely related to basketry techniques (2:101). In these designs, the fragmentation of the animal bodies is extreme, the ambiguous faces have almost lost their power to disturb in the welter of detail. It is only the strict symmetry which prevents a descent into total chaos.

After a period of decline, native American artists have emerged who produce a new art on the foundation of the old. A blanket design by Shona Hah of the Lelooska family in 1974 combines the traditional animal art with a classical running spiral border (2:99 below).

2:101   The 'Chilkat Dancing Blanket' is a cloak with a deep fringe. The symmetrical design is here based on the Eagle crest, but the dominant impression of the design is of staring eyes. North-west Coast, North America. 19th cent.

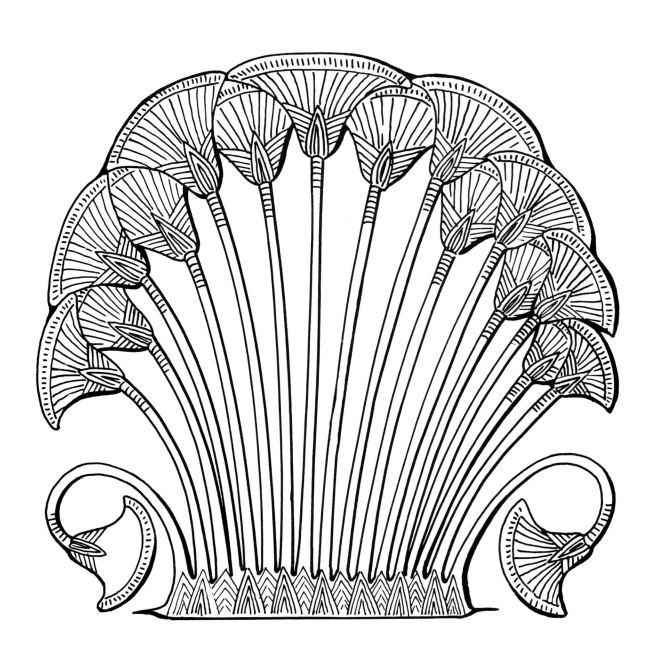

3

Three motifs from ancient Egypt: the lotus, the papyrus and the lily

Highly stylised plant and plant-like motifs are common in painted scenes in the tombs and temples of ancient Egypt. These motifs also decorate objects of both ritual and daily use.

The lotus and the papyrus motifs had already developed their highly conventionalised forms in the third millennium BC, forms which remained largely unaltered throughout the Dynastic period which lasted from c.3000 to 343 BC. The motifs were, however, clearly based on plants which played an important role in the community. Illustrations on the walls of tombs suggest that lotus flowers were much in evidence in daily life in ancient Egypt; they are displayed among animals, fruit and household goods, draped over piles of offerings and tied in garlands (3:1,10). The papyrus grew wild in dense groves and was also extensively cultivated. Every part of the plant was used: the root and stem base were eaten; the stems, tied in bundles, were made into rafts and boats and were used in house construction. The rind of the stem was turned into fibres from which baskets, mats and ropes were woven. The writing material which bears its name was made from layers of the pith cut in thin strips (3:2,13–15).

Dynastic Egypt was divided into two major regions. The hieroglyphic sign for the North or Lower Egypt was in the form of a stylised papyrus plant while the sign for the South or Upper Egypt was the lily. The lily motif was probably not based on an actual plant and it is better described as a pseudo-flower or flower-like motif (3:3,16–19).

The lotus, papyrus and lily motifs spread to Western Asia and the Aegean where they were transformed into some of the most versatile decorative motifs in world art. The lotus motif kept its form relatively unaltered, especially in the form of the lotus-and-bud border, while the papyrus and lily motifs were two of several elements which contributed to the development of the important palmette motif with its far-reaching applications in many areas of decorative art. The lotus and the palmette became major motifs in the repertoire of decorative devices in Greek art and architecture (3:23–28; 4:10). Subsequently the lotus element in these motifs became less clearly defined as palmette-like forms dominate later designs.

Knowledge of Egyptian art in post-Roman Europe was very limited. Some Egyptian motifs were incorporated in Roman art, and the sphinx appeared in the bestiary compiled in the second century AD (2:30, 5:34) and reappeared from time to time thereafter. It was the beginning of an antiquarian interest in Egypt from the middle of the eighteenth century,

3:1 Produce presented as offerings on a wall-painting in a tomb at Thebes. Bundles of lotus blossom are draped over baskets and boxes. Egypt. *c.* 1425–1417 BC.

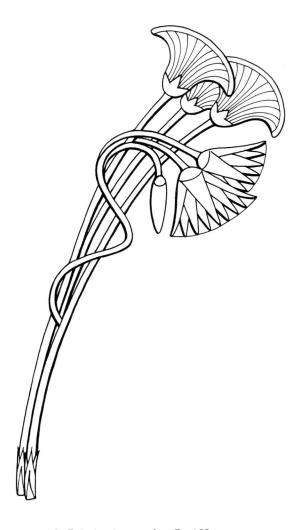

3:2 Painting in a tomb at Beni Hasan demonstrates the difference between the papyrus motif – the three umbels on straight stems with leaf-sheaths at the base – and the lotus motif represented by two blossoms and a bud on curving stems. Egypt. *c.*1971–1928 BC.

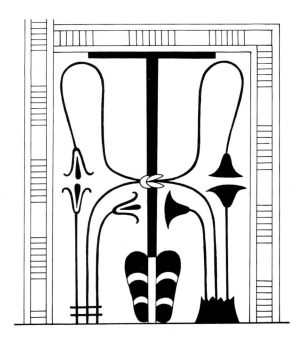

3:3 The symbol of the unification of Upper and Lower Egypt is represented on the side of a statue of Amenophis III. On the left is the lily of Upper Egypt, on the right the papyrus of Lower Egypt. The sign which stands between the heraldic plants is the lung-and-trachea which means 'to unite'. Egypt. *c.*1400 BC.

3:4 On a medal which commemorates the conquest of Egypt in 1798, Napoleon wears a wreath of lotus flowers instead of the more usual laurel wreath for victory. As a result of his campaign – and increasing antiquarian interest – motifs from ancient Egypt became fashionable in Europe. Paris 1808.

3:5 Detail of the links from a gold necklace, made in Paris by F. Boucheron c.1880. The design is an adaptation of the Egyptian lotus bloom and bud. Such designs were available in pattern books.

and publications of its antiquities, which introduced the motifs and styles of ancient Egypt to a European public. In the aftermath of Napoleon's Egyptian campaign of 1798, objects from ancient Egypt were brought back and exhibited in Paris and elsewhere, contributing to the Egyptian fashion in motifs and decoration of the Directoire and Empire styles of furniture and furnishings. In these designs it is the more exotic motifs such as pyramids, sphinxes, obelisks and scarabs which provide an Egyptian flavour; the supporting ornaments are, however, usually the ubiquitous palmette and acanthus scrolls rather than the stiff Egyptian lotus borders (**4:11**). Napoleon, however, is wearing a wreath of lotus flowers on a medal, one of a series of a hundred and four struck to commemorate the Egyptian campaign, all of which bear Egyptian motifs (**3:4**). In a period of renewed interest, lotus flowers and buds are links in a fringe necklace of gold made by F. Boucheron in Paris c.1880. In France, designs like these were taken from pattern books illustrating designs adapted from archaeological objects rather than from the objects themselves (**3:5**). In England, however, objects in the British Museum were copied. Josiah Wedgwood regarded Egyptian motifs as especially suitable for use on the black 'basalt' ware he developed as early as 1767. The British victory at the Battle of the Nile in 1798 and the subsequent import of Egyptian antiquities to England gave a further impetus to the Egyptian fashion in furniture and architecture; one that was still much in evidence at the Great Exhibition in London in 1851. The discovery of Tutankhamun's tomb in 1922 set off another surge of Egyptian-inspired designs, not only in jewellery, but also in architecture. Many cinemas bear witness to this exotic style.

Such antiquarian interest in Egypt was strong elsewhere in Europe. In Denmark, for example, a revival of Egyptian motifs reveals a different approach. When the Ny Carlsberg Glyptotek in Copenhagen was extended in 1901–6 to house collections of Egyptian and Classical antiquities, the architect, Hack Kampmann, extended the academic eclecticism of the original building and completed it in a style which represented the new individualism and national romanticism of the early twentieth century. The mosaic floors of the new galleries were decorated with motifs taken from the antiquities to be displayed there. While the designs reveal Kampmann's personal respect for the ancient arts, they are, at the same time, executed in the free style of Art Nouveau draughtsmanship, as demonstrated by a comparison between his design and a similar composition on a painted tomb ceiling from Egypt (**3:6**).

3:6 *Left* The design of papyrus in the art nouveau style, laid in mosaics on the floor of the Egyptian sculpture gallery in the Ny Carlsberg Glyptotek in Copenhagen in the early 20th century can be compared with, *right*, a painted ceiling design from Medinet Habu, Egypt. *c.*1198–1166 BC.

The Egyptian lotus motif

The Greek word *lotus* has been applied to a variety of different plants. The 'lotus-eaters' of the Odyssey were probably eating bread made from the fruit of the jujube tree (*Zizuphus lotus*) and drinking its fermented juice. In Britain the genus *lotus* is represented by the birds-foot trefoil (*Lotus corniculatus*).

Two major decorative motifs, both known as lotus motifs, are based on types of water-lilies but are otherwise quite distinct. One originated in Egypt, the other in India in association with the rise of Buddhism in the sixth century BC (chapter 6 *The Indian Lotus*). The Egyptian lotus motif took two highly stylised forms. One was based on the white-flowered *Nymphaea lotus* distinguished by a slightly curved outline of the open flower-head, rounded petals and ribbed calyx leaves; the edge of the round leaf is scalloped (**3:7**). In its conventional form it is often only the slightly curved outline of the flower-head which distinguishes this motif from that based on the blue lotus. Other features, like the striped calyx leaves, are not always represented. The blue-flowered *Nymphaea caerulea* has pointed, spotted calyx leaves and narrow, pointed petals; the round leaf has a smooth edge (**3:8**). The conventional form shows the triangular outline of the open flower-head with an arrangement of thin petals between three calyx leaves; there is usually a bud on either side of the flower (**3:9**).

Lotus petals by themselves also became a decorative motif, used particularly in representations of floral decorations and garlands. Elaborate garlands of lotus flowers, petals and other plants and fruit were

3:7 The white lotus, *Nymphaea lotus* L.
(Drawing by Marjorie Blamey.)

3:8 The blue lotus, *Nymphaea caerulea* Sav.
(Drawing by Marjorie Blamey.)

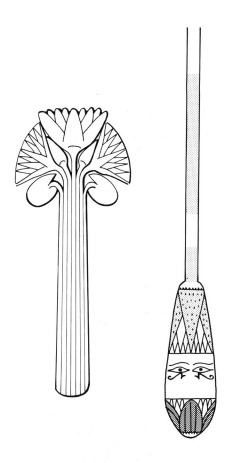

deposited with mummies and have been preserved in their original positions (**3**:10). Representations of domestic architecture in tombs show pillars with capitals in the shape of lotus flowers and buds. These are light and slender and suggest wooden structures with single shafts. In funerary monuments and temples, pillars of stone with lotus capitals usually take the form of a bundle of stems (**3**:11).

The lotus had some ritual significance: the flowers of water lilies close at night and open at sunrise, a feature which came to symbolise a resurgence of life and the sun itself. The motif became associated with the sun-god Horus; the morning sun was pictured as rising from the lotus flower and settling back into the flower at night. (The same symbolism attaches to the Indian lotus motif.) When associated with Isis, the lotus became a fertility symbol. Lotus motifs decorated many objects in daily use as well as those intended for funerary and ritual purposes.

The blue lotus motif developed into a motif of great decorative potential, removed from its origins as a relatively realistic rendering of a water-lily. Many borders and overall designs painted on the walls and ceilings of tombs and temples throughout the Dynastic period include lotus blossom alternating with buds or other plant elements (**3**:12). Some of the many rosette-like motifs in these designs may represent the lotus flower seen from above (**3**:12 *above*). The arcaded stems, and the alternate arrangement of flower and bud, are important features in the further development of this motif beyond Egypt (**3**:24–29).

3:9 *Left* The differences between the two lotus motifs are illustrated in a bunch of flowers carved in low relief in a tomb at Saqqara. The blue lotus motif with buds and leaves surrounds the more rounded form of the white lotus. *c.*2400–2345 BC. *Right* The two motifs are used to decorate the pointed and rounded ends of the steering oar of a model boat from a tomb of the early 2nd millennium BC. The 'eye-of-Horus', a lucky sign, completes the design.

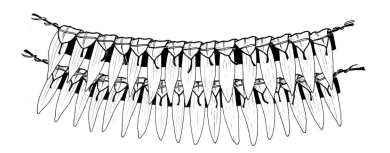

3:10 *Above* Reconstructed method of stitching petals and leaves together in strands for garlands. *Below* The painted collar on Queen Nefertiti's bust has rows of lotus petals interspaced with a row of mandrake fruit. Egypt. *c.*1379–1362 BC.

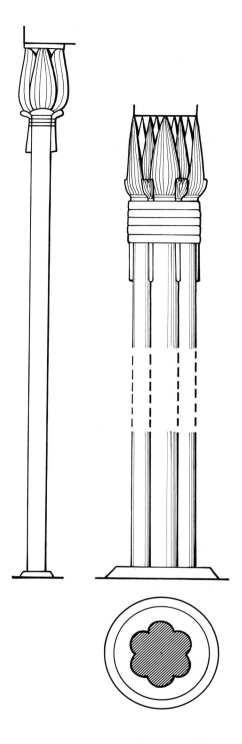

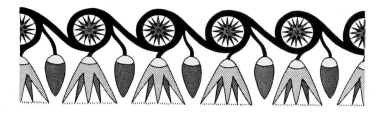

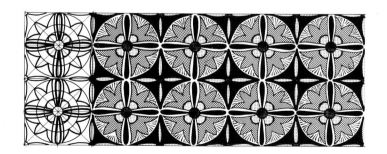

3:11   The lotus pillar is distinguished by a straight shaft and by the equal length of both calyx leaves and petals in the capital. *Left* A painted representation of a pillar from a domestic scene in a tomb of the early 2nd millennium BC. *Right* A stone pillar in a tomb at Abusir from *c.*2430 BC.

3:12   Painted designs from tombs. The overall pattern *below* is made up of roundels on a square grid, each a design of four lotus flowers separated by buds. Egypt. *c.*1425–1379 BC.

The papyrus motif

The papyrus plant, *Cyperus papyrus*, no longer grows in Egypt, but was in the past abundant in the wetlands. It is still found in the upper reaches of the White Nile and in Central Africa. Papyrus grows wild in dense groves; it has a leafless stem of triangular cross section with leaf-sheaths at the base and flowers carried on long fronds in a large umbel at the top. The plant can reach a height of five metres (**3:13**). In nature the papyrus has a ragged look, the large umbels swaying on slender stems which often bend to the ground or break.

In Egyptian art and architecture it became at the outset a highly stylised and disciplined motif (**3:2**). At the beginning of the Old Kingdom, in the mid-third millennium BC, the papyrus plant can be identified as the basis for the design of engaged pillars in the Stepped Pyramid complex at Saqqara, built by the great architect and innovator Imhotep (**3:14** *left*). Stone pillars in the form of highly stylised papyrus stems and umbels, or bundles of papyrus, in tombs and temples, suggest that such light materials were used in domestic architecture (**3:14** *right*). The papyrus motif symbolised the North or Lower Egypt (**3:3**). The stylised form of the papyrus can also be seen in the conventional depictions of papyrus groves. These are rendered as ribbed or striped designs, topped by umbels and buds arranged, as in the lotus-and-bud motif, in regular sequence. In a decoration on a wooden bed in Tutankhamun's tomb, the papyrus grove motif is treated in chased gold (**3:15**).

3:13 *Cyperus papyrus* L. (Drawing by Marjorie Blamey.)

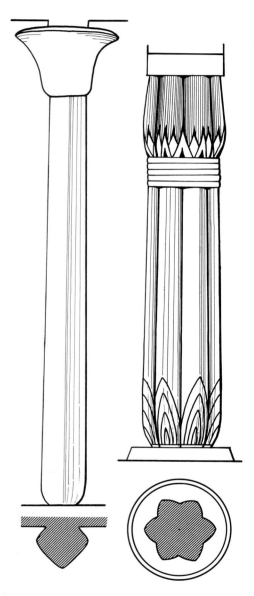

3:14 Stone pillars from the mid-3rd millennium BC. The papyrus pillar is distinguished by the swelling towards the base of the stem, where leaf-sheaths are often indicated, and by capitals where the outer leaves are no more than half the length of the fronds. *Left* from Saqqara, *right* from Abusir.

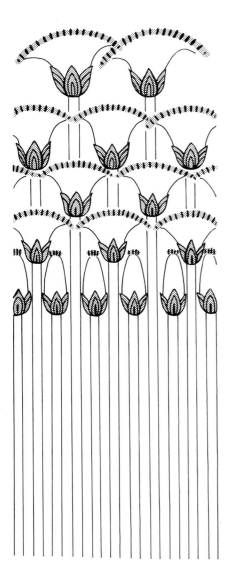

The 'lily of the South' motif

The name 'lily of the South' refers to the use of this motif to represent Upper Egypt, or the South, particularly in the context of the composite symbol for the Unification of Upper and Lower Egypt, an event which *c*.2920 BC marked the beginning of the Dynastic period. Lower Egypt or the North was represented by a papyrus plant (**3**:3). Upper Egypt was at first represented in the Unification symbol not by a lily, but by a sedge-like design, retained in the hieroglyphic sign for the South (**3**:16). Soon, however, another symbol – 'the lily of the South' – appears in its place. As a decorative motif it is seen in its most typical forms on many objects in Tutankhamun's tomb (**3**:17).

It has been assumed that, since the lotus and papyrus motifs were based on common contemporary plants, the lily was also based on a single identifiable plant. In the *Flora of Egypt* (vol.III, 1954, p.276 and IV,1969, p. 148–56) it is suggested that *Kaempferia aethiopia*, an iris-like flower, may have been the model for this design. Specimens held at the Herbarium at Kew Gardens do not convincingly support this identification. Other plants have also been put forward as likely candidates, but none are entirely satisfactory. It seems more likely that the lily motif is an artificial creation, a flower-like motif rather than a stylised flower.

There has been speculation about the identity of the sedge-like design of the first versions of the symbol for the South (**3**:16). Some have identified it with different species of sedge or rush, and it is arguable that this design developed into a lily-like form. Perhaps the plant forms of hieroglyphs for Upper Egypt, (**3**:16 *right*)

3:15   *Above* A motif from a bed in the tomb of Tutankhamun, Valley of the Kings, Egypt. *c*.1361–1352 BC.
Left Details of a papyrus grove from a wall painting in the tomb of Amenemhat at Thebes *c*.1504–1450 BC.

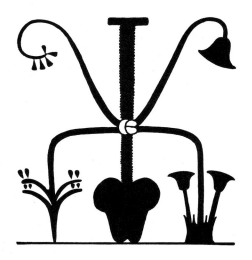

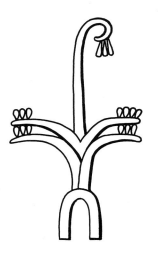

3:16 *Left* The Unification symbol from the Old Kingdom in the mid-3rd millennium BC shows a sedge-like plant on the left representing the South or Upper Egypt, while the papyrus plant on the right represents the North or Lower Egypt. *Right* An Old Kingdom version of the hieroglyphic sign for Upper Egypt.

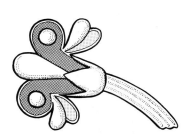

3:17 *Above* Detail from a breast ornament *Left* Three borders with lily designs in gold cloisonné inlaid with red, blue and green stones on the handle of a dagger in the tomb of Tutankhamun, Valley of the Kings, Egypt. *c.*1361–1352 BC.

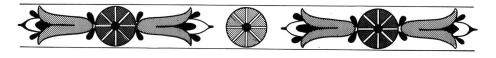

3:18 The designs on two royal head-bands suggest the stylised curving stems and the tiny flowers of the hieroglyphic sign **3:16** *right*. The head-band *above* is painted on a statue of Queen Nofret (*c.*2610 BC). The head-band *below* is in gold, inlaid with red, blue and green stones. It comes from the tomb of Princess Khnumet at Dashur (*c.*1929–1895 BC).

also inspired the decoration of two royal head-bands, where the motif is associated with rosettes which, in this context, can be interpreted as papyrus umbels seen from above (**3**:18). Decorative designs like those illustrated (**3**:19) also have elements which may have contributed to the ultimate form of the lily motif. The 'lily of the South' motif can, in this interpretation, be regarded, not as a new symbol, but as a flower-like development of the original symbol.

3:19 *Above* A motif from a temple shrine at Abusir. *c.*2470 BC. *Below* Gold discs inlaid with red and green stones, from a head-band in the tomb of Princess Sit-Hator-Iunet at Lahun (*c.*1842–1797 BC), are made up of flower-like elements which may have played a part in the development of the lily motif.

Egyptian plant-like motifs in the art of the ancient Near East and the Aegean

Although Egypt was generally self-sufficient in its art, trade and exchange of ideas with the ancient Near East was nevertheless taking place even before the Dynastic period (i.e. before 3000 BC). These contacts grew in strength during the Second Intermediate period (*c.*1783–1626 BC) when Egypt was ruled by Asiatic dynasties. In the New Kingdom, Egypt established an empire in the Middle East, and during the period of the eighteenth dynasty in particular (*c.*1550–1307 BC) Egyptian art became influential and prestigious as high quality objects were sent as gifts by the Pharaoh to foreign rulers. At the same time Egypt became more influenced by foreign art.

Egyptian art was, then, at no time entirely isolated and there was, throughout the Dynastic period, exchange of influences between Egypt, the ancient Near East and the Aegean. The lotus, papyrus and lily motifs entered the repertoire of decorative devices used in the highly creative areas outside Egypt. A seal

impression (**3**:20) produced in Syria, perhaps at Byblos, in the seventeenth century BC displays a blend of motifs drawn from various traditions, typical of an art produced in an area receptive to many influences. The Egyptian style of the figures, the *ankh* and the cartouche with hieroglyphs indicate an understanding of the Egyptian idiom, while the lotus tree, made up of Egyptian plant forms, is nevertheless a Middle Eastern motif – the 'sacred tree'.

The Minoan civilisation in Crete became a focal point of art and culture in the east Mediterranean in the second millennium BC. Its artistic achievements are especially well expressed in pottery where new motifs, or new workings of old motifs became widely known by way of an extensive trade network. One of many ingredients in the Minoan repertoire of plant-like designs can be identified as the Egyptian papyrus motif, the fan of fronds being added to the voluted base of flower-heads already developed from palm, lily and abstract spiral designs (**3**:21, **4**:13–16).

Many centuries later, after the period of the 'Sea Peoples' when disturbances and migrations created a kind of Dark Age in the Eastern Mediterranean, an ivory panel found in the North-West Palace at Nimrud shows a lotus tree which still has distinctive Egyptian plant elements in its design (**3**:22).

3:20 Impression of a cylinder seal. Seals from the same workshop in Syria have been found in Cyprus, Crete and later in Carthage, evidence of the extensive trade network through which artistic products from Syria were disseminated in the 2nd millennium BC.

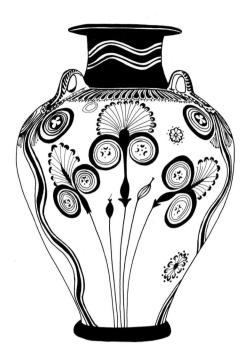

3:21 Painted pottery from Knossos. In the apparently quite realistic design of swaying papyrus umbels, the formal Egyptian arrangement of alternate flowers and buds has been retained. The large volutes emphasise the importance of spiral designs in Minoan art (**4:**13,14). Crete, second half of the 15th cent. BC.

3:22 Ivory panel of Phoenician craftsmanship from the North-West Palace at Nimrud. The 'tree' has the lily motif at the base, papyrus shoots flanking the main stem and a lotus flower at the top. Assyria. 9th cent. BC.

The lotus motif in Greece

Lotus and palmette motifs appear in Greece in the seventh century BC as a result of increasing contact and trade with Egypt, at a time of expansion when Greek colonies were being widely established around the Mediterranean. The art of the East Greeks reflects these influences particularly clearly, and Cyprus, Syria and Palestine served as points of transmission for this trade. Designs like those on a jug from Cyprus and on a stone floor at Nineveh (**3:**23–24), both of which feature the lotus motif, are believed to have been inspired by patterns on Syrian and Phoenician textiles. (It is often suggested that textiles played an important part in spreading the knowledge of motifs in the ancient world (p.16)). A lotus and palmette design on a bone plaque, from burials in the High Altai Mountains in southern Siberia in the fifth century BC, for example, allows a rare insight into the wide range of contacts which existed between people and places at this early period (**2:**77). Finds in these graves included fine textiles, tapestries, silks etc., imported from the Middle East, which had been preserved in the perma frost. The designs on such imported textiles suggest an avenue along which knowledge of Near Eastern motifs, like the lotus and palmette, could have reached this remote area.

In Greece, however, it was largely through the medium of vase-painting and architecture that the lotus and the palmette became important and influential motifs. In Athens potters took advantage of the fine local clay to produce pottery of superior quality. The designs of these vessels are primarily pictorial, but purely decorative bor-

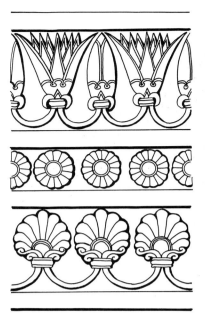

3:23 Painted jug from Cyprus. The design shows the lotus flower motif seen from above with a bull sniffing a lotus flower below. 7th cent. BC.

3:24 Detail of borders with lotus-and-bud, rosette and palmette motifs, carved in low relief on a stone floor in the North Palace of Ashurbanipal at Nineveh, Assyria *c.*645 BC. It is assumed that the designs are modelled on carpet patterns.

3:25 Painted borders on Greek vases of the 6th and 5th cent. BC illustrating changes and variations on lotus-and-bud and lotus-and-palmette designs.

ders include many variations on the theme of twists, meander, lotus and palmette chains and scrolls, versions of patterns used in contemporary architecture.

The basic lotus-and-bud motif on arcaded stems was subject to change and experimentation during this period of intense creative activity. The lotus-and-palmette variant became particularly influential and successful (**3:25**). Acanthus leaves were added to the bases of the lotus and palmette elements, increasing the plant-like look of the border which was thus sufficiently changed in appearance to be given a new name, *anthemion*, or honeysuckle (**3:26**; **4**:10). Confusingly, this name attaches itself variously to the whole ornament, to the lotus or to the palmette element alone. There is no reason to believe that there was a conscious attempt to portray the honeysuckle; the name is used in the sense of the motif being honeysuckle-like.

3:26 Detail of an ornament known as *anthemion* from the Erectheion on the Acropolis, Athens. Late 5th cent. BC.

The egg-and-dart mouldings of the Ionic order

The Ionic capital, and the motifs which decorate it, developed in Anatolia as part of an architectural tradition which produced voluted capitals in a wide area (**4**:22,23). An important group of mouldings in the Ionic order of architecture are ultimately derived from the lotus-and-bud motif (**4**:23). The egg-and-dart (known also as egg-and-tongue, egg-and-anchor, etc.) typically decorates the *ovolo* (or *echinus*), a convex moulding (**3**:27–28 *above*). The water-leaf (leaf-and-dart, heart-and-dart etc.) decorates the *Cyma reversa* (or *Lesbian cyma*), a moulding which in section describes a curve, convex in its upper parts, concave below (**3**:27–28 *above*).

The drum from a capital of the Aeolian type in the Temple of Athena at Bayrakli in Anatolia is another – and more obvious – example of a leaf design ultimately derived from the Egyptian lotus-and-bud motif (**3**:29).

3:27 The Ionic order illustrated by a capital and base from the Temple of Athena at Priene, Ionia, south-west Turkey. 4th cent. BC.

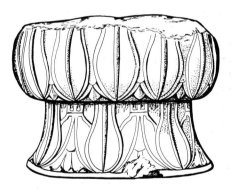

3:28 *Above* Detail of moulding from the Erectheion on the Acropolis, Athens: The leaf-and-dart and egg-and-dart motifs between bead-and-reel borders. *Below* A painted border from a Greek vase of the mid-6th cent. BC illustrates the relationship between these designs and the original idea of the Egyptian lotus-and-bud motif.

3:29 Drum of an Aeolian capital, decorated with a leaf-design which demonstrates its ultimate dependence on the ancient lotus-and-bud motif. Bayrakli, Turkey. End of the 7th cent. BC.

4

The Palmette

Palmette motifs can be defined as fans of graded spines or lobes supported by opposed spirals or similar features (**4**:1,2). This simple definition gives no indication of the complicated background to the motif. It is not possible to trace a definite single point of origin. The palmette motif emerged gradually in the east Mediterranean area as the ultimate distillation of the most successful features of several motifs; it is an infinitely versatile decorative formula consisting of a symmetrical spiral base (in this context often known as volutes) and the fan-shaped uprights.

The name palmette suggests that the motif was derived from representations of palm trees. Names given to motifs are, as a rule, a poor guide to their origins, but the stylised date-palm motif can be said to have contributed certain features to the development of the palmette. The date-palm *Phoenix dactylifera* was one of the oldest domesticated plants in the ancient world. It is probably native to India and perhaps to south Iraq and Arabia. The people who depended on the products of the palm moved westwards and brought the knowledge of the tree to Western Asia, Egypt and Northern Africa. In view of its importance it is not surprising that the tree often had a sacred image in these areas. The presence of date-palms in pre-Dynastic Egypt is indicated by images like that of a highly stylised palm on a slate palette of *c*.3100 BC (**4**:3). In Egypt the date-palm motif acquired certain characteristic features: three straight leaves at the top, curved fronds symmetrically arranged on either side of the trunk, dates hanging down below the fronds, and suckers at the base. Three trunks often rise from the same base (this is the image of a female tree, and the motif was seen as a female symbol) (**4**:4).

In the second millennium BC, the ancient Egyptian motifs, lotus, papyrus, lily and palm, became widely used in Western Asia. Together with the spiral in its many forms (the dominant indigenous motif) they were used and manipulated for a variety of decorative purposes (**4**:5; **3**:20). Minoan Crete became an important focal point of art and culture in the Mediterranean in the mid-second millennium BC and the date-palm was one of several Egyptian motifs which were given new forms by its potters (**4**:13–15).

In the ancient Near East the palmette motif continued to develop in areas less affected by the recessions suffered in the east Mediterranean area from about the thirteenth to the eighth centuries BC (**4**:6,7, **3**:22). Towards the end of this period voluted capitals in monumental stone architecture appeared over a wide area of the Near East and the Mediterranean (**4**:8). The varied forms of these capitals feature the double volute

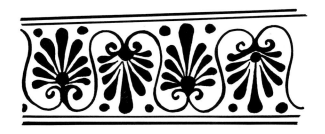

4:1 Engraved border on ivory with rows of rosettes and linked palmettes and pomegranates. Nimrud, Assyria. 9th cent. BC.

4:2 Painted linked palmette border from an *epinetron*. Athens, Greece. 520 BC.

4:3 Detail of the design on a slate palette from Abydos. The tree illustrated is the male date-palm, identified by the inflorescence at the top. Egypt. *c.*3100 BC.

4:4 Clusters of dates hanging below the curved fronds of the female date-palm, together with the three leaves at the top and the suckers at the base, are typical features of the stylised date-palm motif. Detail from a temple relief, Deir el-Bahri, Egypt. *c.*1503–1482 BC.

4:5 The Egyptian motifs of palm, lily, papyrus and lotus leaves on a dagger sheath in Tutankhamun's tomb are somewhat foreign to the typical form in Egyptian art and more like those found in contemporary Western Asia. Egypt. *c.*1361–1352 BC.

4:6 Detail from a relief in the North-West Palace at Nimrud, Assyria. The tree is made up of a large central palmette, surrounded by a garland of small, linked palmettes. *c.* 865–860 BC.

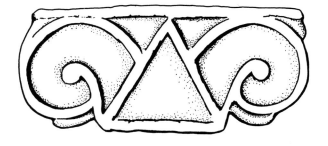

4:7 Ivory panel found in the North-West Palace at Nimrud, Assyria. Made up of different plant details like lily and lotus, the main motif is palmette-like. Phoenician workmanship. *c.*9th cent. BC.

4:8 Double volute motif on a capital from Megiddo, Palestine. 10th–8th cent. BC.

which owes something both to the palmette motif and to the ancient Egyptian lily motif as seen, for example, on the ivory plaque from Nimrud (3:22). It has been suggested that there may have been a widely disseminated tradition associating palm and floral motifs – and symbolism – with wooden supports in buildings of the preceding periods. On a number of sites in Mesopotamia dating from the nineteenth and eighteenth centuries BC, pilasters made from shaped brick imitate palm trunk and other surface patterns. A foundation stone tablet, for instance, recording the dedication of a new image of Shamash, the sun-god, in his temple at Sippar, shows a supporting pillar in the form of a palm trunk (4:9).

The palmette was a major motif in the art and architecture of classical Greece (4:10,17–23). With the establishment of the Roman Empire, in the first century BC, a well-defined style of art and architecture came to dominate a large geographical area until the end of the fourth century AD, leaving a legacy to western as well as oriental art which still permeates our perceptions of what is appropriate as ornament.

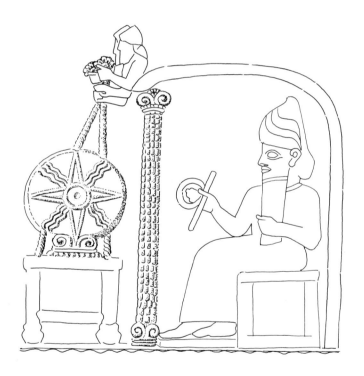

4:9 In this drawing of part of the design on a foundation tablet, some features are emphasized – the palm-trunk pillar with a voluted capital and base (which supports the canopy above the sun-god) and the sun-disc with its double-volute support. Sippar, Babylonia. *c.*900 BC.

4:10 Lotus and palmette border (in the stylised form known as *anthemion* (3:26)), carved in low relief on a pediment moulding. Temple of Apollo at Bassae, Greece. *c.* 425 BC.

4:11 From Thomas Hope, *Household Furniture and Interior Decoration*, 1807, pl. 41. *Above, left and centre* Ornament on pediment and top of library table. *Right* Ornament on pediment of dressing table. *Below* Ornament to table.

The versatility and decorative potential of the palmette has been extensively exploited. With the revival in Europe of the Egyptian and Greek taste as expressed in Neo-Classical architecture in the eighteenth century, books like Thomas Hope's *Household Furniture and Interior Decoration*, published in 1807, became instrumental in introducing Classical motifs to the homes of fashionable people. The book illustrates ornaments which were used in the formal rooms he created as settings for his extensive collection of ancient Greek, Roman and Egyptian artefacts (4:11). His carefully researched designs (and others based on his ideas) appeared in contemporary pattern books which were widely used and became very influential. The palmette was, with the acanthus, the most important element in these designs and both remain major motifs in architecture, furnishings and furniture design (4:12).

The motif sometimes known as the split palmette scroll is discussed with the acanthus in Chapter 5, *Leaf Borders, Leaf Scrolls and The Acanthus*.

4:12 Lotus and palmette border on a Victorian glazed ceramic tile. England. Late 19th–early 20th cent.

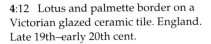

Rising lobes and supporting spirals: the Minoan contribution?

The Egyptian lotus eventually emerged in Greece as a most important decorative motif while the palmette took the place of the papyrus and lily motifs as its companion and foil. The processes of experimentation have been observed in the development of border designs on Greek vases of the sixth and fifth centuries AD (**3:25**). In the much earlier Minoan pottery it is also possible to observe innovative processes at work on the palm motif which led to the gradual emergence of decorative features such as rising lobes between supporting spirals (**4:13**).

The date-palm is thought to have been introduced into Crete by the Egyptians, and it is typical of the way Minoan potters developed existing motifs – by reference to the natural world around them – that their version of the palm motif does not include clusters of dates since this fruit does not ripen in Crete. To achieve an effect similar to that seen in its Egyptian archetype, the bottom fronds are instead strongly voluted (**4:14**, cf.**4:4**). Naturalistic and stylised elements are curiously mixed in these designs, which reflect the style of wall-painting in the great palaces. A vase from Knossos decorated with lilies, for instance, looked so naturalistic that Sir Arthur Evans in *The Palace of Minos at Knossos* (vol.II, 2, p.456, fig.267) identified the species of plant as the Pancratium lily. Yet the composition is closely based on the date-palm motif: three stems rising from a leafy base, three straight buds at the top, two symmetrically voluted petals with three stamens in each flower-head (**4:15**, cf.**4:4**). The date-palm motif continued to contribute various stylised forms of decoration in Mycenaean art (**4:16**, **3:21**).

4:13 A highly decorated jar from Knossos; the addition of three lobes at a point where two opposed curves meet suggests that palmette-like motifs could arise from these animated spiral and scroll designs. This is particularly apparent in the detail under the handle, *right,* Crete. *c.*18th cent. BC.

4:15 Painted vase from the Palace at Knossos, Crete. *c.*1700–1600 BC.

4:14 Painted jar from the Palace at Knossos. The inflorescence of the male date-palm is indicated by red speckling; the highly emphasised and voluted bottom fronds replace the hanging dates. Crete. *c.*1700–1600 BC.

4:16 The date-palm motif, with inflorescence at the top and voluted fronds, can still be identified in a highly stylised form in the design on a Mycenaean vase from Deiras, Greece. *c.*1450–1400 BC.

The palmette in Greek, Etruscan and Roman art

From the twelfth century BC, for some four hundred years, the eastern Mediterranean area and much of Western Asia suffered a period of disturbances and migrations followed by a so-called Dark Age. In the period between 1200 and 1100 BC the Mycenaean civilisation gradually collapsed. This period coincides with the transition from the Bronze Age to the Iron Age. In Greece, however, there was not a complete break with the past and prosperity and growth began to return towards the beginning of the eighth century BC. The palmette motif was one of several which appeared in Greece in the late eighth century BC as the result of increasing contact with Western Asia, where the motif had in the meantime continued to develop. A design like that on a pedestalled *krater* from Rhodes is typical of the form of the palmette in what is known as the 'orientalising period' (4:17).

Experimentation with decorative motifs of this period can be studied in detail on a considerable body of pottery from Athens (4:18; 3:25). A design, carved on the side of a stone pedestal in the Temple of Athena Polias at Priene, displays some of the features, old and new, which were part of the Classical repertoire of decorative motifs. The whole composition is organised according to the ancient Egyptian formula of alternate flower-and-bud; spiral scrolls and palmettes take on the role of tendrils, stems and flowers, whilst acanthus leaves represent a new motif which helps to create the illusion of a growing plant (4:19; 5:6; cf.3:26,4:10). Very florid palmette scrolls became the fashion in pottery of the fourth century BC. These motifs separate figural scenes or decorate the areas round or below handles (4:20).

The Ionic order of Greek architecture developed, in circumstances which are unclear, as one of several variations of the idea of supporting volutes and upright fans (4:21). The antecedents of the Greek capital must be sought in Near Eastern designs in the seventh century BC. Two types of capital, based on double volutes, the Aeolian and the Ionic, emerged in the eastern Greek territories of Anatolia (4:22,23). While the Aeolian forms appear a little earlier than the Ionic (at the end of the seventh century BC) there is no evidence to suggest that it was the prototype for the Ionic capital. Rather, it would seem most likely that the two capitals were more or less contemporary products of the long Near Eastern tradition of supporting double volutes (3:22). The Ionic order is known from the middle of the sixth century and came to its fullest development in the fourth century BC.

In the eighth century the Greeks began to establish colonies in Italy, colonies which in time led to the rise of well-organised city states along the

4:17 The border of a *krater* from Rhodes displays typical Near Eastern motifs: the two confronted goats, the palmettes, running spirals and twists. c.650 BC.

4:20 The palmette motif separates two figural scenes on a red-figured situla from the Greek colony at Ruvo in Apulia, Italy. Late 4th cent. BC.

4:18 Painted palmette scroll and linked palmette borders from Athenian pottery. Greece. c.520 BC.

4:19 Detail of a design on a stone pedestal in the temple of Athena Polias at Priene. South-west Turkey. c.4th cent. BC.

4:21 Ornament at the top of a funerary stele illustrates one of many variations on supporting volutes and upright fans. Traces of red and blue paint indicate that this kind of ornament was originally picked out in bright colours. Perinthos, Turkey. End of 6th cent. BC.

4:22   Aeolian capital from Larisa,
Anatolia, Turkey. First half of the 6th cent.
BC.

4:24   Border from a bronze mirror with a
slanting palmette scroll (**2:28**). Said to
have come from Atri, Abruzzi, Etruria,
Italy. 500–475 BC.

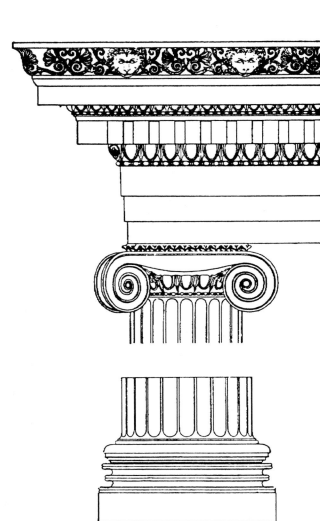

4:23   The Ionic order, the Temple of
Athena at Priene, Ionia, south-west
Turkey. The temple was dedicated in
334 BC.

4:25   Detail of a palmette scroll under the
handle of an amphora. Vulci, Etruria.
Italy. 400–360 BC.

southern coasts of the peninsula and in Sicily. The indigenous populations of this region had been less affected than the eastern Mediterranean area by the problems following the fall of the Mycenaean civilisation. They had strong links to the north, particularly with Central Europe which had experienced a period of rapid development during a flourishing Bronze Age. The people now known as the Etruscans inhabited part of west-central Italy; with the establishment of the Greek colonies and through contact with the other Mediterranean trading nations – the Phoenicians in particular – they came to share in the high culture of the Eastern Mediterranean. Towards the end of the fifth century, and in the fourth century BC, the Etruscans began to face the rising power of Rome in the south and at the same time developed closer contacts with the Celts who had settled in the Po Valley in the north. The palmette motif on Etruscan objects of this period demonstrates their continued dependence on the Greek styles, while the emphasis on the spiral scroll element of this motif and on diagonal compositions perhaps show Celtic influence (**4:24–26**; cf.**7:5–9**).

The versatility of the palmette motif was explored and exploited as one of the most important decorative devices in architecture by the Romans, who built on the Greek lotus and palmette borders, but also created new variations on the versatile palmette (**4:27**). The lotus element becomes less frequent, but the acanthus continues to accompany the palmette, giving plant-like features to this abstract motif.

The knowledge and use of the palmette has never been entirely lost. In its original Greek and Roman forms the palmette was reintroduced in Europe with the revival of Egyptian and Greek taste and neo-classical architecture in the eighteenth century (**4:11**).

4:26 Detail from a terracotta plaque from Lanuvium, Latium. Plaques like this protected exposed wooden beams in roofs. The terracotta would have been painted in bright colours. Italy. *c.* 4th cent. BC.

4:27 Two panels at the base of a column of the temple at Didyma, Turkey. 1st cent. AD. The panels exemplify the kind of variations on the palmette which have made this motif exceptionally popular.

5
Leaf borders, leaf scrolls and the acanthus

To set leaves and flowers on either side of a stem is a simple decorative idea, which was not unknown before it was adopted and developed into major motifs in sixth-century Greece (5:1,2). It cannot, therefore, be taken for granted that all subsequent examples of this design are derivative. In reality, however, the extensive use of specific leaf borders and scroll motifs in the art and architecture of ancient Greece and Rome has caused these particular motifs to exert a great and enduring influence on the decorative arts of the civilised world.

The symbolic use of wreaths and flowers in Greek society and mythology led artists to produce a number of border motifs of stylised leaves, some of which developed into formalised decorative motifs for more general use (5:3–5,17–24). Alongside these quite naturalistic borders were those highly stylised motifs derived from the ancient Egyptian lotus and the palmette (3:25,26,28, 4:10,18). In the fourth century BC, both large and small leaves began to appear in association with scroll and palmette motifs to produce designs which render these abstract motifs more plant-like (5:6, 4:19).

The ornamental leaf motif, known as 'acanthus', has long been associated with the plant of that name (5:31). The Roman architect Vitruvius wrote in the first century BC on the origins of the Corinthian capital. He tells the story of the sculptor Kallimachos who seeing curving acanthus leaves growing around a basket of toys left on the tomb of a small girl, created the first Corinthian capital. The story, although clearly an invention, is interesting in that it shows the early connection between this ornamental leaf motif and the plant. But the connection is tenuous and the motif rarely corresponds very closely to the species to which it is attributed. Throughout most of its long history, the leaf ornament generally known as 'acanthus' is in fact an imaginary leaf adapted to many uses, including flower-like arrangements with no reference to any living plant (cf. 5:31 and, for example, 5:7–16).

In the art and architecture of the Christian church the acanthus became a useful supporting decorative motif: very often secondary to a motif of significance, it has no symbolic associations of its own (5:35–7; 9:34,36). The vine scroll was, however, incorporated in Christian iconography (5:23,25–29; 2:50; 7:23).

Acanthus, ivy and vine scrolls became disseminated throughout the Hellenistic world and the Roman Empire, particularly in being used as enrichments on buldings and in designs on wall-paintings and mosaics (5:9,10,33,34). They merged into a general simple leaf scroll which

5:1   *Above* An early example of a leaf
scroll motif on a cylinder seal impression.
Below On another seal impression calves
are seen feeding on the leaves represented
in the scroll design. Susa, south-west Iran,
*c.*2900 BC.

5:2   At one time called 'sacred ivy' and
thought to relate to Egyptian religious
symbols, this leaf scroll from Mycenae is
now thought to owe more to spiral motifs
than to observations from nature. Greece.
c. 1550–1500 BC.

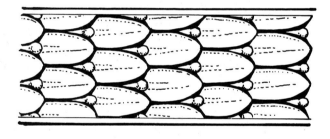

5:3   Ivy scroll encircling the neck of a
Greek vase made in Apulia, southern
Italy. *c.* 370–360 BC.

5:5   Ornament of overlapping bay-leaves on the main
staircase of the British Museum, London. In this Greek
revival building by Robert Smirke, the ornament (which
in Greek architecture usually covers bold convex
mouldings) is used as a flat frieze. Mid-19th cent.

5:4   Detail of a vine scroll motif on a Roman lead coffin from Sidon,
Lebanon. Late 2nd or 3rd cent. AD.

5:6 Carving at the top of a marble stele. The realistic acanthus leaves combined with half-palmettes and spiral scrolls create an effect of a living, though imaginary plant. Athens, Greece. *c.* 390–365 BC.

5:7 Corinthian capital from the monument of Lysicrates in Athens, Greece. 334 BC.

5:8 A carved panel at the base of a column in the temple at Didyma illustrates one of the uses made of the leaf motif in Roman architectural decoration. Between curling leaves and buds is a motif sometimes known as an acanthus 'flower', a flower-like arrangement of leaves. Turkey. 1st cent. AD.

5:9 Detail of a sculptured Roman frieze from Aphrodisias in Caria, Anatolia. Scrolls rise from a calyx of leaves and hold winged cupids in their coils. Turkey. *c.* AD 200.

became a part of Buddhist art in India and greatly influenced decoration in China (**5**:38–42). The leaf scroll remains a universal motif in the East. In the Islamic world the motif known as the arabesque developed from this version of the leaf motif into an intricate and varied ornament which, while without religious overtones, has nonetheless become synonymous with the art of Islam (**5**:43–47, p.13).

In Medieval Europe the same imaginary leaf was a dominant supporting motif in all areas of decoration. In twelfth-century ivory carving and manuscript illumination, for example, the leaf scrolls achieve the status of major decorative motifs (**5**:11–12). It is to art of this period that William Morris (one of the founders of the English Arts and Crafts movement in the second half of the nineteenth century) looked for inspiration in an attempt to infuse new ideals of excellence and craftsmanship into industrial design and interior decoration. Flower patterns for wallpaper were based on studies from illustrations in medieval Herbals. In ornamental borders for a volume of Chaucer, however, it is clear that it is the imaginary acanthus leaf and flower of the medieval tradition with their versatility and decorative possibilities, which have been his models (**5**:13).

Glazed ceramic tiles of the period reflect a return to the art of other periods in order to invigorate Victorian designs perceived by the Arts and Crafts movement as tired and decadent. Medieval tile patterns were faithfully copied, while, on another tile, a design of arabesque leaves is generally Islamic in character (**5**:14,15). The all-purpose leaf also lent itself to the sinuous lines of Art Nouveau (**5**:16). It remains a mainstay of modern designers.

5:10 *Left* A leaf scroll rising from a vase. At the top a rosette of leaves and fruit. From a mosaic pavement in Carthage, Tunis. Roman. 4th cent. AD.

5:11 *Right* Leaf scrolls in an openwork interlaced tree design, carved in bone. Anglo-Norman Romanesque. 12th cent. AD.

5:12 Decorated initials and design details from the Winchester Bible. England. 12th cent. AD.

Incipit secunda pars ✿ ✿ ✿ ✿ ✿ ✿ ✿ ✿

FER FRO THILKE PALHYS HONUR-
ABLE
Theras this markys shoop his mariage,
Ther stood a throop, of site delitable,
In which that povre folk of that village
Hadden hir beestes and hir herbergage,
And of hire labour tooke hir sustenance,
After that the erthe yaf hem habundance.

AMONGES thise povre folk ther
dwelte a man
Which that was holden povrest of
hem alle;
But hye God som tyme senden kan
His grace into a litel oxes stalle:
Janicula men of that throop hym calle.
A doghter hadde he, fair ynogh to sighte,
And Grisildis this yonge mayden highte.

But for to speke of vertuous beautee,
Thanne was she oon the faireste under sonne:
For povreliche yfostred up was she,
No likerous lust was thurgh hire herte yronne;
Wel ofter of the welle than of the tonne
She drank, and for she wolde vertu plese,
She knew wel labour, but noon ydel ese.

But thogh this mayde tendre were of age,
Yet in the brest of hire virginitee
Ther was enclosed rype and sad corage,
And in greet reverence and charitee
Hir olde povre fader fostred shee;
A fewe sheep, spynnynge, on feeld she kepte,
She wolde noght been ydel til she slepte.

And whan she homward cam, she wolde brynge
Wortes, or other herbes, tymes ofte,

5:13 *Left* A page from the Tale of the Clerk of Oxenford in the Chaucer *Canterbury Tales* which was designed and produced by William Morris at his private Kelmscott Press, 1896.

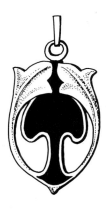

5:16 A small silver and enamel pendant from *Yule-Tide Gifts 1909*. Liberty & Co., London.

5:14 Glazed tile in a four-tile pattern. Copy of medieval design. Maw & Co., Shropshire, England. Second half 19th cent.

5:15 A repeat pattern in glazed ceramic tiles. Created by William De Morgan, it is a new design, using the arabesque leaf to achieve an Islamic/oriental effect, enhanced by the colour scheme in blue and green. Sands End Pottery, Fulham, London 1888–1897.

Laurel, olive, vine and other realistic leaf borders in Greek ornament

5:17 Conventionalised form of leaves and berries of *above* laurel, *centre* olive and *below* myrtle. Details from Athenian vases. Greece. 4th cent. BC.

Among the ancient Greeks, wreaths of leaves and flowers were used as marks of distinction; they were worn by victors of wars, or public games, and as emblems of office. Wreaths were made from plants which had particular significance and which were also attributes of specific characters in the Greek pantheon and mythology. The plants were those common to the Mediterranean: laurel, olive, myrtle, ivy, vine, oak and so on. In Greek vase-painting characters portrayed in figural scenes may wear wreaths of leaves as attributes to aid identification. In addition, simple borders of leaves and berries encircle the necks and bodies of vessels as though they were stylised wreaths (**5**:3,17).

Among the most frequently used leaf borders are those based on laurel, olive, ivy and vine. The bay tree or laurel *Laurus nobilis* is native to the Mediterranean region; in the classical world it was sacred to Apollo, Dionysus and various other deities; its symbolic meaning included triumph and victory (**5**:18). The olive *Olea europaea* was probably native to the Eastern Mediterranean, but had been widely cultivated in the ancient world for its important oil (**5**:19). Olive trees are represented as early as the second millennium BC on wall-paintings in Knossos and on Minoan pottery (**5**:20). All the leaf borders developed conventionalised forms, and it is not always possible to distinguish one from another (**5**:21). Indeed the context may be a better guide to the identity of a particular leaf than its shape: leaves and berries in a wreath design in association with Athena, for example, would be interpreted as olive, while in architectural ornament

5:18 Bay tree or laurel *Laurus nobilis*, an evergreen shrub with aromatic leaves. (Drawing by Marjorie Blamey.)

5:19 Olive *Olea europea, Above* A branch of the cultivated tree *Below* The wild olive *Olea oleaster*. (Drawing by Marjorie Blamey.)

overlapping leaves covering a convex moulding are known as bay-leaf whatever their shape (**5**:5,22). Ivy and the vine are both associated with Dionysus (Bacchus), god of wine and ecstasy. They are common motifs in vase painting and decorate many cups and vessels used at the table and in the popular Dionysian cult which involved copious wine drinking (**5**:3,23).

Another motif featuring plants and fruit are swags suspended between *bucrania*, the horned skulls of rams, oxen or bulls (**5**:24). In Greek and Roman art, the motif embellishes altars, funerary monuments and temples, reflecting the significance and popularity of animal sacrifice. This was one of the motifs which was extensively used in interior decoration in Renaissance and eighteenth-century Europe in the context of Classical revival.

5:21 A Roman clay lamp is decorated with a wreath of leaves and berries, which could equally be identified as any one of the three plant motifs in **5**:17. Italy. *c.*AD 50–100.

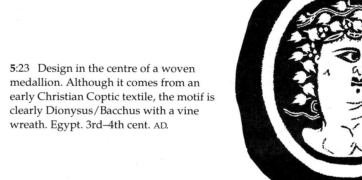

5:23 Design in the centre of a woven medallion. Although it comes from an early Christian Coptic textile, the motif is clearly Dionysus/Bacchus with a vine wreath. Egypt. 3rd–4th cent. AD.

5:20 A border of olive leaves and flowers painted on a cup from Knossos, Crete. *c.*17th cent. BC.

5:22 Reverse of Athenian silver tetradrachm. The owl represents Athena, thus the leaves and berries in the corner can be identified as olive. Greece. *c.*450–406 BC.

5:24 A swag of corn, nuts, fruit and leaves between horned skulls carved on a marble cinerary urn. Athens, Greece. *c.*AD 120–140.

5:27   Vine scrolls on stone crosses from Hexham,
Northumberland. Anglo-Saxon. 8th–9th cent. AD.

5:25   Tapestry woven band from an early
Christian (Coptic) burial. Egypt. 4th–5th
cent. AD.

5:26   A vine scroll surrounds the rim of a silver gilt paten. In the
centre is a Latin cross and the inscription 'O Lord, Remember
Bishop Paul, a Sinner'. Byzantine, 6th–7th cent. AD.

The vine scroll and the tree in Christian art

Christianity became the sole religion of the Roman Empire in AD 380. It had for some time co-existed with other beliefs and, for most of the fourth century, Classical designs and motifs were used to illustrate Christian as well as non-Christian themes. A well-loved motif like the vine scroll, which celebrated wine drinking in the cult of Bacchus, for example, acquired a Christian interpretation as a symbol of Christ, although clearly not always used in such a connotation in the early Christian period (**5:23,25**). In Christian iconography, the vine scroll came to be associated with the saying of Christ 'I am the true vine' (John, XV:1). Bordering a Christian cross and inscription, on a Byzantine paten it is clearly a Christian symbol (**5:26**). Vine scroll designs on Anglo-Saxon crosses are interpreted as Christian symbols referring to the Biblical scenes which are sometimes part of their decoration (**5:27**; **7:23**). Birds and animals are sometimes set within the vine scroll (**2:50**).

The vine scroll is sometimes symmetrical, branching from a central stem. This brings it close to a related motif, the tree, often rising from a vase, and sometimes inhabited by birds or other animals (**5:28**; **0:14–17**). This motif is labelled 'tree of life', a term used freely for such designs wherever they occur. Trees have indeed been the subject of worship. In India, for example, there is considerable evidence of a tree cult going back to a pre-historic past. The fig tree is venerated among both Hindus and Buddhists. A motif of Persian origin with a tree between peacocks is widespread in Christian contexts (**5:29,30**). In Christian iconography the tree mo-

tif may refer to Jesse's dream 'There shall come forth a rod out of the stem of Jesse and a branch shall grow out of its roots' (Isaiah XI:1). These examples serve only to emphasize that there is no single 'tree of life' motif, trees offer an easy symbolism which has been exploited in many cultures.

5:28 Design woven in wool on linen from an early Christian (Coptic) burial. Egypt. 5th–6th cent. AD.

5:29 Design on a marble sarcophagus in the Church of Saint-Pierre, Vienne, Isère, France. 6th–7th cent. AD.

5:30 A ring of the Anglo-Saxon king Æthelwulf (839–858), inscribed with his name, also bears a design of a (?)cross between peacocks. Wiltshire, England.

The Acanthus

5:32 *Left* Corinthian capital from the temple of Castor and Pollux in the Forum at Rome, 1st cent. AD. *Right* Composite capital from the arch of Septimius Severus in the Forum at Rome. Italy. 2nd cent. AD.

Varieties of the acanthus family grow wild in southern Europe; two species have been singled out as likely models for different forms of decorative leaf motifs: *Acanthus mollis*, with broad, blunt tips to the leaves and *Acanthus spinosus* with comparatively narrow leaves and pointed lobes terminating in spines (**5:31**). The acanthus leaf motif was from its beginnings a supporting motif, its chief role being to render more plant-like traditional designs which were abstract and formal (**5:6**), to support volutes in architectural enrichments and to form the calyx from which spiral scrolls arise (**5:7,9**).

The acanthus leaf is the main ornamental element of the Corinthian capital, introduced in Greek architecture in the early fifth century BC as a variation on the capitals of the Ionic order (**3:27**; **4:23**). The spirals which support the abacus at the top – the volutes – spring from a double row of acanthus leaves (**5:7**). The Corinthian capital was further developed and elaborated in Roman architecture, where a composite form, combining Corinthian and Ionic features was also introduced (**5:32**). The acanthus motif was from the first closely associated with the palmette. It has been suggested that the acanthus motif is more closely described as an acanthus-like version of the palmette motif. Gombrich (1984 p.187–8 discusses this aspect of the acanthus motif and concludes:

whether or not the palmette can be watched as turning itself into an acanthus, it is still likely that the plant motif was received into the repertory of Greek ornament because it could so easily be assimilated to the traditional palmette …

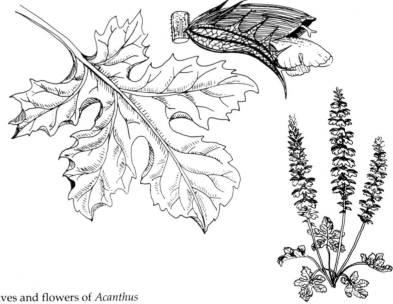

5:31 Leaves and flowers of *Acanthus mollis, above,* and *Acanthus spinosus, below.* (Drawing by Marjorie Blamey.)

The schematic motifs which Greek designers had derived from the ancient Orient were returned to life in the great awakening that can be observed in all aspects of Greek civilisation. The 'animation' of the scroll into a living plant with a resemblance to a familiar weed is part of that evolution.

The large leaf was added to plant scrolls like ivy and vine. In a frieze from Aphrodisias in Caria, large acanthus leaves form a calyx from which spring scrolling stems, which in turn

5:33 Leaf scroll from a border in a mosaic floor from Hinton St Mary, Dorset, England. Roman. 4th cent. AD.

5:34 Design from the corner field of a large mosaic pavement found in London on the site of the Bank of England. Inside the plaited border is a cross of stylised leaves. The three-petalled flowers in the corners may be identified as versions of the ancient lotus motif. Roman. 3rd cent. AD.

enclose figures (**5**:9). Large leaves are folded over the stems while small leaves form bell-like collars where the stems divide.

The stylised form of the acanthus half-leaf is very similar to that of the half-palmette, emphasizing further the close association between the two motifs. This motif is variously, and confusingly, known as either acanthus or a half-palmette scroll. Considering the highly stylised nature of the leaf shapes, the more general name of leaves and leaf scroll will be used here for the simple forms of this group of motifs (**5**:33,34).

At the beginning of the fourth century AD, the Roman Empire was divided, with Byzantium (Constantinople) as capital of the Eastern region. In the fifth century the Western Empire fell to the Germanic tribes who gradually overran its provinces in Europe. From different homelands, some with late Roman and some with oriental traditions of decoration from the larger area between eastern Europe and Asia, they introduced new and stimulating ornamental ideas into the indigenous art which had been fairly uniform under the Romans. In the course of the sixth and seventh centuries Christianity was gradually introduced in the new kingdoms, which arose out of the old Roman provinces. Major motifs in the art of the early Christian church were intricate ribbon interlace together with stylised leaves (**9**:34–36). The leaf was new to Germanic art. Here animal motifs had long dominated, but the leaf soon became established (**5**:35). It emerged in the eighth century in western Europe as a *leitmotif* in the art of the Carolingian empire (**5**:36). As such it influenced the art of the rest of the region and was particularly adopted by the Anglo-Saxons. Its first significant appeerence here is as a border to a presentation page of a copy of Bede's *Life of St Cuthbert* probably presented to Chester-le-Street in 934 (**5**:37). It then became the determining feature of the richly illuminated manuscripts of the Anglo-Saxon Winchester style (**5**:12).

5:35 A gold foil mount from a Langobard grave. Animal motifs and leaf scrolls formed a very successful partnership. Switzerland. 7th cent. AD.

The all-purpose leaf in the East and the 'arabesque'

The acanthus, ivy and vine scrolls became disseminated throughout the Hellenistic world and the Roman Empire, particularly as enrichments on buildings and in designs on wall-paintings and mosaics (5:7–10, 32–34). Trading links by sea, as well as overland routes, maintained their dispersal through the Indian sub-continent, Central Asia, China and the western world.

New functions for buildings and art associated with Buddhism made use of architectural features and ornamental detail derived from a western Hellenistic heritage. A capital carved on a pilaster as part of a building portrayed on a stone relief from Gandhara in Afghanistan (modern north-western Pakistan), on the important trade route between the Indian sub-continent and the west, is clearly a simplified version of the

5:36 Detail of a border which surrounds the lion's mask on the bronze knocker of the west door of Aachen Cathedral. The stylised leaves barely conceal that this is the Classical lotus and palmette border. Germany. c.AD 800.

5:37 Detail of a border from the frontispiece to Bede's *Life of St Cuthbert*. Several of the characteristic features of the Classical acanthus motif are further developed here, not only the calyx from which scrolls rise, but the bell-like collars where scrolls divide (cf.5:9). ?Winchester, England. c AD 934.

Corinthian capital (**5**:38,cf.**5**:7). The region of Gandhara, became an important area in the development of Buddhist art, in which architectural ornament reflect western Classical art (**5**:39). A leaf scroll on another stone panel from Gandhara demonstrates the simple form which resulted from the rendering down of these motifs to basics – the scrolling stem and the simple leaf (**5**:40). When, however, the Indian lotus becomes entwined in the coils of the scroll, new rich and varied forms demonstrate the versatility of this formula (**6**:11,13).

With the expansion of the Buddhist faith into Central Asia and China, the leaf scroll was associated with various aspects of the architecture of temples and shrines. These have forms closely related to the classical pattern (**6**:15), but change and develop as the scroll becomes an important element in Chinese decorative art (**5**:41,42; **6**:16,19,20).

In the art of Islam the complete ban on representational art in religious contexts resulted in a concentration of artistic endeavour on geometric designs. As a complement to these angular forms are intricate leaves and scrolls of an entirely imaginary nature (**9**:42). The earliest, and rare, illuminations of the Koran, feature the leaf scrolls and a palmette-like flower (**5**:43). Leaf scrolls already current in Asia and China, were brought together in Islamic art to create a distinctive style, not only in Koran illumination, but also in other media such as carpet designs, pottery and metalwork (**5**:44–47). Fine engraved and inlaid metalwork produced by Muslim craftsmen in Venice at the end of the fifteenth century introduced these designs to Europe where they came to be known as 'arabesque' or 'moresque'.

5:38 A detail of the capital on a pilaster of a building depicted on a stone relief has the large leaves and volutes typical of the Corinthian capitals of Greece and Rome. Hadda, Gandhara, north-west Pakistan. *c*. 2nd–3rd cent. AD.

5:39 *Above* A vine scroll from Gandhara, north-west Pakistan. 2nd–3rd cent. AD.

5:40 Leaf scroll on a carved stone panel from Gandhara, north-west Pakistan. 2nd–3rd cent. AD.

5:41 Leaves and 'flowers' set in a scroll pattern. In these abstract forms, there can be no distinction between the stylised leaf and the idea of the half-palmette. From a cave temple at Xiangtangshan, China. 6th cent. AD.

5:42 The design in the centre of a dish is a flower-like rosette made up from elements from the Indian lotus, the acanthus and half-palmette. Henan or Shaanxi ware, China. First half of 8th cent. AD.

5:43 A leaf scroll border from the Koran written and illuminated by Ibn al-Bawwab in Baghdad. Iraq. *c.* AD 1000.

5:44 The decorative possibilities of these flower-like designs are to this day continually exploited. This example from the inside of a 12th-cent. ceramic bowl from Iran.

5:45 A typical arabesque pattern. Block-printed on leather for bookbinding boards. South Arabia/Yemen. 15th cent. AD.

5:46 Detail of a border from a Koran written and illuminated in Cairo in AD 1304.

5:47 Extended drawing of the design engraved on a dish cover. It features counter change, a much used decorative device in Islamic art. Iran. *c.*AD 1600.

6

The Indian Lotus

Two major flower motifs, based on water-lilies, have greatly influenced decorative art in many cultures until the present day. One, the Egyptian lotus originated in Egypt in the third millennium BC and is the subject of Chapter 3. The second found its characteristic form as a motif in Buddhist art. Though quite distinct and unconnected, the two motifs share the same simple symbolism. The flowers of water-lilies close at night and open with the sun in the morning, suggesting death followed by rebirth and renewal. Such symbolism associated with the Indian lotus predates its place in Buddhist iconography, but it is in Buddhist art that the lotus first became an important motif, decorative as well as meaningful.

The Indian lotus motif is based on the species of water-lily which is typified by *Nelumbo nucifera* (**6**:1). This is a larger and more striking plant than the blue and white Nymphaea water-lilies of Egypt (**3**:7,8). The flower of the Indian lotus is bright pink, white or blue, it is 15–20cm in diameter, and stands high above the surface of the water. The petals are a pointed oval and are set in three rows; in the centre is a large pistil, covered by a perforated casing – a gynvecium – which may be as large as the palm of a hand. The pistil is surrounded by a thick fringe of stamens. The large, circular leaf is floppy and stands out of the water on a long stem. All parts of the plant at one time or another inspired decorative motifs.

Although Buddhism was probably founded in the sixth century BC in India, nothing can be associated with Buddhist art before the third century BC. The main Buddhist monument, the *stupa*, is a domed structure surrounded by highly decorated railings pierced by gateways. Carved decoration on these monuments depicts scenes from the legends of the life of the Buddha in real or symbolic forms. But motifs derived from the Indian lotus also appear prominently in sophisticated and stylised forms, suggesting a long history of use in materials which have not survived (**6**:2,11,13).

Contact between the classical world and the Indian sub-continent was maintained both by sea, and by the land route through the Middle East and Central Asia. It was along the east/west land route, which linked the Middle East and India with China and the Far East, that Buddhism spread from India first into Central Asia in the early centuries AD and then into China. With Buddhism came the lotus rosette and lotus scroll together with other features of Buddhist architecture and objects associated with the Buddhist faith.

Plant ornament was rarely used in ancient China before the third century AD, indeed it was not until the tenth and eleventh centuries that

6:1 The Indian pink, white or blue lotus, *Nelumbo nucifera*. (Drawing by Marjorie Blamey.)

flower patterns become widely used in secular decoration. After that, however, the Indian lotus, in more or less stylised forms and in flower scrolls, is a major motif on porcelain (**6**:3,17–19). It was from these sources that the motif became well known and ultimately much copied and popular in Europe (see also p.16ff. and p.91 on the influence of Chinese taste in Europe).

The motif took on different forms in the art of Islam where the lotus flower head, the floppy leaf and the scroll can be traced in the flower-like border patterns, much used in carpet and other textile designs, and in the bizarre vegetation on Iznik plates and tiles (**6**:4,21–23). It was through its use in textile design, and in particular with the popularity of the so-called pomegranate pattern, that this all-purpose flower became a persistent motif in European decorative art (**6**:5; **0**:12–17).

The growth of interest in oriental and ancient art in the nineteenth century led to the inclusion of exotic motifs in pattern books used by artists and craftsmen (on pattern books see p.19ff.). The oriental form of the Indian lotus motif was reintroduced as, for example, on a comb with an openwork lotus design in 'Persian Style' made in Paris in the 1890s by Louis Wiese, a jeweller who specialised in reproducing the styles of past periods (**6**:6). In England, the Indian lotus lent itself to the sinuous lines of the Art Nouveau style of design in forms which are still familiar today in furnishing fabrics, wallpapers, and carpets (**6**:7–9).

6:2 The Indian lotus rosette or medallion carved in stone on the Sanchi Stupa I. The three slightly different blooms are interspersed by flowers seen in profile. Madhya Pradesh, India. 1st cent. BC/1st cent. AD.

6:3 Detail of the cut design on a mould for a Ding ware dish. Lotus flowers in the centre, and peony flowers in the surrounding border, are set on scrolling stems while the leaves also take on flower-like forms. Song dynasty, China. AD 1189.

6:4 *Above* Flower scroll border from the frontispiece of a Koran painted in Egypt. AD. *Below* Scroll design of fantastic flowers on a painted border tile from Iznik, Turkey. Ottoman Empire. 2nd half of 16th cent. AD.

6:5   The Indian lotus flower in a stylised form, embroidered in ivory on the blue silk of a skirt border. Norway. 18th cent.

6:7   Glazed tile with a lotus motif surrounded by the sinuous scrolls of the Art Nouveau style. Malkin, Edge & Co, Staffordshire, England. Early 20th cent.

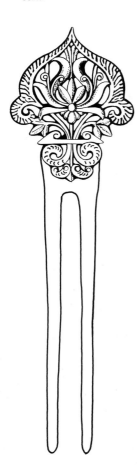

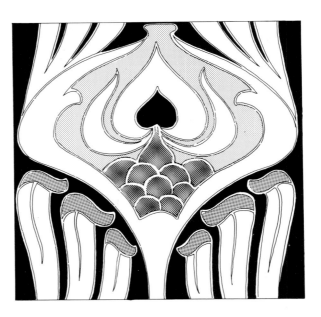

6:8   The motif is highly stylised on another English tile, made by Doulton, Staffordshire. Early 20th cent.

6:6   Hair comb of bone with gold mount. Louis Wiese, Paris 1890–1900.

6:9   A small silver and enamel pendant in Liberty & Co., London, Yule-tide Gift catalogue of 1909, is another stylised version of the Indian lotus.

The Indian lotus motif in Buddhist art

The Indian lotus gave rise to several motifs in Buddhist art. Images of the Buddha and Bodhisattvas are often shown sitting or standing on highly stylised lotus flowers and the lotus is one of the Buddha's auspicious signs (6:10). The lotus rosette or medallion is the flower seen from above and is seen, for example, on the gateway structure of the *stupas* at Sanchi and Amaravati (6:2,11). The petals of the lotus rosette on the base of a small gold reliquary from Bimaran illustrate the shape which became a feature of many lotus-related motifs (6:12).

Contacts with the west took place along the trade routes which led from Europe and the Middle East to the Indian subcontinent and through Central Asia to China. These contacts began before the brief invasion by Alexander the Great in 326 BC, and were later much reinforced in the period of the Roman Empire. Influences from classical motifs associated with the decoration and enrichment of buildings can be seen in Buddhist architecture. In Gandhara, in a strategic position along the trade routes on the border between Afghanistan and Pakistan, the acanthus, ivy and vine scrolls were adapted to forms which became very influential in Buddhist art (5:38–42). The Indian lotus motif was incorporated in a scroll design on the same model as many roughly contemporary Roman vine scrolls or acanthus ornaments. The more free-flowing lotus scrolls from the Amaravati stupa are variations on the same theme (6:11,13,14). The scroll rising from a vase is a variant of the vase and flower motif which was also very popular in Roman decoration. The Indian lotus motif, in one of its later forms, became associated with the vase and flower motif in, for example, European folk art (0:15 and p.21-2)

Buddhism, together with the style of architecture and objects associated with the faith, spread to China along the trade routes through Central Asia. A rare find of wooden architectural fragments from a Buddhist shrine in the Tarim basin in Central Asia illustrates the extent of classical influence. A wooden beam, for example, is carved with a stylised bay-leaf moulding, leafscrolls, rosettes and a reef-knot – all common motifs in the western Classical tradition (6:15).

6:10 Different versions of the 'lotus throne'. *Above* Gandhara, *c.*2nd–5th cent. AD. *Centre* On a Chinese blockprint from AD 947 the Bodhisattva Avalokiteshvara (the lotus bearer) stands on a lotus flower and holds another in his hand. *Below* The pedestal of the bronze figure of the seated Buddha from South India has a double lotus petal motif. 13th cent. AD.

6:12 The lotus rosette on the base of a small gold reliquary from Bimaran, Gandhara, north-west Pakistan. 2nd–3rd cent. AD.

6:11 Detail of lotus designs on stone pillars from the Great Stupa at Amaravati. The lotus rosette shows the gynvecium and stamens of the Indian lotus in realistic detail. Different aspects of the bloom, bud and leaf in stylised forms are set in the loops of scrolling stems. Andhra Pradesh, India. 1st–2nd cent. AD.

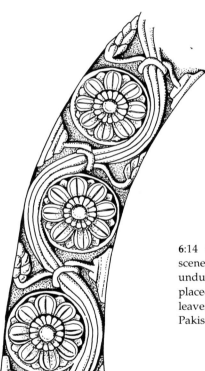

6:14 On an arched border framing a scene from the life of the Buddha is an undulating plant scroll with regularly placed lotus rosettes with highly stylised leaves and buds. Gandhara, north-west Pakistan. c.2nd cent. AD.

6:13 Detail of lotus designs on stone pillars from the Great Stupa at Amaravati. Rising from a vase, the scrolling stem carries in its loops different views of the lotus bloom, the bud and the leaf. Andhra Pradesh, India. 1st–2nd cent. AD.

6:15 Carved wooden beam from the Buddhist shrine at Loulan, in the Tarim Basin in Central Asia. c.3rd cent. AD.

The Chinese flower scroll and the fantastic flower of Islam

6:16 The central panel of the painted decoration on the ceiling of a Buddhist cave temple at Dunhuang, Gansu province, China. The lotus rosette is surrounded by a leaf and flower scroll. Sui dynasty. AD 581–618.

Having been imported into China the Indian lotus and the scroll motifs (of western classical origin) were initially used exclusively as decoration, together with figures and other enrichments, in Buddhist temples and shrines and on metal vessels associated with worship. In designs painted on the ceilings of cave temples at Dunhuang in Gansu, in the far western provinces of China, for example, the lotus rosette is a frequent motif (**6**:16); here it is surrounded by a design in which different aspects of lotus flowers are set on scrolling stems together with small stylised leaves. These are not the leaves of the lotus plant in nature (**6**:1), but a pseudo-leaf typical of the leaf scroll motif of the western classical tradition (**6**:15).

There had been no previous tradition of plant decoration in China, so that when ceramics fired at high temperatures began to be produced for domestic purposes in the sixth century AD, the imported lotus motif in more or less stylised forms dominates the designs (**6**:17,18). More realistic lotus plants, which may have relied on observations from nature, occur painted on later Chinese porcelains.

The flower scroll motif, however, retained throughout its long history in Chinese porcelain decoration the essential elements of its Buddhist architectural heritage. Flower-heads, which can be identified as lotus blooms by reference to this motif's gradual stylisation in Buddhist art, are set in regular sequence within the coils of the scroll (**6**:19, cf. **6**:15,16). Leaves remain small, stylised and unrelated to the leaf shapes of the natural plants (**6**:1). Little attempt is made to produce flowers in the scroll

6:17 Lightly incised under the glaze of a porcelain bowl, is a design of stylised lotus blossoms, scrolling stems and small conventionalised leaves. The three-lobed feature may represent the natural leaf, curled and seen from the side. Song dynasty, China. 11th–12th cent. AD.

6:18   Design of lotus leaves, lightly incised under the glaze. Yue ware, China. first half of 10th cent. AD.

6:19   Flower scroll with lotus flowers and small conventionalised leaves. In the centre a stylised peony. Plate, painted in blue on white porcelain. Jingdezhen, Jiangxi province, China. 2nd half of 14th cent. AD.

6:20   Peony scroll, painted in blue on a white porcelain jar. Jingdezhen, Jiangxi province, China. c.AD 1350.

6:21   The Indian lotus set in an intricate scroll and inlaid with silver and gold on a writing box from Egypt. c.AD 1300–1350

which look like those of a living plant. (The shape of the flowers is at times reminiscent of the flower-like arrangements created from acanthus and half-palmette-like leaves which were also a part of the repertoire of motifs in Buddhist cave temples (**5**:41)). When the peony became a fashionable plant, it replaced the lotus bloom in the scroll. As was the case with the lotus, this is a highly decorative motif, but not a good likeness of the living plant (**6**:20).

From the tenth century the kilns at Jingdezhen, in Jiangxi province, China, began large scale production of fine porcelain which has continued to this day. Markets for the trade in fine porcelain were concentrated in different regions at different times, but the influence of China's porcelains has been sustained and world-wide. Chinese porcelain reached Europe in some quantity in the fourteenth century where it was used as gifts by Europe's nobility. Large-scale imports began in the early seventeenth century alongside other oriental items such as silk and laquer.

Chinese decorative art also influenced the art of Islam. It first became important with the Mongol conquests in the thirteenth century, conquests which produced powerful dynasties which ruled empires stretching from China to Asia Minor and Egypt. The emergence of rich and powerful courts encouraged all types of arts and crafts. In the hands of Islamic craftsmen, the lotus motif was the subject of further stylisation and became increasingly fantastic, while still tending to the rather rigid geometrical compositions favoured in much Islamic art (**6**:4,21,22). In the lavish art of the Ottoman Empire, highly coloured tiles and ceramics were decorated with many kinds of flowers, sometimes in natural profusion. Such designs are, however, often more disciplined than is at first apparent, while among the naturalistic garden flowers are fantastic variations of the lotus and peony blooms and leaves first developed in the East (**6**:4,23).

In Europe, both the Chinese and the

Islamic forms of this all-purpose flower motif became incorporated in textile designs, and in the pattern books which greatly influenced design and taste from the fifteenth century onwards. It has become one of the most favoured flower motifs in European folk art and survives as a major motif today (**6**:5–9; **0**:12,13,15).

6:22   The hexagon shape of blue and white painted tiles from the Mosque at Edirne determines the compositions of stylised flowers and leaves. Turkey. 15th cent. AD.

6:23   On brightly coloured plates produced at Iznik some of the flowers are fantastic versions of the lotus, with the gynvecium developed in the shape of pomegranates. This form of the lotus motif is known as 'pomegranate' when it occurs in textile designs (**0**:12,13). Turkey. 16th cent. AD.

7

The Celtic Scroll

'The Celtic scroll' is here used as a convenient label for a distinctive group of motifs, characterised by sinuous spiral scrolls, sometimes asymmetrical or with a threefold symmetry. The group is discussed separately from other spiral-based ornament, dealt with in Chapter 1, because of its complicated and important role in the development of art styles in Europe. Scroll motifs of this kind are associated with the Celtic peoples of the Iron Age who, from the fifth century BC, inhabited an area which at its most extensive reached from the Balkans and Western Asia in the east to Italy in the south and the British Isles in the west (7:1,5–11). The motif was ultimately based on Mediterranean lotus and palmette borders and scrolls and found its most mature form in the outlying western fringes of the Celtic world in the British Isles (7:2,12–17). In Ireland and parts of Britain, the scroll became one of the main elements in early Christian medieval art, together with animal and ribbon interlace from Germanic, Roman and Anglo-Saxon sources (7:3,18–23; **9**:37–40; **2**:48,49).

Since the word 'Celtic' is used in contexts where it can mean rather different things, a brief outline of the history of the Celts may be useful. The common working use of iron was introduced to central Europe sometime in the eighth century BC and spread across Europe over a number of centuries as a result of the movement of peoples from the east. In the past this has been interpreted in terms of large-scale migrations – now it is more generally thought of in the context of smaller groups of invaders settling among existing populations, possibly as overlords. Whether these incomers were Celts or not is uncertain.

In the early fifth century BC the settlements of these groups were replaced by people who are clearly identified by archaeologists as 'Celts'. They, like their predecessors, represented a wealthy, aristocratic, horse-riding, war-like society with wide trading connections reflected in the art recovered in rich burial deposits. The Celts are labelled after a people who are generally thought to have emerged in a central European area around the Middle Rhine and north-east France in the first half of the fifth century BC. In the fourth and third centuries BC some tribes moved southwards into Italy (where they sacked Rome *c*.387 BC) and eastwards into the Balkans and Anatolia. Celtic groups also spread into western France and the British Isles. In all these areas they absorbed some of the traditions of the older inhabitants among whom they settled as tribal chieftains. They are unlikely to have thought of themselves as a cohesive people with a collective name. To add to the confusion we do not know if this group of people spoke a language related to the languages now

7:1 Units of three linked spiral scrolls make up a plant-like border. Detail from a design on a bronze flagon, found in the grave of a Celtic chieftain at Waldalgesheim, Mainz-Bingen, Germany. Mid-4th cent. BC.

7:2 Units of three linked spiral scrolls make up a design which, with minor variations, is repeated three times in the design on a bronze mount from Brentford, London. 3rd–1st cent. BC.

7:3 Decorated letters from the Book of Kells, Ireland. Early 9th cent. AD.

known as 'Celtic'. The name 'Celt' derives from that given by classical writers from the sixth century BC onwards to the people living north of the Alps (*Keltoi* in Greek and *Galli* or *Celtae* in Latin). The name was not used at this time to describe the language spoken by such people, and at no time did the classical writers apply this name to the people living in the British Isles or in Ireland.

The ancient Celts decorated such functional objects as domestic vessels, horse-trappings and weapons with designs which appear generally abstract, though plainly often based on plant-like forms. Since such objects are clearly of high status and value, these striking designs have led to much speculation about their possible symbolic meaning. Ian Stead (1985, p.7), expresses in bleak but salutary terms his doubts about the chances of success in this quest:

> Sensitive and appreciative modern writers have made valiant efforts to interpret its (Celtic art's) meaning, but the imagination of modern man is an unreliable guide to the aims, beliefs and feelings of his primitive forebears. Only the Celtic artist and his patrons could explain Celtic art, and as they never set pen to paper the knowledge died with them.

The Celts in Continental Europe were gradually engulfed by the expansion of the Romans, a process which began in the early third century BC and reached its furthest limits in the British Isles about the time of the birth of Christ. During the period of Roman occupation, the Celts in Wales, Scotland and northern England and in Ireland remained, if not totally unaffected by their Roman neighbours, still unconquered.

The link between the surviving Celtic languages of Western Europe and the description and name of the ancient 'Celts' was not made until the eighteenth century when it emerged as a result of a growing interest in antiquity in Europe and particularly in Britain. In the nineteenth-century Celtic revival in Ireland, the entire style of the art in its early medieval forms – regardless of its separate motifs – became symbolic of national identity (**7**:24). In the Arts and Crafts Movement and the Art Nouveau art style at the turn of the century, these motifs were also a major source of inspiration for designs (**7**:4,25–26; **9**:21).

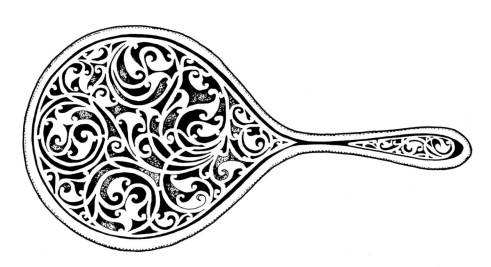

7:4 Design on the back of a mirror in a silver and tortoiseshell toilet set (cf.**7**:17). Liberty & Co, London. *c*.1925.

The Celtic scroll motif in Continental Europe

7:5 The openwork drinking horn mount in gold from a Celtic chieftain's tomb in Eigenbilzen, Belgium, has a border of a lotus and palmette motif, very close to classical prototypes of this ancient motif (cf. **3**:25). 5th cent. BC.

The art style which is labelled 'Celtic' appears rather suddenly in Western Europe in the fifth century BC with a focus in the Rhineland, but with a wide distribution in Central Europe (**7**:1,5–9). The early Iron Age societies in Europe were wealthy and wine-loving. Established trading links with the Mediterranean – through Italy with the Etruscans and with the Greek colony at Marseilles on the south coast of France, for example – were already extensive and included the import of richly decorated objects associated with the storing and drinking of wine.

Etruscan art included many motifs which originated from Western Asia and the Near East. Among the motifs which appear in the art of Europe as a result of influences from, and trade with, these areas were sphinxes, griffins, bulls and lions. It was, however, the subsidiary and supporting borders of palmette and lotus motifs which became the subject of vigorous development by the Celtic tribes as they moved south of the Alps into northern Italy in the early fourth century BC. Throughout the next couple of hundred years, variations on these motifs mark the progress of the rapid expansion of the Celts south into Italy, as well as both eastwards and westwards in Europe (**7**:1,5–7; **4**:24–26).

A distinctive Celtic style emerged as designs developed more abstract forms, in which paired and opposed scrolls became a dominant motif with a strong emphasis on diagonals and triangles (**7**:1,7). The ingenious way in which three linked scrolls are manipulated is the most typical single feature of Celtic art (**7**:2,8,26).

A tendency to ambiguity is another

7:6 The shape of a pot from Saint Pol-de-Léon, Finistère in Brittany, is modelled on metal vessels in contemporary Etruscan art. The design, linked by oblique scrolls recalls the palmette-scroll motif. 4th cent. BC.

7:7 Detail from a bronze disc, embossed in gold and inlaid with coral and enamel. Auvers-sur-Oise, France. No longer plant-like, opposed scrolls now dominate an increasingly abstract design. Early 4th cent. BC.

characteristic of this art. There is often doubt about the real nature of a motif: whether a curving lobe is a leaf or a fleshy scroll, or whether a face is a face, or merely a juxtaposition of leaves and scrolls which ambiguously suggests eyes and nose (7:9,10). Likewise, complicated designs obscure the regular compass-drawn grids on which patterns are constructed. There may also be an ambivalence between patterns and their background (7:11,17).

7:8 Variations on three linked spirals: *Above* and *centre* Designs on a band of gold leaf and a border of iron on a bronze helmet from Amfreville-sous-les-Monts, France. *Below* Drawing of a detail of the design on a gold bracelet from Waldalgesheim, Mainz-Bingen, Germany. Second half 4th cent. BC.

7:9 Palmette scrolls, as well as elusive faces, are evoked in a typical Celtic scroll design on the bronze mount of a scabbard. Filottrano, Italy. Late 4th cent. BC.

7:10 A mask from a bronze shield found in the River Witham, Lincolnshire, is an ambiguous figure made up of plant-like elements. England, early 3rd cent. BC.

7:11 Openwork bronze disc from a burial at Somme-Bionne, France. Designs like these were produced on a compass-drawn grid. 5th cent. BC. (From Megaw 1989,61.)

The Celtic scroll motif in the British Isles

There is little evidence to suggest when Celtic peoples reached the British Isles or to indicate where they came from; it is probable that at least two separate groups of Celtic settlers reached Britain and Ireland from the Continent at some stage. It is now thought unlikely that large numbers were involved in these movements. It is assumed that trade and other forms of contact with the Continent were also responsible for the introduction of iron working and later for other innovations including Celtic taste in art.

From the middle of the third century BC, at a time when the Romans began their expansion through the Celtic lands of Europe, the Celtic style of decoration took an independent direction in the British Isles, developing its motifs in ever more sophisticated ways. Much of the earliest Celtic art in the British Isles is found on weapons and horse-trappings. Many were found in circumstances which suggest ritual depositions, often in rivers, rather than in burials, for the religion of the Celts was associated with water – rivers, streams, lakes and bogs. This was a high-status art, indicating the presence of an aristocratic warrior class, and can best be seen on a number of swords, scabbards and shields (7:2,12–16). On these objects the Celtic scroll motif is fully mature, having successfully transformed a repertoire of mainly classical ornament into an art style with an identity and vocabulary of its own. Its main features comprise linked or opposed spirals and scrolls with sinuous and attenuated trailing tendrils. There is an ambiguity in apparently abstract designs: scrolls may look like birds'

7:12 Linked and opposed scrolls: a detail from the design on a bronze scabbard from Lisnacrogher, Ireland. 3rd cent. BC.

heads, faces or plant tendrils (7:10,14), while contrasting surface textures or colours tease the eye as to what is the motif and what is the background (7:15–17). The back of a bronze mirror from Holcombe, Devon, is typical of the best of these designs (7:17). The layout of the design on the back of the mirror is based on a compass-drawn grid. The areas engraved with a 'basketry' pattern can be seen as the primary design, but they can also be interpreted as the backgroud to the plain pattern; if the mirror is hung up by its handle, a mask is revealed at its base.

Throughout the Roman occupation of Britain (from the middle of the first century to the end of the fourth century AD) the art of the native Britons survived in the north and west of the British Isles. At this time, the Celtic scroll was re-interpreted to serve new circumstances and media, influenced to some extent by the close proximity

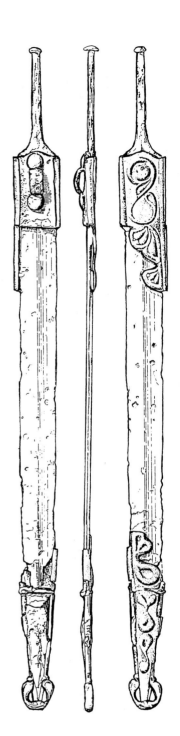

7:13 Scabbard mount on a sword, from Shepperton Ranges. England. 2nd cent. BC. (Drawing by David Williams.)

7:16 Bronze harness mount inlaid with red enamel in a scroll design based on a compass-drawn grid. Polden Hill, Somerset. England. 1st cent. AD.

7:14 The design in repoussé on the flange of a round shield boss in bronze. The River Thames at Wandsworth. England. 3rd–2nd cent. AD.

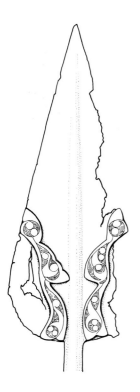

7:17 Bronze mirror from Holcombe, Devon. England. 1st cent. BC–1st cent. AD. (Drawing by Philip Compton.)

7:15 Iron spearhead. Recovered from the River Thames. England. 2nd–1st cent. BC.

7:18 Scroll design on a hanging-bowl mount in bronze and enamel from the burial of an Anglo-Saxon king at Sutton Hoo, Suffolk. England. c.AD 625–32.

7:19 The design on a bronze disc, inlaid with red enamel from Lagore, Crannog, Co. Meath. Ireland. 7th–8th cent. AD.

7:20 Decorated letter from the Lindisfarne Gospels, Northumberland, England. c. AD 698.

of Roman culture and, more importantly, by the introduction of Christianity in the fourth century. The departure of the Romans, and the arrival of the Anglo-Saxons, brought the vigorous Germanic animal art to England. The high quality of the indigenous Celtic art, which became a major contributor to the art style which developed among the Christian Anglo-Saxons, is evident in such 'hanging bowl' designs as the scroll on a mount in the royal burial at Sutton Hoo (7:18).

Just as in an earlier period, the Celtic artist had skilfully adapted a variety of motifs to make striking designs on swords and shields, so did the later insular scribe blend a repertoire of motifs from Continental and Mediterranean sources into a lively and versatile style well suited to the miniature scale of an illuminated letter or embellishment (7:3,20,21; 2:49; 9:37–40). The contribution of the Celtic scroll to this style takes the form of a linked spiral scroll motif, often based on ruled or compass-drawn grids which determined the layout of manuscript pages. Grids also served to aid the transfer or copying of motifs and their reduction and enlargement for different purposes. Grids impose a rigid, symmetrical composition, a tendency which the spiral scroll motifs obscured and relieved (7:22).

The taste for spirals also invaded the other elements of this style; drawing into tight spirals the branches of the vine scroll, the ear of an animal or ribbons in an interlace pattern (7:20,23). In the course of the eighth century the scroll motif became less common in a style in which the ribbon and animal interlace dominated. With the temporary settlement of Scandinavians in the British Isles, Viking art styles entered the repertoire of the indigenous art: this in turn was overtaken by the Romanesque in the late eleventh century.

7:21 Spiral scroll motifs from a carpet page in the Book of Durrow. Northumbria, England. Second half 7th cent. AD.

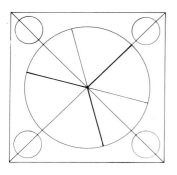

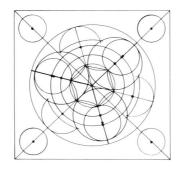

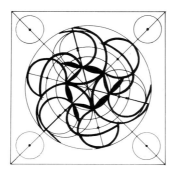

7:22 Analysis of a small square from the Lindisfarne Gospels illustrates the use of a compass-drawn grid which could be traced on the back of the vellum page.

7:23 Vine scroll carved on an Anglo-Saxon stone cross from Bakewell, Derbyshire. The tight spirals leave little room for the grapes. England. 8th–9th cent. AD.

The revival of Celtic art in Ireland

In the eighteenth and nineteenth centuries the Gothic revival in art and architecture resulted from a growing interest in the history of the Middle Ages. A major heroic and romantic heritage was perceived to be of Celtic origin.

The interest in the literary and antiquarian remains of ancient Celtic culture began in the middle of the eighteenth century. It was particularly stimulated by the publication in 1762 of *Ossian*, the poems of a Celtic hero, which James Macpherson claimed to have translated from an ancient text, but which he had composed on the basis of Highland folklore. *Ossian* did, however, capture the imagination of Europe – particularly of Germany and France – and drew attention to Irish heroic poems, mostly written down in the early Middle Ages but supposedly drawn from earlier oral sources.

The development of Irish antiquarian studies began in the first half of the nineteenth century, through the publication of topographical drawings of monuments in the field and the study and collection of objects and manuscripts by the Royal Irish Academy. The publication of this material led to the conviction that the customs, music-making, story-telling and so on of the poor Irish-speaking peasants could be identified as the last traces of the ancient 'Celtic' culture.

With a growing sense of national identity, and a need for a visual expression of Irish nationality, attention turned to models from what was seen as the golden age of Irish art – early medieval art as represented by the Book of Kells, the Tara brooch and such great monuments as the Irish High Crosses. Emblematic motifs –

7:24 'These admirably executed imitations (of the Tara brooch) can be had in various styles, from us, or our agents, at a price from two to seven guineas each'... (From Waterhouse & Co pamphlet, 1852.)

7:25 Scroll design by Henry van de Velde in the style of Art Nouveau on a bound copy of W.Y. Fletcher, *English Bookbinding in the British Museum*, 1895.

the shamrock, wolfhounds and round towers were everywhere imitated. Interlace and knot patterns, as well as spiral scrolls, began to be used wherever ancient Ireland was evoked to demonstrate the splendours of the Irish heritage.

This style of ornament also proved a popular and commercial success. Reproduction jewellery, manufactured by Waterhouse & Co. in Dublin, for example, illustrates how such undertakings were seen to extend in meaning beyond mere business. In a pamphlet of 1852 George Waterhouse tells that the Royal Irish Academy had allowed him access to its collections of brooches and other items of jewellery to

… take correct drawings of the best patterns, which eventually led us to an extensive manufacture of them; and from that period a steady and increasing demand … Ireland can now boast to the continued use of peculiarly national ornaments, worn by her princes and nobles in ages long since past.

Waterhouse himself was the initial purchaser of one of the most striking

of these brooches which he named the Royal Tara Brooch (although it did not come from Tara), copies of which were foremost amongst his range of products (7:24).

Towards the end of the century, a second wave of a Celtic revival became associated with the Arts and Crafts Movement. As with *Ossian*, the interest in Celtic design now influenced the wider art world. The designs were taken out of the hands of the commercial imitators and were used freely and creatively in new media like stained glass, textile and embroidery. Designs in the style of Art Nouveau sometimes evoke the earlier Celtic designs by which they were inspired (7:25,26). More often, however, it is the idea of interlace in conjunction with the sinuous lines which creates successful designs in this style (7:4; 9:21). (On the more recent attempts at encouraging the use of 'Celtic' motifs in modern design by George Bain and others see p.183ff.)

7:26 In a design of a brooch, triangular features are linked in ways which recall early Celtic designs (cf.7:8). (After an advertisement for Liberty & Co, London.) Archibald Knox, England. *c*.1900.

8

The rosette and intersecting circles motif

The term 'rosette' is used to describe a large and varied number of motifs. In its simplest form it is a design of radiating petals, a flower seen from above. It is usually a very stylised motif, without symbolic significance, and is used in a supporting or minor decorative role. Such simple motifs were created independently in many places at different times. The motif is so universal that it would be impossible to cover its detailed development here. This chapter, therefore, concentrates on a discussion of one of its earliest and most important appearances – in Western Asia. It is here that radiating motifs can be traced back to the fifth millennium and where the rosette, or star, was a significant motif (**8**:1,6,13–16).

In Egypt the lotus flower, seen from above, became a rosette motif which was sometimes realistic but more often highly stylised (**8**:2, **3**:12 *above*,). The lotus rosette became further stylised as the motif became a part of the art of the ancient Near East, where rosette motifs already had a long history (**8**:3). (On the lotus rosette in Indian art see Chapter 6, **6**:2,11,12).

Rosette designs are also produced by compass-drawn intersecting circles (**8**:4,5. On other geometrical constructions used in ornament see Chapter 9, **9**:22–24). Abstract constructions are frequently the framework for area-filling designs, but the six-pointed and four-pointed stars are also isolated from the grid pattern and may be given a floral character (the six-pointed star is sometimes known as the 'marigold' motif). The geometrical principle used to divide the circumference of a circle into equal parts was well understood in Western Asia in the first half of the second millennium BC; it is, for example, the subject of a mathematical problem on a clay tablet (Barnett, 1957,p.64 and n.7). Designs based on these grids are, however, known from much earlier times (**8**:6).

Rosettes and intersecting circle motifs were widely used in Egypt and in the art of the Mediterranean (**8**:7–10, **1**:31,35). Rosettes became a part of the Greek and Roman repertoire of decorative motifs and the possibilities and permutations of the intersecting circles were enthusiastically explored in Roman mosaics (**8**:11). In Europe the rosette is a universal motif. From the early Middle Ages to the present day, rosette motifs have been used in all kinds of decoration – in architecture, furniture, furnishings and metalwork. A page from Meyer, *Handbuch der Ornamentik*, 1898, illustrates some architectural uses of this ornament (**8**:12). Like the acanthus leaf the rosette is a universal and convenient device providing, for example, a central feature in a design, a decorative head to a functional peg or nail, or cover for the cross-over points in a lattice.

8:1 Details of rosette designs from cylinder seal impressions. Mesopotamia. *Left* and *centre c.*2900 BC, *right c.*2600 BC.

8:2 A rosette flower based on the white lotus, *Nymphaea lotus* painted inside a glazed bowl. (cf.**3**:7) Egypt. *c.*1400–1320 BC.

8:3 Stylised lotus rosette incised in the fragment of an ivory bowl. Megiddo, Palestine. 12th cent. BC.

8:4 The circumference of a circle can be divided by its radius into six equal parts. Circles of the same size, drawn from these points, produce a grid which forms the basis for many rosette and star designs.

8:5 In this grid the circumference is divided into four equal parts.

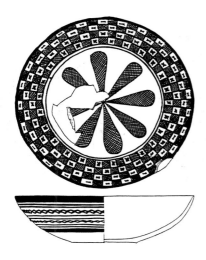

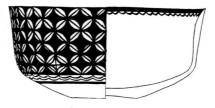

8:6   Pottery of Tell Halaf type painted in red on a buff slip. Arpachiyah, Iraq. 5th millennium BC. (After Mallowan and Rose 1935 fig.53,1; 60,3.)

8:7   Cylinder seal impression from northern Syria. 18th–17th cent. BC.

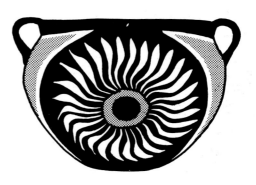

8:8   Kamares ware cup with a painted rotating rosette motif. Minoan Crete. 17th–16th cent. BC.

8:9   Rosettes and intersecting circles were important motifs in Mycenaean decorative art. Ear-ring and gold foil disc from Shaft grave III at Mycenae, Greece. c.1550–1500 BC.

8:10   Painted ceiling patterns in the tomb of Amenemhat, Thebes, Egypt. *c.*1470–1379 BC.

8:11   Two of many variations on the intersecting circles design used in Roman mosaics. Antioch, Turkey. 2nd–mid-6th cent. AD.

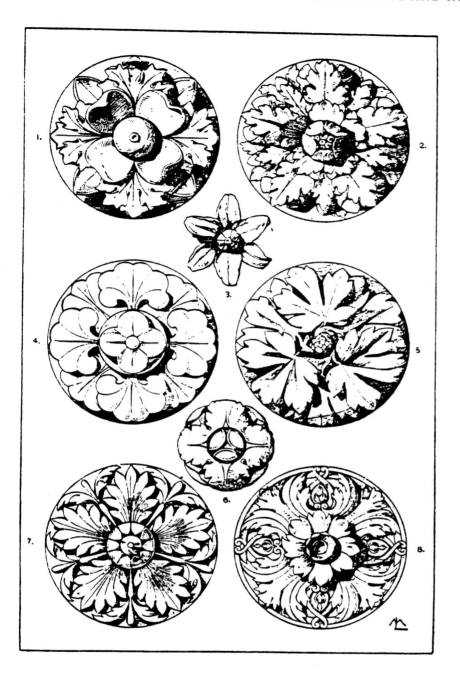

8:12 1 Greek rosette, 2–3 Roman rosettes,
4 Romanesque keystone from the
Monastery of the Holy Cross in Vienna.
13th cent., 5 Early Gothic keystone from
the Sainte-Chapelle, Paris. 1240, 6 French
renaissance of Louis XIII (1610–1643),
7 Italian renaissance, from the door of the
Baptistry in Parma, 8 Ceiling rose in
plaster, French late 19th cent. (From
Meyer 1898, Taf.115.)

The rosette and star motifs in the ancient Near East

Rosettes and intersecting circle patterns have a long history in Western Asia. They occur, together with other designs, as early as the fifth millennium BC on the fine painted pottery from Tell Halaf in Syria and at other sites where similar pottery was produced (8:6). It is not known if the motifs had a special significance in this context.

In the third millennium BC, however, the rosette or star represented divine figures or ideas. Scenes on cylinder seals provide information about the siginficance of motifs which occur in connection with deities and heroes. The rosette flower, as well as the rosette star, has been identified as the symbol of the fertility goddess Inanna in Sumerian art, while the heavenly bodies, sun, moon and star, represent the sun-god Shamash, the moon-god Sin and the goddess Ishtar in the form of the star-disc and crescent (8:13, 4:9). In the rich finds from the royal graves at Ur the rosette, or star, is a very common motif on all sorts of objects, suggesting that it was not just a divine symbol but a good-luck sign in general (8:14). The continued function of the rosette as an amulet or charm is apparent in the low reliefs which panel the walls of the North-West Palace at Nimrud. The king, the crown-prince and mythological attendants, wear bracelets which are interpreted as a protective device, placed, as is the custom with amulets, on a vulnerable part of the body (8:15).

The rosette was also a purely decorative motif, used in conjunction with other semi-floral lotus and palmette ornament (3:24, 4:1). On a stone pavement from Nimrud, the borders of lotus and rosettes surround panels of intersecting circles (8:16).

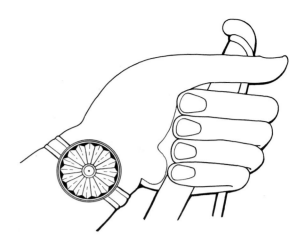

8:13 The star disc, often shown resting in the cradle of the moon, represents the main astral bodies and their respective deities. Mesopotamia. *Above* second half 3rd millennium BC, *below* 18th–17th cent. BC.

8:15 A detail from a panel in low relief in the North-West Palace at Nimrud. The crown-prince and mythological attendants all wear rosette-shaped bracelets on both wrists, probably as amulets. Assyria. 865–860 BC.

8:14 Gaming board made of wood, inlaid with shell, lapis lazuli and red limestone. The squares with a rosette were perhaps 'lucky', while the eyes on other squares may have represented the 'evil eye'. The small lozenge-shaped engravings on the side of the board, however, are also eyes – the *oculi* motif – associated with ancient hunting magic. The Royal Cemetery at Ur, Iraq. *c.*2600 BC.

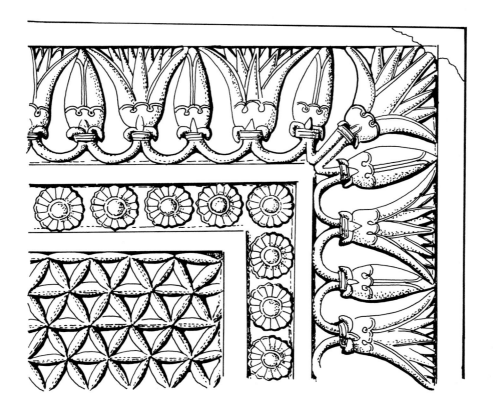

8:16 Detail from a stone pavement.
Nimrud, Assyria. 9th cent. BC.

9

Twists, plaits, interlace and geometrical constructions

The motif known as twist, cable, *guilloche* or *entrelac* can be traced back to the beginning of the Neolithic period when pottery began to appear in the archaeological record. Before the technique of potting developed, containers were made of other materials among the most important of which were fibres – woven, twined, knotted and plaited into baskets and nets – hollowed out wood and bark or stitched-together skins. The twisting and plaiting of fibres to make cord, nets and baskets was, with knotting, weaving and all other ways of manipulating fibres, among the earliest human activities. Incidentally these activities produced patterns which were imitated decoratively in other materials from the earliest times: a thin bone disc of Palaeolithic date from France, for example, bears a motif which recalls leather stitching (**9**:1).

The earliest painted pottery often has decoration which imitates the patterns which are formed when different strands are used in the plaiting of baskets (**9**:2). The twist pattern, in its simplest form, was produced by the impression of a cord in soft clay. Potters all over the world, from Neolithic times to the present, have made use of this convenient method of decoration, making patterns by impressing cords, plaits, knots, combs, shells or nails into the clay of a pot while it was still soft (**9**:3; **1**:21 *left*). The motifs which are the subject of this chapter, however, imitate twisted cord by creating the illusion of strands passing over and under each other. Such a motif occurs on a group of clay stamps, from the early Neolithic settlement Çatal Hüyük in Central Anatolia, Turkey. A flint dagger from the same site, however, has a bone handle in the shape of a coiled snake, suggesting that the interpretation of the stamp design as entwined snakes is a possibility in this context (**9**:4; on other stamp designs from this site see **1**:14).

Snakes occur frequently in the art of the ancient Near East. A cylinder seal impression from Susa, capital of Elam in south-west Iran, for example, has a design of two interlaced snakes. A similar design on a knife handle from Egypt emphasises the widespread use of this and other interlacing animal motifs in the ancient world (**9**:5, **2**:15,16). A decoration of interlaced ribbons on a vessel from Mari in south-central Iran can also best be interpreted as a design of snakes by comparing it with similar vessels where snakes have the same surface decoration of coloured inlay (**9**:6). In other instances, however, an interlaced snake can develop more casually when a head is added to an abstract plaited motif (**9**:7). We are not in a position to judge to what extent a twist or coil – without a head – suggested a snake to the initiated observer.

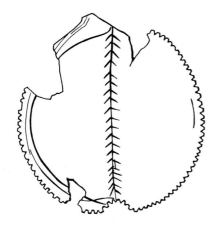

9:1 Bone disc, cut from a scapula. France, *c.*12 000 BC.

9:2 Pottery. *Above* From Hacilar in Anatolia. Second half of the 6th millennium BC. *Below left* From Tell al-Ubaid, Iraq, 5th millennium BC, *below right* from Susa in south-west Iran. First half of the 4th millennium BC. The painted designs recall typical basket patterns.

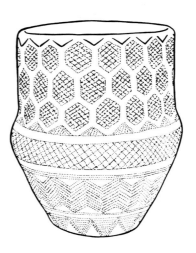

9:3 Pottery with impressed cord decoration from the Neolithic and Early Bronze Age in Europe. *Left* From V. Hoby, Skåne, Sweden. Late 3rd millennium BC, *centre* from Ilford, Dorset, England, *right* from Prague, Czechoslovakia. *c.* 2000 BC.

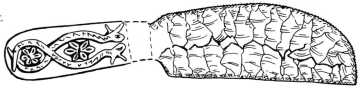

9:4 *Left* Flint dagger with a bone handle carved to represent a coiled snake. *Right* Incised design on a stamp of baked clay, approx. 7 x 3 cm. Çatal Hüyük, Anatolia, Turkey. First half of the 6th millennium BC.

9:5 *Above* Cylinder seal impression from Susa, south-west Iran. *Below* Flint knife with ivory handle. Egypt. 4th millennium BC.

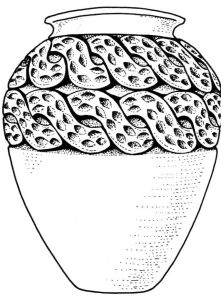

9:6 Vase carved from green steatite. The indentations in the twisted band design originally held coloured inlay perhaps to emphasize their snake-like appearance. Votive offering in the temple of Ishtar, at Mari, south-central Iran. First half of the 3rd millennium BC.

9:7 The normally abstract plait motif on a cylinder seal impression, has taken on the character of a snake by the apparently casual addition of a head. Mesopotamia, *c.*2300 BC.

Later, however, twist patterns associated with the art of northern Syria in the second millennium BC, clearly imitate cords, knots and plaits (**9**:8,9). Craftsmen of Phoenicia and Syria, where twist and plait motifs continued to be popular, used a wide range of tools to work ivory. To produce the ornament on ivory plaques found at Nimrud (part of tribute and loot collected from a wide area by the Assyrian rulers in the ninth century BC) a pair of compasses were used to construct a regular pattern of circles and curved lines (**9**:10). The use of the compass as the basis for decorative motifs had already developed in the ancient Near East as early as the second millennium BC. Linking circles could also be used to produce rosettes (**8**:4,5) and winding band motifs such as the so-called 'pulley-pattern' (**9**:11). Initially most commonly used on small bone and ivory objects, the compass-drawn rosettes, winding band, and concentric circle patterns became important motifs on metal objects of the Bronze Age, not only in the Mediterranean but throughout Europe (**1**:13,37–39; **7**:11,22; **8**:9).

The twist was among several motifs of Western Asian origin which provided the inspiration for vigorous experimentation with decoration in pottery and architecture in Greece from the eighth century BC (**2**:25; **4**:17). The established orders of temple architecture required enrichments which developed standardised forms. Among the motifs developed were various twists and interlaces. A reconstruction of the decoration in painted terracotta on a sixth-century Doric building from Olympia, for example, shows a double twist as a major motif (**9**:12). Later larger-scale motifs of the same kinds were painted directly onto the stone. Carved enrichments were also embellished with colour, as on the Temple of Athena at Pergamon where the deeply cut strands of a plaited ornament originally held coloured inlay (**9**:13). The plait is constructed on the same principles as that in ivory from Nimrud (**9**:10).

Twists, plaits and interlacing motifs are decorative conventionalised motifs and have, with few exceptions, no symbolic meaning. They do not, as a rule, appear to portray real plaits in a functional capacity. Knots, however, by virtue of the obvious symbolism of joining and uniting as

9:8 *Left* The simple twist is also known by other names such as the cable, or *guilloche*. *Right* Examples of some of the many variations on twist and plait-like motifs. Details from cylinder seal impressions, Syria 19th–18th cent. BC.

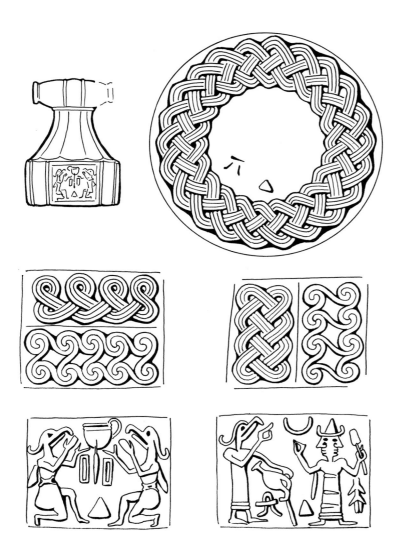

9:9 A stamp seal from Anatolia *c.*1600 BC. The four panels and the base, drawn separately and enlarged, could all be used as seals.

9:10 The simple twist and a more complicated plait, constructed using a compass. Both motifs are found on ivory plaques from Nimrud, Assyria. 9th–8th cent. BC.

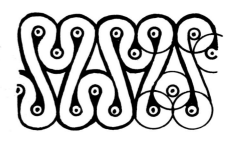

9:11 'Pulley-pattern' from an ivory
handle. Atchana, Hatay, Turkey.
14th–13th cent. BC.

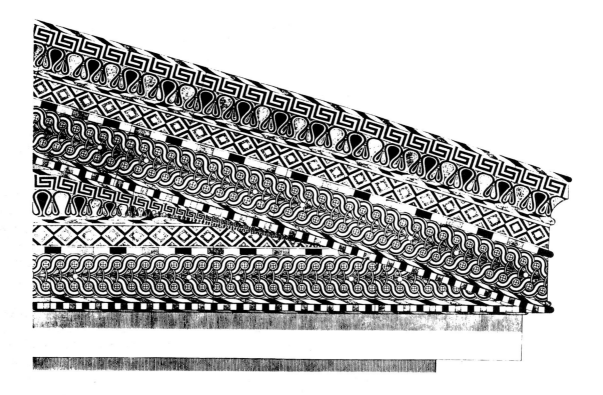

9:12   Reconstruction of terracotta
decoration of the Treasury of Gela,
Olympia. Late 6th cent. BC. (Drawing by
Hans Schlief.)

9:13   Plait ornament, deeply cut in the
marble, to allow the inlay of a coloured
substance. Temple of Athena, Pergamon,
Anatolia. 3rd cent. BC.

well as by their practical uses in everyday life, are universal motifs in art and have a multitude of realistic as well as symbolic applications. Among knots, the reef knot, and its companion the Granny, are by far the most common (9:14). From the third millennium BC onwards the sign which symbolised the Unification of Upper and Lower Egypt shows the plants representing the two regions tied by a reef knot around the lung-and-trachea hieroglyph which means 'to unite' (9:15; 3:3,16). Bracelets and necklaces in ancient Egypt have knot-shaped gold clasps. In more recent times knot motifs in jewellery were given as love tokens – as they still are today.

The reef knot is sometimes known as 'the Knot of Herakles' (Hercules) after the knot with which Herakles tied the skin of the Nemean lion around his shoulders by its paws on many representations of this popular story (2:28). The reef knot motif on jewellery became the fashion at the time of Alexander the Great, who liked to compare himself to the heroic Herakles (9:16).

The 'endless' or 'mystic' knot is one of the auspicious signs of the Buddha. It is not a true knot, but a one-strand interlace design. It is a universally popular design and has lent itself to many different symbolic interpretations (9:17).

The important building projects in stone which began in Greece and continued to expand with the requirements for both public and private building by the Romans, encouraged decorative motifs based on geometrical constructions which shared the disciplines of proportion and size with the structures they embellished. Geometrical constructions were exploited to the full in the designs of Roman mosaic (9:27,28; 1:46–48; 5:34; 8:11).

In the fourth century AD the Roman Empire was divided. Constantinople became the new capital of the eastern regions. In the fifth century the western Empire suffered defeats by Germanic tribes who gradually overran its provinces in Europe. Alaric, king of the Visigoths, moved south into Italy and sacked Rome in AD 410, and the last Roman Emperor was replaced by Theodoric, king of the Ostrogoths in AD 493. As a result a number of new kingdoms arose in the old Roman provinces. The Visigoths settled in Spain and south-west France, the Ostrogoths and Lombards in Italy, the Franks in Belgium and north-east France, while the British Isles were invaded by the Jutes, Angles and Saxons from Denmark and northern Germany. The invading forces were probably not very large and became a ruling class for the defeated indigenous and Roman populations. The Germanic peoples introduced their own ornament into the erstwhile Roman Empire. The consequences of the introduction of barbaric art styles were profound for the later development of Christian art in Europe. The colourful technique of *cloisonné* (cell-set patterns of semi-precious stones or glass), for example, was introduced into the new kingdoms (9:18, 2:40). When, in the course of the sixth and seventh centuries these kingdoms became Christian, the Church made lavish use of this colourful method of decoration in which simple interlacing patterns as well as interlacing animals were popular motifs (9:30–33; 2:45,46).

In the eastern Empire, more intricate interlace motifs developed as a consquence of a general trend towards abstract decoration under the influence of official prohibitions against realistic representations of the

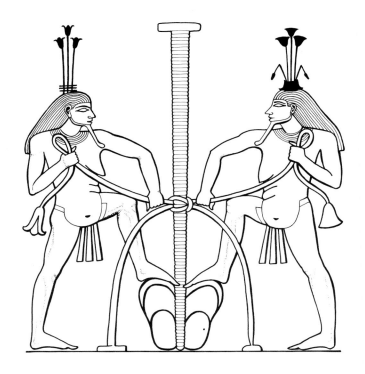

9:14 *Left* The reef knot consists of two half knots, one left and one right, tied one on top of the other. Other names for this knot are Square, True, Hard, Flat, Common and Ordinary. *Right* The Granny knot consists of two identical half knots. This knot is also known as False, Lubber's, Calf and Booby knot.

9:15 Engraved on the throne of Sesostris I are the signs which symbolise the unification of Upper and Lower Egypt. *c*.1971–1928 BC.

9:16 The centre piece of a diadem in gold is a 'Knot of Herakles' motif inlaid with large garnets. No prov. Hellenistic, *c*.2nd cent. BC.

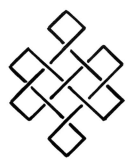

9:17 The 'endless', or 'mystic' knot. A much used symbol of continuity and infinity, it is also one of the auspicious signs of the Buddha.

human figure in the early Church. A large body of textile fragments recovered from the graves of the Copts (an early Christian Community in Egypt) illustrate the movement away from naturalistic designs to new subjects such as elaborate interlace. The developed ribbon interlace became an important part of Church architecture and remained a major motif of enrichment throughout Europe to the Romanesque and beyond. (9:19,34–36; 5:11,12).

With the rise of Islam, and after the death of Muhammad in AD 632, his followers came out of Arabia to conquer Syria and Egypt (then part of the Byzantine empire). In AD 642 the Sassanian empire fell to the Muslim Arabs and by the eighth century North Africa and Spain became a part of Islam, along with areas in the east in Transoxiana and the Indus Valley. This rapid expansion influenced the development of a specifically Islamic art. The conquered areas consolidated their own strong artistic traditions, particularly the traditions of the Byzantine and Sassanian empires. The followers of Muhammad brought no particular art style out of Arabia, but only the script, which was regarded as an expression both of art and religion and of ideas about art and its purpose. Islam itself became the unifying influence which adapted the art of the conquered territories to the needs of the new religion. Designs based on geometric construction and interlace were acceptable to both Christians and Muslims. It was in the art of Islam, however, that geometric decoration achieved a high degree of elaboration and sophistication and, in some contexts, a symbolic content (9:41–46).

In early medieval manuscript painting, ribbon interlace was one of three motif groups which created the distinctive Hiberno-Saxon style (9:20,37–40) (the other two being animal interlace, p.67ff. and 2:49 and spiral scrolls p.158ff. and 7:3,20–21). At the time of awakening antiquarian interest in the ancient culture in Ireland, in the middle of the nineteenth century, collections of objects and manuscripts held in the Royal Irish Academy were studied and published. The ornament of this metalwork and these manuscripts inspired a new art which was perceived – somewhat inaccurately – as representative of a Celtic identity and the ribbon interlace and intricate knot patterns have remained synonymous with Celtic art ever since (9:40; 7:24). In the late nineteenth and early twentieth centuries, the Arts and Crafts movement and the designers of Art Noveau made use of its many possibilities in new designs (9:21,7:4,25,26).

Throughout its long use in ornament, traced here as a continuous tradition from Syrian cylinder seals in the first half of the second millennium BC to the present, interlace takes the form of a repeating symmetrical motif. When it becomes part of an interlacing animal design there may be exceptions to this general rule (2:44). An art style based on interlacing and geometrical motifs in free asymmetrical designs evolved in Central Africa. In the kingdom of Kuba, embroidered textiles were decorated with designs made up of a limited number of interlacing and geometrical motifs which formed asymmetrical and irregular compositions of great sophistication. There is no reason to believe that outside influences were involved in the creation of this art; the individual motifs, twist and plaits, chevron, and cross, are universally available. The people of Kuba, and probably originally of a larger area in the Congo basin, transformed these simple motifs into a rich and varied art style (9:47–49).

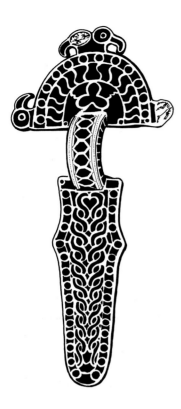

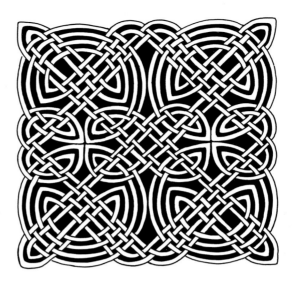

9:20 Ribbon interlace from the
Lindisfarne Gospels, Northumberland,
England. *c*. AD 698.

9:18 Ostrogothic gold brooch inlaid with
garnets and emeralds. Desana, Piedmont,
North Italy. *c*.AD 500.

9:19 Tapestry woven strip, indigo-dyed
wool on linen. Coptic, Egypt, 5th cent. AD.

9:21 Border design for a frame. Pen and
ink drawing. Archibald Knox, one of the
chief designers of jewellery, pewter and
silver ware for Liberty & Co. London.
Early 19th cent. (From Tilbrook and
House 1976.)

Geometrical constructions as a basis for ornament

In ancient Mesopotamia (as in ancient Egypt) simple geometry was used in the measurement of land, in the construction of buildings and in astronomical calculations. The Greeks developed this knowledge: Euclid included all known geometry in the first systematic treatise on the subject written around 300 BC in the mathematical school in Alexandria. Decorative designs based on geometrical figures are basically simple: they may easily be constructed with only a compass and a rule and by the application of certain procedures which produce triangles, squares, hexagons and stars. Such designs can easily be reduced and enlarged. Examples of some of the most common constructions and most useful properties for the purpose of geometric design are illustrated (**9:22–24; 8:4,5**).

The Golden Mean is a ratio or proportion which is found in relationships in the pentagram, the five-pointed star (**9:24**). The pentagram was the symbol of the school of the Greek philosopher Pythagoras (569–500 BC), for whom number relationships were of great importance. The Golden ratio was used in Greek architecture, and the belief that it was also applied by the Greek sculptor Phidias in his work led to the adoption early this century of ϕ(Phi) to designate it. In the Middle Ages, and during the Renaissance, mathematicians saw a special significance in this ratio and it has attracted much attention from those interested in number magic generally. The belief that this is a proportion which gives special aesthetic pleasure is widely held but hard to prove (**9:25**).

The intricate use of geometric construction in Islamic art and architecture produced patterns which greatly influenced European art, especially through the media of textiles and metalwork. Leonardo da Vinci published a series of knot patterns in about 1495 which he had adapted from the intricate Islamic metalwork then being produced in Venice. Inscribed 'The Academy of Leonardo da Vinci', it is thought that the complex knot patterns were destined to serve as models for artists of various crafts (**9:26**). These, and examples of interlace from other sources, were included in the pattern books which, from the second half of the fifteenth century, were distributed throughout Europe providing a library of decorative motif (p.19ff.).

The construction of ribbon interlace has more recently been the subject of interest. In the 1950s, George Bain, a school arts master published methods of construction which would allow the use of 'Celtic' motifs such as ribbon, animal and figure interlace, spiral scrolls and calligraphy to be taught in schools in Scotland. This was done in an idealistic fervour to foster a pride in a Celtic heritage. About his methods of construction he writes:

If the methods and their stages that are shown in this book are not those used by the ancients, then they can only prove to have been simpler, perhaps more ingenious but not more difficult … When some of the methods of the Celts as shown in this book have been assimilated … things happen with the ease that a mouth opens when a spoon is raised to it.

[8th impression 1981, p.21,17]

This will produce a rueful laugh among those who have tried to use his methods, better suited to somebody already an accomplished artist than the ordinary person he claims to address. An amended version of his method has been published by his son Ian (1986). More recently Aidan Meehan (1991–92) has produced a series of books which perpetuate the 'Celtic' mythology which has become attached to these motifs and encouraged their use in modern design.

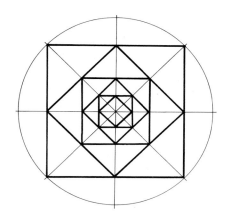

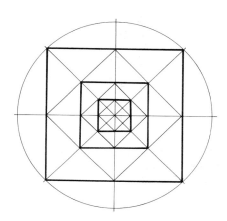

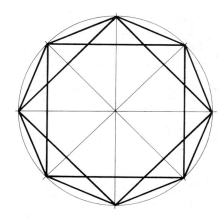

9:22 Some constructions and properties of squares, octagons and eight-pointed stars. *Above* In this figure the areas of the concentric squares are progressively halved. *Centre* The bold lines show the squares where the areas are progressively quartered. *Below* The eight-pointed star and the octagon.

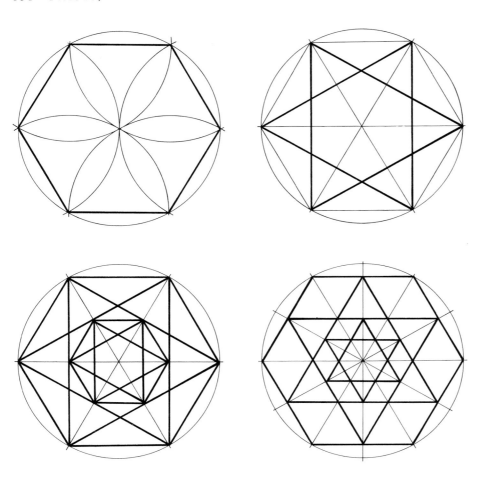

9:23 Some constructions and properties of triangles, hexagons and six-pointed stars. *Above left* The circumference of a circle can be divided into six equal parts by its radius. A hexagon is produced when the six points set off on the circumference are joined by straight lines. *Above right* When alternate points are joined by straight lines two triangles make up a six-pointed star. *Below left* The ratio between the diameters of hexagons based on concentric six-pointed stars drawn from the hexagons' corner is 1:2. *Below right* When the concentric stars are drawn from the hexagons' midpoints, the ratio between the heights of the hexagons is also 1:2.

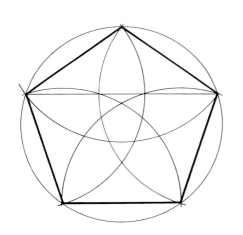
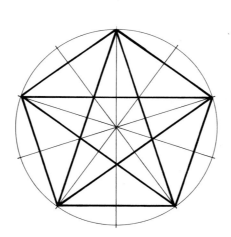
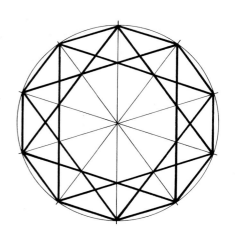

9:24 Some constructions and properties of the pentagon and the five- and ten-pointed star. This figure had particular interest because ratios within it conform to the ratio known as the Golden Mean. *Left* The ratio of the diagonal to the side in a regular pentagon is 1:1.618 or φ, the Golden Mean. *Centre* As a result, many parts of the five-pointed star also conform to this ratio. *Right* The decagon and the ten-pointed star.

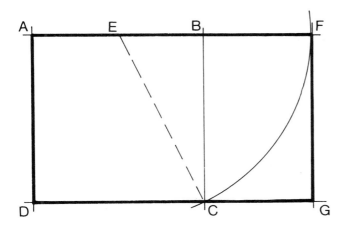

9:25 Method of construction of the Golden rectangle: bisect the side AB in a square ABCD in E. With centre E and radius EC draw an arc of a circle cutting AB produced in F. Draw FG perpendicular to AF meeting DC produced in G. Then AFGD is the Golden rectangle. Is it really more pleasing than rectangles of other proportions?

9:26 Knot pattern from 'The Academy of Leonardo da Vinci', a collection of engravings published c.1495. Italy.

There is no knowing what methods were used in antiquity to construct these designs. The grids which can sometimes be traced on the back of manuscript pages merely indicate methods used in these particular instances (**7:22**). In other media, such as stone sculpture for example, other means for establishing important guidelines were no doubt applied; it has been suggested that a stencil, cut out of leather, may have been used for this purpose. In my drawing of manuscript borders (**9:38**), the construction lines were originally necessary to allow me to copy the patterns accurately. They have been retained to aid the understanding of a complex design. Other construction lines could equally well have been used and led to the same result.

For the purposes of classification of complex interlace motifs in stone sculpture, a workable system based on variations of four-strand plaiting has been devised (Adcock in Cramp 1984). It must not, however, be assumed that actual plaiting was in the mind of the carver of the designs, the layout of which must have been geometrically based.

Motifs based on geometrical constructions and interlace in Roman, early Christian and Medieval art

Patterned mosaic flooring developed in Greece in the third century BC. The same repertoire of motifs was applied to wall-paintings, stucco panels and floor mosaics. The designs of decorative borders and figurative panels included motifs taken from architectural detail as well as from textiles. Roman interiors closely followed Greek fashions in design. As the Empire expanded to include an area reaching from North Africa and the Near East to Europe south of the river Danube and west of the Rhine, including much of Britain, public as well as private buildings were decorated with designs in a fairly uniform style.

Mosaic pavements and panels were laid with stone, tile or glass cut into cubes known as *tesserae*. Recycled materials, such as broken stone and tile from a building site, were often used for this purpose. It is assumed on practical grounds that there was some form of pattern book from which clients could choose designs for their floors – but of these nothing survives. The overall layout often took the form of a framework or grid, which could be scaled up or down to fit differently shaped rooms. The construction lines became the framework for the decorative borders, while the spaces between them were filled with decorative panels. These panels were sometimes of finer materials and were perhaps prefabricated while the borders and surrounds were locally produced. The construction of the general layouts was based on well-known geometrical principles and could be executed from a base line with the use of set squares and compasses. They range from simple concentric circles and squares

9:27 One quarter of a complicated design on a grid of octagons and squares, repeated mirror fashion in the remaining quarters. Reconstruction of a mosaic paving from Boxmoor, Hertfordshire, England. Mid-2nd cent. AD. (From Neal, 1981, fig.8.)

9:29 Twists and plaits in Roman mosaics are frequently shaded by a sequence of colours. The outside strands in the plait on a Roman mosaic in London, for example, are made up of three rows of *tesserae*, red, yellow and white, while the crossing strands, in the centre, have one white and two grey rows which, together with the black outlines, diminish the effect of a realistic plait, but not its decorative impact. London. 3rd cent. AD.

9:28 Detail of a mosaic panel with an eight-pointed star set in a square frame of borders with twists, plaits, meander and wave scrolls. In the centre is a representation of Venus, surrounded by a leaf scroll. The lower panel has a design of dolphins. Kingscote, Gloucester, England. Late 3rd–early 4th cent. AD. (After Neal 1981.)

(**1**:47; **5**:34) to complicated constructions involving the rotation, overlapping or interlacing of the motifs (**9**:27,28; **1**:48; **8**:11). The over/under feature, when applied to geometrical constructions, contributed a three-dimensional effect, which was sometimes enhanced by shading (**9**:29, **1**:46).

At the beginning of the fourth century AD the Empire was divided, the eastern region having Byzantium (Constantinople) as its capital, while Rome remained the capital of the west. The Empire in the west was already in decline when, in the course of the fifth century, groups of Germanic peoples invaded Europe from the east. Roman art in the provinces had been uniform. The influx of Germanic peoples from very dissimilar cultural backgrounds not only introduced new artistic ideas to the region, but also led to a rich variety of responses to these ideas in indigenous art. A style of colourful gold jewellery inlaid in *cloisonné* with coloured stones or glass, for example, had its centre in south-east Europe where it represented the late Roman and oriental styles in the larger region between eastern Europe and Asia. In ornament created in this technique, cells divide the surfaces into fret patterns of simple shapes, steps and twists. Associated with this art was an eagle motif which became highly influential in Europe (**9**:18, **2**:40). This style of ornament followed the Goths westwards out of the Pontic region of south-east Russia, and the Lombards southwards from their homelands in Pannonia (**9**:30). It was a gaudy art which greatly appealed to the pagan tastes of the other Germanic tribes of the west (**9**:31,32, **2**:45,46). It also became an important and enduring element in Christian decorative art. Reliquaries and book covers were encrusted with precious stones, and manuscript illumination imitated the pattern of *cloisonné* cells in fret designs. The gold, black, green, blue and red colours of the jewellery were imitated by the early Anglo-Saxon scribes (**9**:33).

9:30 Langobard silver-gilt brooch; the animal heads have eyes inlaid with garnets. Sakvice, Moravia, Czechoslovakia, 5th–6th cent. AD.

9:31 The eagle heads, set in a 'rotating' pattern, on a gold pendant are inlaid with garnets in *cloisonné*. Faversham, Kent, England. 7th cent. AD.

9:32 Examples of cell patterns in *cloisonné*, taken from various mounts in the royal burial at Sutton Hoo. The stones set in the cells of gold are garnets. Suffolk, England. First quarter 7th cent. AD.

9:33 Decorative details in manuscripts sometimes copy *cloisonné* designs. Shading indicates different colours, usually gold, black, red, green and blue. From the top: Book of Durrow, Lindisfarne Gospels, Book of Kells. England and Ireland 7th–9th cent. AD.

The Byzantine empire reconquered Italy as the Ostrogothic kingdom collapsed in the sixth century. Thus was introduced an art which had developed away from classical realism to a more stylised linear style in figure representation and abstract ornament. The simple twist and plait of the Roman mosaics evolved into intricate ribbon interlace which, together with a very stylised acanthus leaf, were major decorative motifs in Byzantine art (**9**:19,34). The Lombards, who already had simple twists in their repertoire, were perhaps the first to make close contact with this developed interlace ornament during their repeated incursions into Italy in the second half of the sixth century (**9**:30,35,36; **5**:35). The decorative potential of this more intricate ornament was soon embraced with enthusiasm by the Germanic peoples over a wide area. In the hands of the pagan peoples of the north, it provided the impetus for an animal style of great vigour (p.67ff. and **2**:36–63).

In western European Christendom, interlacing motifs also inspired a new art which was expressed in the rich jewellery and weapons of the kings and courts and in the furnishings and vessels of the new Church. The royal burial at Sutton Hoo represents a transition between pagan and Christian in England. A pagan burial, it contained objects from Christian continental Europe and Byzantium. The style of decoration in the jewellery, much of which was produced in England, reflects the kind of artistic taste which was current at the time amongst the elite (**2**:44–46, **7**:18,19) – a style which is also apparent in early manuscript decoration (**2**:47–49; **7**:20–22). With the coming of Christianity, Bibles and service books were urgently needed. At the time of the Conversion in Britain, after AD 598, books brought from the Continent were copied and embellished with designs which at first centred on the initial letters of important passages, but soon involved borders and whole pages of decoration.

Ribbon interlace was primarily used

9:34 Detail from an openwork marble choir screen from San Vitale, Ravenna, Italy (consecrated 547 AD).

9:35 A Lombard strap mount from a horse harness in gilt bronze from Vaszkeny, Hungary. 6th cent. AD.

9:36 Carved wood tablet in the chapel of Institution Saint-Martin, Angers, France. Probably made in Italy. 6th–7th cent. AD.

9:37 Ribbon interlace from the
Lindisfarne Gospels, Northumberland,
England. *c.*AD 698.

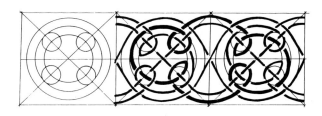

9:38 Borders from the Book of Durrow.
The construction lines are not original but
are here shown to aid the unravelling of
the designs and their transformation, by
the use of colour. Colour is indicated by
different shading. Northumbria, England.
Third quarter of the 7th cent. AD.

to fill a border, a panel, or the space between more important motifs (**9**:20,37,40). Manuscript pages were ruled as a guide to lay the text, while the area to be decorated was divided into geometrical grids with ruler and compass. The rigid discipline of these grids controlled the scrolls and interlacing ribbons drawn on them. It is a measure of the draughtsman's skill that this is rarely apparent or intrusive.

Ribbon interlace, although used earlier, sprang from an ornament based on geometrical constructions in Roman mosaics, and continued to have architectural application in the early Church. It was therefore ideally suited to the discipline of the grids of the manuscript pages. In Anglo-Saxon manuscript art, this ornament was used with skill and ingenuity. David Wilson (1984, p.34) describes the interlace in borders of the Book of Durrow (**9**:38), written in Northumbria in the third quarter of the seventh century, thus:

The artist makes skilful use of his patterns and colours. First he constructs a pattern and then he breaks it up into fields by changing the colour register, so that there are two ways of looking at the result. At the same time he gives an impression of false symmetry by following certain lines of construction, but misleads the eye by the use of different colour on the same ribbon.

The motifs of the manuscripts are also found in other art associated with the church. Stone crosses, which served many purposes as grave markers or covers, memorials or (where they have pictorial scenes) as aids to preaching, favour a rich variety of ribbon interlace in some areas, particularly in the north of Britian. The Picts, who at the beginning of the seventh century were living in much of northern and eastern Scotland, incorporated a developed ribbon interlace in their distinctive art (**9**:39).

In Ireland, the superlative skill of the metalworkers transformed the motifs they had in common with Anglo-Saxon art with unparalleled refinement. A draughtsman working

with pen and ink cannot hope to do justice in a drawing to the very fine, sharp interlace on the best of these masterpieces of the jeweller's art. A detail from a decorated letter in the Book of Kells illustrates the same use of interlace as an elegant and versatile filling motif (**9**:40).

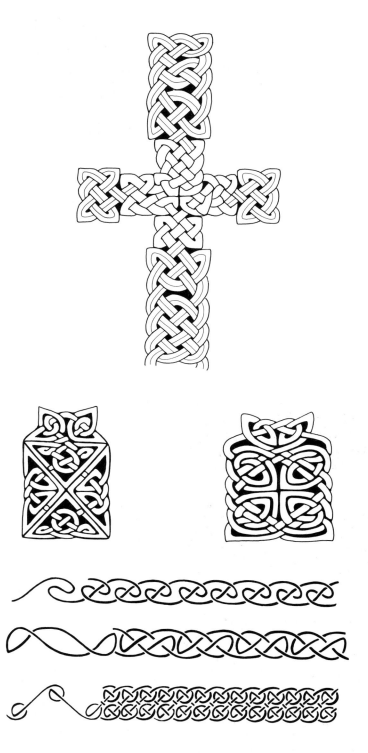

9:39 Interlace and knot patterns from the art of the Picts. *Above* from stone crosses, *below* from decoration on metalwork. The explanatory drawings reveal some of the different methods used to produce these designs. Scotland. 8th cent. AD.

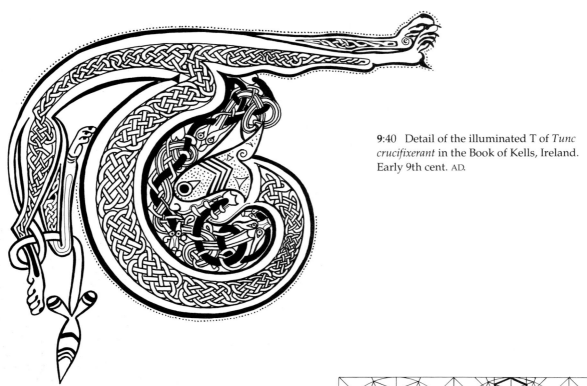

9:40 Detail of the illuminated T of *Tunc crucifixerant* in the Book of Kells, Ireland. Early 9th cent. AD.

9:41 An example of some of the ways a design based on an octagon grid may be varied by allowing the lines to become an interlace or by colouring the shapes produced by the grid. (After El-Said and Parman 1976).

Geometric interlace in Islamic art

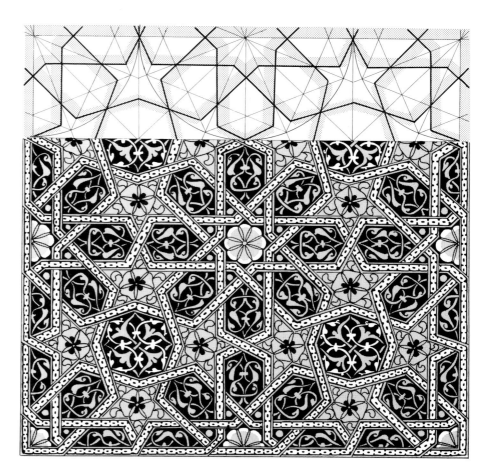

A ban on representational art in religious contexts, in mosques and in the illumination of the Koran, meant that the artistic genius of the Islamic world concentrated on the refinement of abstract decorative art (including the decorative use of script). Geometry was a highly important science in Islam and its figures and constructions became permeated with symbolic, cosmological and philosophical significance. In architecture strict adherence to geometrical principles in plans and elevations formed the basis for the harmony and discipline which all Islamic art strives to achieve. Geometrically-based patterns cover the walls of mosques and an infinitely large number of variations were based on the grids produced by a limited number of basic constructions, (for example, **9**:22–25 and **8**:4,5). In these contexts such designs sometimes became imbued for the initiated with metaphysical and religious significance.

Variations were created not only by using different constructions, but by emphasising the different shapes which can be drawn from the construction lines, or by allowing the lines or bands of the figures to pass over and under each other to produce an interlace, and filling the spaces in the geometrical framework with stylised leaf and floral designs (**9**:41,42, on the arabesque see p.13,139 and **5**:43–47). Designs of this kind were used in Roman mosaics and in the art of the early Christian church (**9**:19,27,28,34–36). Simple interlacing twists and plaits are motifs which Islamic and Christian art have in common and they appear not to be involved in

symbolism in either religion. Interlacing borders of very similar design decorate both Gospels and Korans (**9**:38,43,44).

In secular contexts rules are less strict and allow for a more individualistic treatment of decoration. The use of geometrically-based grids however, remains the basis for many designs (**9**:45,46).

9:42 Design on a page of an illuminated Koran based on an octagon grid. Egypt, 15th cent. AD.

9:43 Interlacing ribbon designs from an illuminated Koran. ? Egypt. 10th cent. AD.

9:45 One of several small designs which decorate a brass ewer, made at Mosul in 1232. The key pattern is based on an octagonal construction. Iraq.

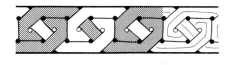

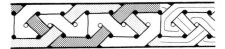

9:44 Ribbon interlace from an illuminated Koran written in Cairo 1304. The interlaced borders are painted gold with red and blue circles at the crossing points. The shading has been added to illustrate the different methods by which a similar effect was achieved. Egypt.

9:46 Detail of a small design, based on a grid of intersecting circles, inlaid in gold and silver on a metal writing box. Egypt. *c.*1300–1350 AD.

9:47 Extended drawing of the carved design on a wooden cup. Late 19th cent. Kuba, Zaire.

9:48 Detail of a dark red ceremonial raffia skirt with pink appliqué design. Late 19th cent. Kuba, Zaire.

The interlacing and geometrical art of the Kuba

The Kuba kingdom, in an inaccessible area of Central Africa on the southern fringes of the equatorial forest (formerly Belgian Congo, now Zaire) was not, as far as is known, visited by foreign travellers until the 1890s. Collections of examples of the art of the region (with tales of a sophisticated Kuba state) were brought back by anthropologists and explorers in the early years of this century.

The interlacing designs of the Kuba are the result of a long independent tradition of specialised patterns. They are the remnant of an art style which in the past may have been current over a larger area in the Congo basin and Central Africa. The Kuba kingdom, however, evolved in the early seventeenth century. In a highly organised society centred on the court, the decoration of objects of daily use, as well as those which represented wealth and status, was held in high esteem. Men produced fine wood and ivory carvings, decorating cups and containers for domestic use with patterns of interlacing and geometrical designs (**9:47**). While some wooden vessels suggest that they were modelled on baskets, and while designs occasionally imitate nets of cords, other interlacing designs are unrelated to actual knotting and plaiting and make up a large body of distinctive motifs. Fibres of the raffia palm were used by the men in basketry and in the weaving of textiles.

The designs applied or embroidered by women on these textiles are of particular interest by reason of their greater range of variation on the same small number of given motifs. Squares of raffia cloth were joined to make up skirts worn on ceremonial occasions by both sexes. Patterns in appliqué made use of a range of angular elements, squares, right-angled crosses, chevrons, and hooks (**9:48**). Other cloths, embroidered in techniques which produced a fine cut pile, were used for display rather than as costume, and were ultimately used in funeral rites (**9:49**). These textiles were also decorated with tightly controlled motifs limited to angular interlace, chevrons, squares, crosses and hooks.

In contexts such as tatoos and certain carvings in wood or horn curvilinear patterns were allowed. The structure of the textile patterns (which are still produced today in the laborious cut-pile embroidery technique) are remarkable in that the interlacing and geometric elements are presented in free compositions which aim to achieve overall balance without symmetry or regular repetition. The admired skills are subtle rather than bold – the unexpected variation on a well-known design, or a new juxtaposition of the approved individual motifs.

Some patterns were traditional and handed down from one generation to another. Patterns were named after their innovator, a king, or other important person. Other names are descriptive or point to an association with some natural or animal feature. Patterns and their names were subject to an almost fanatical interest and public debate. The story is told about missionaries to this area in the 1920s who showed off their motorbike to the Bakuba king. The king was unimpressed by this testimony to western technology, but he and his court were fascinated by the tyre marks left by the wheels in the sand. The pattern of the treads was copied and has entered the repertoire of designs used by Kuba craftsmen; it is known by the name of the king who first saw and appreciated it.

Symmetry and orderliness in ornament is a deeply rooted preference in the Western world. This is no more so than in interlacing ornament which from the time of the twists and plaits on Syrian seals in the second millennium BC has proceeded with pedantic over/under accuracy. The asymmetry and irregularity of the interlace in the Kuba textiles appear wilful – almost shocking. The underlying regular weave has not tempted these free-hand embroiderers to follow the easier path of using this grid to create regular repeats. The more difficult task of controlling a free design, with a self-imposed limitation to a small number of given motifs, is a deliberate choice, all the more difficult since women related by kin may have cooperated to complete a single textile.

Compare the woollen tapestry strip from a Coptic grave in Egypt (**9**:19), and the raffia mat (**9**:49) from a different African tradition: it is the same motif, each quite perfect of its kind. The Kuba textile stands for many other approaches to aesthetic satisfaction which have not found a place in this book.

9:49 *Left* Detail of an embroidered cut-pile raffia textile in yellow and black *Below* In this embroidered raffia mat, the cut-pile design is in shades of gold and rust on a plain yellow ground. This pattern has a descriptive name, *imbol* ('basket work or 'knotting'). Late 19th cent. Kuba, Zaire.

Notes on the illustrations

Introduction

0:1 Petrie, Flinders, *Decorative Patterns of the Ancient World*, London 1930, pl.xxxi.

0:2,3 Barley, N. and Sandaruppa, S., *The Torajan Ricebarn*, British Museum Occasional Paper 72. London 1991.

0:4 On site.

0:5 Simpson, E., 'The Phrygian Artistic Intellect', *Source Notes in the History of Art*, vol.vii, 3/4,fig.3,7.

0:6 Boehmer, R.M., 'Phrygische Prunkgewänder des 8. Jahrhunderts v. Chr. Herkunft und Export', *Archäologischer Anzeiger*, h.2,1973. Bellinger, L., *The Bulletin of the Needle and Bobbin Club*, 46,1,1, 1962, 10–16.

0:7 In the temple treasure of Shosoin, Japan. Geijer, A., *A History of Textile Art*, London 1979.

0:8,9 Kent and Painter 1977, nos. 312,317. *British Museum*, London, WAA 133033, 124095.

0:10 Geijer 1979, pl.24b, Vollbach 1969, pl.21. *Victoria and Albert Museum*, London. 8579-1863.

0:11 Geijer 1979, pl.30, Vollbach 1969, pl.70, *Cathedral Museum*, Mainz, Germany.

0:12 From a painting by Masolino da Panicale in the Brancacci Chapel, Carmine Church, Florence.

0:13 *Victoria and Albert Museum*, London.

0:14 Wascher, H., *Alte bemalte Spanschachteln*, Rosenheim 1983, fig.11 and p.47.

0:15 *Narodni Museum*, Prague. Peesch, R., *The Ornament in European Folk Art*, New York 1983.

0:16 Bringeus, N-A., *Sydsvenska bonadsmålningar* in *Böcker om Konst*, Lund 1982, p.277.

0:17 *Museum of American Folk Art*, Exhibition catalogue, *American Folk Art, Expressions of a New Spirit*, New York 1983.

0:19 Sketches from shawl fragments in the *Victoria and Albert Museum*, London. See also Irwin, J., *Shawls, A Study of Indo European Influences*. Victoria and Albert Museum Monographs no. 9, figs.1-8. London 1955.

Chapter 1

1:1 Golomshtok, E.A., 'The Old Stone Age in European Russia', *Transactions of the American Philosophical Society*, New series., vol.xxix, pt.2, Philadelphia. 1938.

1:2 de Saint-Périer, R., 'La Grotte D'Isturitz II', *Archives de l'Institut de Paléontologie Humaine, Memoire 17*, 1936, fig.51 and 'Les baguettes sculptées dans l'art paléolithic', *L'Anthropologie*, vol.xxxix, p.63–4, 1929.

1:3 *State Hermitage Museum*, St Petersburg, Russia.

1:4 Cherry, S., *Te Ao Maori, The Maori World* (Exhibition Catalogue) Dublin 1990, no.109. *The National Museum of Ireland*, Dublin 1886,377.

1:7 Collon 1987, no.835.

1:9 *British Museum*, London. Details from Catalogue of vases E.44, B.364, B.15.

1:11 *National Museum of Antiquities*, Bucharest, Romania.

1:12 Davidson, J.L. and Henshall, A.S., *The Chamber Tombs of Scotland*, I, no. 72, Edinburgh 1963.

1:13 Müller, S., *Nordische Altertumskunde*, vol.I, Abb. 138, Strassburg 1897.

1:14 *Museum of Anatolian Civilizations*, Ankara, Turkey.

1:15,16 Piggott, S., *Ancient Europe*, fig.18,47. Edinburgh 1965.

1:17 *Left and top right*, Schutz, H., *The Prehistoric Germanic Europe*, fig.33, pl.1b, New Haven and London 1983, first published 1937; *below right*, von Tompa, F., *Die Bandkeramik in Ungaren*, pl.xxxiii, Budapest 1929.

1:18 Sandars 1985, fig.187.

1:19 *Petrie Museum, University College London*, London. UC 6349, 9806.

1:20 Vainker 1991, fig.3. *British Museum*, London. OA 1966.2–23.

1:21 Pearson, R. (ed.), *Ancient Japan*, (Exhibition Catalogue Sackler Gallery), Smithsonian Institution, Washington DC 1992, nos. 49,52.

1:22 O'Kelly, M.J., *New Grange, Archaeology, Art and Legend*, Kerbstones K1 and K67. London 1982.

1:23 Evans, J., *The Prehistoric Antiquities of the Maltese Islands: A Survey*, London 1971; Ridley, M., *The Megalithic Art of the Maltese Islands*, Poole 1976.

1:24 Wiencke, M.H., 'Banded pithoi of Lerna III', *Hesperia*, xxxix, 1970.

1:25,26 Thimme 1977, fig.109, no.401.

1:27,28 *Above*, Levi, D., *Festòs E la civiltà Minoica*, Tavole 1:2, pl.xxx d no.1039, lxxi, xxxvi f 383;11. 1:28 *Below*, Evans 1928–35, vol.II:2, fig.312c. *Archaeological Museum*, Herakleion, Crete.

1:29,30 Karo 1930–33, no.625, fig.121–3, pl.lxiii, no.675, pl.lxi, no.347, pl.vi, stele 1429. Marinatos 1960.

1:31 Marinatos 1960, pl.161.

1:32 Wilson E. 1986, 92–4. *British Museum*, London.

1:33 Tomb of Wahka II, Qaw el-Kebir. 12th Dynasty, Middle Kingdom. Wilson E. 1986, 25–6.

1:34 Davies N. de G., *The Tomb of Menkheperresonb, Amenose and another*, pl.iv. Wilson E. 1986, 72.

1:35 Tomb of Nebamun, no. 90, Thebes. Wilson E. 1986, 58.

1:36 *Above, British Museum*, London. GR 1877.12–7.10. *Below*, Ahlberg, G., 'Prothesis and Ekphora in Greek Geometric Art', *Studies in Mediterranean Archaeology*, vol. xxxii, Göteborg 1971, figs.7, 18, 29.

1:37 Mazsolics 1973, Abb.8.

1:38 *Above*, Montelius, G.O.A., *Minnen från vår forntid*, vol.I, Stockholm 1917, fig.904a. *Below* and 1:39 *below*, Müller, S., *Nordische Altertumskunde*, vol. I, Strassburg 1897, abb.107, 214–19. 1:39 *above*, National Museum, Copenhagen, Denmark.

1:40 *British Museum*, London. CM BMC Priene 2.

1:41 Hibbs, V.A., *The Mendes Maze: A libation table for the Genius of innundation of the Nile (II–III AD)*, New York University PH.D. 1979. *Musée du Louvre*, Paris.

1:42 *British Museum*, London. GR 1896.6–15.1.

1:43 *Above*, Willetts, R.F., *Everyday Life in Ancient Crete*, London 1969, fig.7 amended from Le Rider, G., 'Monnaies crétoises du Ve Au 1er Siècle Av J-C', *Études Crétoises, tome XV*, École Française d'Athens, Paris 1966, pl.xxiv 27. *Below, British Museum*, London. CM BMC 5.

1:44 *British Museum*, London. CM 1896.7–3.308.

1:45 Rancken, A.W., 'Kalkmålningar i Sibbo gamla kyrka', *Finskt Museum*, vol.42, 1935, p.29. Kraft 1985, fig.6.

1:46 Campbell 1988.

1:47 Neal 1981, no.2.

1:48 Neal, D.S., *Lullingstone Roman Villa* (English Heritage), 1991.

1:49 Marshall, Sir J., *Mohenjo Daro and the Indus Civilization*, London 1931., vol.iii,pl.cxiv nos. 512,514.

1:50 *Above, Sadberk Hanim Museum*, Istanbul. *Centre and below, Museum of Anatolian Civilizations*, Ankara, Turkey.

1:51 *National Archaeological Museum*, Athens

1:52 Nylén, E., *Bildstenar*, Visby 1978, 27. Nylén 1988.

1:53 *Cambridge Museum of Archaeology and Ethnography*. Wilson E. 1983, 87.

1:54 Davis B.L. *German Army Uniforms and Insignia 1933–1945*, London 1971.

Chapter 2

2:1 Mallowan and Rose 1935, figs. 73–75.

2:2 After Mellaart 1967, fig.45.

2:3 Collon 1987, no. 904. *British Museum*, London. WA 89308.

2:4 Teissier 1984, no. 557.

2:5 Curtis, 1989. *British Museum*, London. WA 123924.

2:6 Kent and Painter 1977, no. 304. *State Hermitage Museum*, St Petersburg, Russia.

2:7 Wilson E. 1988, 15. *Keir Collection*, London.

2:8 After Stanfield J.A. and Simpson, G., *Central Gaulish Potters*, London 1958, pl.26, no.319.

2:9 Neal 1981, no.61. *British Museum*, London. PRB 1965.4–91.

2:10 *British Museum*, London. MLA 1860.10–2.130, Mosaic 57b.

2:11 Eames 1980, nos. 9113–9120.

2:12 Fong 1980, no.32. *Institute of Archaeology*, Beijing, China.

2:13 *Museum of Anatolian Civilizations*, Ankara, Turkey.

2:14 *British Museum*, London.

2:15 Collon 1987, no. 885.

2:16 Aldred 1980, fig.7.

2:17 Collon 1987, no.158. *British Museum*, London. WA 104486.

2:18 *Museum of Anatolian Civilizations*, Ankara, Turkey.

2:19 *Above* Boehmer R.M. and Güterbock,H.G., *Glyptik aus dem Stadtgebiet von Bogazköy*, Berlin:Mann 1987, Taf.v, no.52. *Below*, Alp, S., *Zylinder- und Stempelsiegel aus Karahöyük bei Konya*, Ankara 1968, no. 59.

2:20 Barnett 1982, pl.26d.

2:21 *Above*, Moscati 1988, p.406. *Musée Royaux d'Art et d'Histoire*, Brussels, Belgium. *Below*, Mallowan 1966, pl.vi, fig.426.

2:22 Barnett 1982, pl.40c.

2:23 Curtis 1989, fig.33 left. *British Museum*, London. WA 132927.

2:24 From Burn 1991, fig.133. *British Museum*, London. GR 1897.4–1.872.

2:25 Williams 1985, fig.25. *British Museum*, London. GR 1873.8–20.385.

2:26 Burn 1991, fig.32. *British Museum*, London. GR 1861.4–25.46.

2:27 *British Museum*, London. Vase E 84.

2:28 *British Museum*, London. Bronze 542. Swaddling J., *Corpus Speculorum Etruscorum*, Great Britain, vol.1, fasc.1, forthcoming.

2:29 *British Museum*, London. Terracotta 616.

2:30 *British Museum*, London. Terracotta D 661.

2:31 *British Museum*, London. Terracotta D 690.

2:32 See 1:48.

2:33 Haseloff 1981, iii, Taf.10. *Rheinisches Landesmuseum Bonn*, Germany.

2:34 Haseloff 1981, iii, Taf.2. *Enns Museum*, Austria.

2:35 Burn 1991, fig.168. *British Museum*, London. Mosaic 29.

2:36 Haseloff 1981, iii, Taf.5. *Nationalmuseet*, Copenhagen, Denmark.

2:37 Haseloff 1981, iii, Taf.7,1. *Arkaeologisk Museum*, Stavanger, Norway.

2:38 Wilson E. 1983, 2. *British Museum*, London.

2:39 Haseloff 1981, iii, Taf.18–20, Wilson E. 1983, 4. *Maidstone Museum and Art Gallery*, England.

2:40 Hubert J. et al. 1960, 240. *Germanisches Nationalmuseum*, Nuremberg, Germany.

2:41 Haseloff 1981, iii, Taf.35. *Statens Historiska Museum*, Stockholm, Sweden.

2:42 Haseloff 1981, iii, Taf.26. *Nationalmuseet*, Copenhagen, Denmark.

2:43 Haseloff 1981, iii, Taf.87. *Rheinisches Landesmuseum Bonn*, Germany.

2:44–46 Wilson D.M. 1984. Wilson E. 1983, 6, 9, 11. *British Museum*, London.

2:47 Wilson E. 1983, 30. *Trinity College Library*, Dublin, Ireland. A.4.5.(57).

2:48,49 Wilson E. 1983, 17, 36, 37. *British Library*, London. Cotton Nero D. iv.

2:50 Wilson E. 1983, 44.

2:51 Wilson E. 1983, 40. The Gandersheim Casket, *Herzog Anton Ulrich Museum*, Brunswick, Germany.

2:52 *Statens Historiska Museum*, Stockholm, Sweden.

2:53 *Universitetets Museum för Nordiska Fornsaker*, Uppsala, Sweden.

2:54 *Statens Historiska Museum*, Stockholm, Sweden.

2:55-57 *Universitetets Oldsaksamling*, Oslo, Norway.

2:58 *Statens Historiska Museum*, Stockholm, Sweden.

2:59 Wilson E. 1983, 51. Braddan Old Church, Isle of Man.

2:61 *Statens Historiska Museum*, Stockholm, Sweden.

2:62 Wilson E. 1983, 52. *Winchester Cathedral Library*, England.

2:63 Wilson E. 1983, 52. *National Museum*, Dublin, Ireland.

2:64–66 Payne 1990. *British Library*, London. 64, 66 Royal MS 12F xiii; 65 Harley MS 4751.

2:68 *British Museum*, London. MLA 78.12–30.333, 54.6–3.2.

2:69 Wilson E. 1983, 94, 95. *British Museum*, London. *Above left*, Lewes Priory, Sussex, *below left*, Chertsey Abbey, Surrey, *right*, Clarendon Abbey, Wilts. Eames 1980.

2:70 *British Museum*, London. Eames 1980.

2:72 Chang, K.C., 'An Essay on *Cong*', *Orientations*, June 1989, fig. 6. Rawson 1987, fig.3.

2:73 Rawson 1987, fig.9a. Fong 1980, no.4. *Hubei Provincial Museum*, China.

2:74 *British Museum*, London. OA 1956.10–16.1.

2:75 Watson 1974, pl.3. *William Rockhill Nelson Gallery, Atkins Museum*, Kansas City, USA.

2:76 Watson 1974, pl.22. *Freer Gallery*, Washington DC.,USA.

2:77–79 *Frozen tombs … 1978.* Griaznov, M., *L'Art Ancien de L'Altai*, Leningrad 1958, Artamonov 1974. *State Hermitage Museum*, St Petersburg, Russia.

2:80 *Above, Nomads: Masters of the Eurasian Steppe*, exhibition catalogue, Natural History Museum of Los Angeles County, 1989. *Below*, Gyllensvärd, B.W., *Chinese Gold and Silver in the Carl Kempe Collection*, Stockholm 1953, no. 23.

2:81 *Above*, Artamonov 1974, no.36. *State Hermitage Museum*, St Petersburg, Russia. *Below*, László 1970, pl.7. *Magyar Nemzeti Museum*, Budapest, Hungary.

2:82 *Right*, See 2:77–79. *Left*, Bunker, E.C., 'Dangerous scholarship: On citing unexcavated Artefacts from Inner Mongolia and North China', *Orientations*, June 1989. *Shaanxi Provincial Museum*, China.

2:83 See 2:77–79. *State Hermitage Museum*, St Petersburg, Russia.

2:84 Artamonov 1974, no.60. *State Hermitage Museum*, St Petersburg, Russia.

2:85 See 2:77–79. *State Hermitage Museum*, St Petersburg, Russia.

2:86 From Loewe, M., *Everyday Life in Early Imperial China 202 BC–AD 220*, figs 40–43.

2:87 Williams C.A.S. 1960.

2:88 Zhongguo meishu quanji, gongyi meishu bian no. 9:-yuqi, PEKING: Wenwu Publishing House, 1989.

2:89 Fong 1980, no.38. *Institute of Archaeology*, Beijing, China.

2:90 Rawson 1984, fig.73. *British Museum*, London. OA 1983.2–1.03.

2:91 Rawson 1984, fig.79. *British Museum*, London. OA 1972.6–20.1.

2:92 Rawson 1984, fig.80. *British Museum*,

London. OA 1983.2–1.01.

2:93   Rawson 1984, fig.126.

2:94   Whitfield and Farrer 1990, no.60. *British Museum*, London. OA 1991.1–1.0169 (Ch.00147).

2:95   *British Museum*, London. Franks Collection 72.

2:96   Sellato, B., *Hornbill and Dragon: Kalimantan, Sarawak, Sabah, Brunei*, Jakarta and Kuala Lumpur 1989. Sketch from a photograph. *Sarawak Museum*, Borneo.

2:97   Sellato 1989, p.104.

2:98   *British Museum*, London. Dr. Charles Hoore Collection 1905–800.

2:99   Wilson E. 1984, 68 *Above*. British *Museum*, London. *Below* Private Collection

2:100   Wilson E. 1984, 75. Holm, B., *Northwest Coast Indian Art, An Analysis of Form*, Seattle 1965. *University Museum*, Philadelphia, Pennsylvania, USA.

2:101   Wilson E. 1984, 72. Samuel, C., *The Chilkat Dancing Blanket*, Seattle 1982. *British Museum*, London.

Chapter 3

3:1   Wilson E. 1986, 3. Tomb of Nakht, no.52, Thebes.

3:2   Wilson E. 1986, 45. Tomb of Amenemhat, no.2, Beni Hasan.

3:3   Wilson E. 1986, 34.

3:4   Obverse design by Julien Marie Jouannin of medal struck in 1809 as a part of Vivant Denon's medallic history of Napoleon. The reverse legend reads L'EGYOTE CONQUISE MDCLXCVIII. *British Museum*, London. I am grateful to Mr P.A.Clayton for drawing my attention to this medal and for providing a photograph.

3:5   *British Museum*, London. Hull Grundy Collection no.982. Tait 1984.

3:6   *Left*, tracing from original full-scale drawings in the archives of the Ny Carlsberg Glyptotek. I am grateful to the curator J.P.Munk for giving me access to the drawings. *Right*, Wilson E. 1986, 75.

3:9   Wilson E. 1986, 44.

3:10   Wilson E. 1986, 46.

3:11   Wilson E. 1986, 54, 55. After L. Borchardt, *Die Ägyptische Pflanzensäule*, Berlin 1897, fig.11 and 9.

3:12   Wilson E. 1986, 57, 67. *Above* From the tombs of Amenhotpe-si-se, Nebamun and Pairy at Thebes; *below*, drawing based on several examples from the 18th Dynasty.

3:14   Wilson E. 1986, 30. *Left*, engaged pillar from Djoser's Step Pyramid at Saqqara. 3rd Dynasty, *c.*2650 BC. *Right*, pillar from the funerary temple of

Nyuserre, Abusir. 5th Dynasty *c.*2430 BC.

3:15   Wilson E. 1986, 28, 29. *Cairo Museum*, Egypt.

3:16   Wilson E. 1986, 34, 36. *Left*, from the throne of a statue of Mycerinus. 4th Dynasty. *Museum of Fine Art*, Boston, USA.   *Right*, Hieroglyph on stela of Wepemnofret, Giza. 4th Dynasty, *c.*2570 BC. *Museum of Anthropology of California*, USA.

3:17-19   Wilson E. 1986, 36, 38. *Cairo Museum*, Egypt.

3:20   Collon 1986, pl.22, 1. *University College London, Petrie Collection*, UC 11616.

3:21   *Archaeological Museum*, Herakleion, Crete.

3:22   Barnett 1957. *British Museum*, London. WA 118148.

3:23   *Cyprus Museum*, Nicosia, Cyprus.

3:24   *British Museum*, London. WA 124962.

3:25   *British Museum*, London. Vase B 76, B 331, B 364.

3:26   *British Museum*, London. Sculpture 409b.

3:28   *British Museum*, London. *Above*, Sculpture 409. *Below*, Vase B 117.

3:29   Akurgal, E., 'The Early Period and the Golden Age of Ionia', *American Journal of Archaeology*, 66, 1962. *Izmir Archaeological Museum*, Turkey.

Chapter 4

4:1   Barnett 1957, pl.cxiv. *British Museum*, London. WA 127065.

4:2   *British Museum*, London. Vase B 598.

4:3   Wilson 1986, 32. *British Museum*, London. EA 20791 and *Ashmolean Museum*, Oxford.

4:4   Wilson 1986, 32. Temple of Queen Hatshepsut.

4:5   Wilson 1986, 39. *Cairo Museum*, Egypt.

4:6   *British Museum*, London.

4:7   Barnett 1957, pl.cxlvii. *British Museum*, London. WA 132696.

4:8   Betancourt 1977, pl.10. *Oriental Institute*, University of Chicago, USA.

4:9   *British Museum*, London. WA 9100.

4:10   *British Museum*, London. Sculpture 505.

4:12   Maw & Co. Shropshire (made after 1883). *British Museum*, London. MLA 1980.3–7,145.

4:13   Evans 1928–35, vol.i, pl.iii. *Archaeological Museum*, Herakleion, Crete.

4:14   Evans 1928–35, vol.i, fig.90; Betancourt 1985, pl.12.1. *Ashmolean Museum*, Oxford, England.

4:15   Evans 1928–35, vol.i, fig.447.

Archaeological Museum, Crete.

4:16   Walberg 1986, fig.8b. *National Museum*, Athens, Greece.

4:17   Williams 1985, fig.23. *British Museum*, London. GR 1860.2–1.16.

4:18   *British Museum*, London. Vase B 211, E 171, B 310.

4:19   *British Museum*, London. Sculpture 1134.

4:20   Robertson 1987. *Lady Lever Art Gallery*, Port Sunlight, Liverpool, England, no. 54.

4:21   *The Anatolian civilisations*, II, 1983, B.123. *Tekirdag Museum*, Turkey.

4:22   *The Anatolian Civilizations*, II, 1983, B23. *Archaeological Museum*, Istanbul, Turkey.

4:23   After Wiegand, Th. and Schrader, H., *Priene…*, Berlin 1904.

4:24   Macnamara 1990, fig.41. *British Museum*, London. Bronze 542.

4:25   *British Museum*, London. Vase F 482.

4:26   *British Museum*, London. Terracotta D 711.

Chapter 5

5:1   Amiet, P., 'Glyptique Susienne', *Memoire de la Délégation archéologique en Iran* 43, Paris 1972, nos. 1034, 1306. *Above*, *Musée du Louvre*, Paris. *Below*, *Musée Iran Bastan*, Teheran, Iran.

5:2   Walberg 1986, fig.8d.

5:3   Cook 1976, fig.98. *British Museum*, London, Vase F 160.

5:4   Walker 1991, fig.58. *British Museum*, London. GR 1921.12–13.2.

5:6   *British Museum*, London. Sculpture 605.

5:9   *British Museum*, London. GR 1921.12–20.125.

5:10   *British Museum*, London. MLA 1857.12–18.139,141.

5:11   Wilson E. 1983, 72. *Victoria and Albert Museum*, London.

5:12   Wilson E. 1983, 71–2. *Winchester Cathedral Library*, England.

5:13   *William Morris Gallery*, Walthamstow, England.

5:14   *British Museum*, London. MLA 1980.3–7,87.

5:15   *British Museum*, London. MLA 1980.3–7,94.

5:16   *Westminster Public Library*, London.

5:17   *Above, Lady Lever Art Gallery*, Port Sunlight, Liverpool, England, no.48. *Below*, Burn L.,'A Dinoid Volute-Krater by the Meleager Painter: An Attic Vase in the South Italian Manner', *Occasional*

Papers on Antiquities 7, Greek Vases in the J.Paul Getty Museum, vol.5. Malibu, California 1991.

5:20 Evans 1928–35, ii, fig.282. *Archaeological Museum*, Herakleion, Crete.

5:21 *British Museum*, London. Lamp Q 1103.

5:22 Cook, 1984, fig.6. *British Museum*, London. CM BMC Athens 42, reverse.

5:23 Vollbach 1969, pl.7. *Textile Museum*, Washington, USA.

5:24 *British Museum*, London. Sculpture 2325.

5:25 Vollbach 1969, pl.5. *Victoria and Albert Museum*, London.

5:26 Temple, R. ed., *Early Christian and Byzantine Art*, The Temple Gallery, London 1990, no.5.

5:27 Wilson E. 1983, 42–3. Cramp 1984, nos. 908, 926.

5:28 Vollbach 1969, pl.18. *Museum für angewandte Kunst*, Vienna, Austria.

5:29 Hubert et al. 1969, no.31.

5:30 Wilson D.M. 1984, 105. *British Museum*, London.

5:33 Neal 1981, no.61. *British Museum*, London. PRB 1965.4–9.1.

5:34 *British Museum*, London.

5:35 Roth 1979, fig.95. *Schweizerisches Landersmuseum*, Zürich, Switzerland.

5:36 Bullough 1980, pl.14.

5:37 Wilson E. 1983, 54. Wilson D.M. 1984, fig.203. Cambridge, Corpus Christi College, 183, fol.iv.

5:38 Rawson 1984, fig.28. *British Museum*, London. OA 1900.5–20.1.

5:39 Rawson 1984, fig.33. *British Museum*, London. OA 1951.5–8.1.

5:40 Rawson 1984, fig.27. *British Museum*, London. OA 1899.6–9.49.

5:41 Rawson 1984, fig.44.

5:42 Watson 1984, no.31. *The Fogg Art Museum*, Cambridge, Massachusetts, USA.

5:43 Wilson E. 1988, 70. *Chester Beatty Library*, Dublin, Ireland.

5:44 Wilson E. 1988, 73. *Ashmolean Museum*, Oxford.

5:45 Wilson E. 1988, 83. *Oriental Institute*, University of Chicago, USA.

5:46 Wilson E. 1988, 78. *British Library*, London. Add. 22406/7.

5:47 Wilson E. 1988, 94. *Victoria and Albert Museum*, London.

Chapter 6

6:2 Marshall, J. and Foucher, A., *The Monuments of Sañci*, II, pl.xxiii. Oxford n.d.

6:3 Vainker 1991, 70. *British Museum*, London. OA 1926,4–21.1.

6:4 Wilson E. 1988, 85–6. *Above, National Library*, Cairo, Egypt, Koran 7. *Below, Çinili Kösk Museum*, Istanbul, Turkey.

6:5 Sjøvold, A.B., *Broderikunst og prydsøm*, Kunstindustrimuseet i Oslo, 1979.

6:6 *British Museum*, London. The Hull Grundy Collection no. 1052A. Tait 1984.

6:7,8 *British Museum*, London. MLA 1980.10–10,5.

6:9 *Westminster Public Library*, London.

6:10 *Above, Exhibition of Gandhara Art of Pakistan*, Exhibition catalogue, Tokyo 1984, I–12. *Centre* and *below*, Zwalf 1985, nos.330, 207. *British Museum*, London. OA 1919.1–1.0242, 1928.10–16.13.

6:11 Barrett 1954, Knox 1992. *British Museum*, London.

6:12 *British Museum*, London. OA 1900.2–9.1.

6:13 Barrett 1954, Knox 1992. *British Museum*, London.

6:14 *British Museum*, London. OA 1980.2–25.1.

6:15 Whitfield and Farrer 1990, no.117. *British Museum*, London. OA MAS 707 (L.B.II.0034).

6:16 Rawson 1984, fig.48a.

6:17 Rawson 1984, fig.109. *British Museum*, London. OA 1947.7–12.59.

6:18 Watson 1984, no.107.

6:19 *British Museum*, London. OA 1975.10–28.6(47).

6:20 Rawson 1984, fig.62b. *British Museum*, London. OA 1960.7–28.1.

6:21 Wilson E. 1988, 84. *British Museum*, London. OA 81.8–2.20.

6:22 Wilson E. 1988, 36.

6:23 Wilson E. 1988, 89.

Chapter 7

7:1 Drawing after H–J Joachim in Megaw 1989, 141. *The Celts* 1991, no.213. *Rheinisches Landesmuseum Bonn*, Germany.

7:2 *The Celts* 1991, no. 642. *Museum of London*, London.

7:3 Wilson E. 1983, 16. *Trinity College Library*, Dublin. A.1.6(58).

7:4 *Silverwork designed and made by Liberty & Co.*, n.d.[1925], *Westminster Public Library*, London.

7:5 The Celts 1991, no. 94. *Musée Royaux d'Art et d'Histoire*, Brussels, Belgium.

7:6 *The Celts* 1991, no.56. Megaw 1989, 131. *Musée des Jacobins*, Morlaix, France.

7:7 Megaw 1989, 139. *Bibliothèque Nationale*, Paris, France.

7:8 *Above* and *centre, The Celts* 1991, no.270. *Musée des Antiquités Nationale*, St Germain-en-Laye, France. *Below*, Drawing after Jacobstahl in Verger, S., 'La genèse celtique des rinceaux é triscèles', *Jahrbuch des Römisch-Germanischen Zentralmuseums Mainz*, 34, 1987. *Rheinisches Landesmuseum Bonn*, Germany.

7:9 *The Celts* 1991, no.277. Megaw 1989, 158. *Soprintendenza archaeologica delle Marche*, Ancona, Italy.

7:10 Stead 1985. *British Museum*, London.

7:11 *The Celts* 1991, no.90. Drawing in Frey, O.H. and Schwappach, F., 'Studies in Early Celtic Design', *World Archaeology*, **4**:3 (Febr.1973), 339–56, amended in Megaw 1989,p.63. *British Museum*, London.

7:12 Raftery, B., *A Catalogue of Irish Iron Age Antiquities*, Marburg 1983, no.262. *British Museum*, London.

7:13 *Chertsey Museum*, Surrey, England.

7:14 Stead 1985, 75. *British Museum*, London.

7:15 Stead 1985, 58. *British Museum*, London.

7:16 Stead 1985, 13. *British Museum*, London.

7:17 Fox, A., 'The Holcombe Mirror', *Antiquity* xlvi, 1972, fig.2. *British Museum*, London.

7:18 Wilson E. 1983, 12. *British Museum*, London.

7:19 Youngs 1989, no.60. *National Museum of Ireland*, Dublin.

7:20 Wilson E. 1983, 17. *British Library*, London. Cotton MS Nero D IV.

7:21 Wilson E. 1983, 13. *Trinity College Library*, Dublin, Ireland.

7:22 Wilson E. 1983, 14. *British Library*, London. Cotton MS Nero D IV.

7:23 Wilson E. 1983, 43.

7:24 The original brooch was found at Bettystown, Co. Meath and is now in the *National Museum of Ireland*, Dublin.

7:25 Schmutzler, R., *Art Nouveau*, London 1977, pl.xi.

7:26 Tilbrook and House 1976, no. 38.

Chapter 8

8:1 *Above*, Wiseman, D.J., *Cylinder seals in Western Asia*, London 1959, pl.9a, 8c. *British Museum*, London. WA 89517, 128840. *Below*, Collon 1987, no.53. *Ashmolean Museum*, Oxford, England.

8:2 Wilson E. 1986, 40. *Musées Royaux d'Art et d'Histoire*, Brussels, Belgium.

8:3 Loud, G., *The Megiddo Ivories*, Chicago 1939. pl.28, no.148. *Palestine Archaeological Museum*, Jerusalem, Israel.

8:7 Collon 1987, no.223. *British Museum, London*. WA 116145.

8:8 Betancourt 1985, pl.9J. *Archaeological Museum*, Herakleion, Crete.

8:9 Karo 1930–33, pl.xxviii no.20, xxxii no.61.

8:10 Wilson E. 1986, 66.

8:11 Campbell 1988, nos. 238a, 239f.

8:12 *Above*, Collon 1982, pl.xxiii, no.162, pl.xlix, no.432. *Below*, Collon 1986, pl.xxxi, no.435. *British Museum*, London. WA 102436, 102493, 21123.

8:14 After a drawing by M. Louise Baker in Wooley C.L., *Ur Excavations, II, The Royal Cemeteries*, London 1934, pl.95. *British Museum*, London.

8:15 *British Museum*, London.

8:16 *Musée du Louvre*, Paris, France.

Chapter 9

9:1 Sieveking 1987, Peccadean Collection no.618, *British Museum*, London.

9:2 *Above left Sadberk Nanim Museum*, Istanbul; *above right Museum of Anatolian Civilizations*, Ankara; *below British Museum, London*.

9:3 *Above*, *Historiska Museet*, Lund, Sweden. *Centre*, *British Museum*, London. *Below*, Piggott 1965, fig.52.

9:4 Mellaart 1967, fig.121,pl.xiv. *Museum of Anatolian Civilizations*, Ankara, Turkey.

9:5 *Above*, Collon 1987, no.24. *Musée du Louvre*, Paris, France. *Below*, Petrie, W.M.F., *Prehistoric Egypt*, London, 1917, pl.xlviii, 3, 4. *Petrie Museum, University College London*, London.

9:6 Parrot, A., *Sumer*, London 1960, fig.168b.

9:7 Collon 1987, no.109.

9:8 *From the top*: Collon 1987, no.216. *British Museum*, London. GR 1900.5.21,2; Teissier 1984, no.552; Collon 1987, no.764. *Ashmolean Museum*, Oxford; Collon 1987, no.234. *Musée du Louvre*, Paris, France. *Right*, Teissier 1984, no.439.

9:9 *British Museum*, London. WA 115654.

9:10 Barnett 1957. *British Museum*, London. WA 132258, 118106,127068.

9:11 Barnett 1957, fig.92. *British Museum*, London. WA 126165.

9:14 Ashley C.W., *The Ashley Book of Knots*, London 1947.

9:15 Wilson E. 1986, 35.

9:16 *British Museum*, London. GR 1867.5–8.537.

9:17 Williams C.A.S. 1960.

9:18 Hubert et al. 1969, 243. *Museo Civico d'Arte Antica*, Turin, Italy.

9:19 Lasko 1971, fig.62. *Whitworth Art Gallery*, Manchester, England.

9:20 Wilson E, 1983, 27. *British Library*, London. Cotton MS Nero D IV.

9:21 Tilbrook and House 1976, fig.235, design no. 80. *Private Collection*.

9:25 Huntley H.E., *The Divine Proportion, A Study in Mathematical Beauty*. New York and London 1970.

9:26 *British Museum*, London. PD 1877.1–13.364.

9:28 Drawing based on Neal 1981, no.63.

9:29 Jones C., *Roman Mosaics*, Museum of London, 1988.

9:30 Menghin W. et al. (ed.) 1988, xiv, 21b.

9:31,32 Wilson E. 1983, 11, 10. *British Museum*, London.

9:33 Wilson E. 1983, 20–21.

9:34 Haseloff, A., *Pre-Romanesque Sculpture in Italy*, Florence 1930, pl.35A.

9:35 Roth 1979, 87b.

9:36 Hubert et al. 1969, 222.

9:37–39 Wilson E. 1983, 28, 29, 24, 25.

9:40 *Trinity College Library*, Dublin. Ireland. A.1.6(58).

9:42 Wilson E. 1988, 30. *National Library*, Cairo, Egypt, Koran 98.

9:43 Wilson E. 1988, 51. *British Library*, London. Add.11735.

9:44 Wilson E. 1988, 53, 52. *British Library*, London. Add. 22407.

9:45 Wilson E. 1988, 40. *British Museum*, London. OA 1866.12–29, 61.

9:46 Wilson E. 1988, 23. *British Museum*, London. OA 81.8–2.20.

9:47 Mack 1990. *British Museum*, London. Torday collection 1909.5–13.70.

9:48,49 *Below*, Mack, J., 'In search of the Abstract', *African Textiles*, Hali, 31, 1986. 'Bakuba Embroidery Patterns: a Commentary on their Social and Political Implications' in D. Idiens (ed.) *The Textiles of Africa*, Pasold Research Fund 1980, p. 162–74.

9:49 *Left*, Picton and Mack 1979. *British Museum*, London. Af.1.2674.

Illustration acknowledgements

The drawings are the copyright of the author except for the following: Marjory Blamey retains the copyright of her botanical drawings 3:7, 8, 13; 5:18, 19, 31; 6:1. Permission to reproduce 0:2, 3; 2:11, 24, 28, 69, 70, 94; 7:17 and 9:26 has been granted by the Trustees of the British Museum. The drawing illustrated as 0:5 is reproduced here by kind permission of Dr Elisabeth Simpson and I am grateful to Dr Hertha Wascher for allowing me to use her drawing as 0:14. 1:15, 16 are reproduced courtesy of Professor Stuart Piggott and Edinburgh University Press. I am very grateful to Claire O'Kelly for allowing me to use the drawings from her original tracings reproduced here as 1:22. 2:71 is reproduced courtesy the Board of Trustees of the Victoria and Albert Museum, London. T. B. Batsford have generously allowed me to reproduce four drawings made by me for a different purpose and illustrated here as 2:86. 4:11 is reproduced courtesy The British Library, 5:13 courtesy William Morris Gallery, Walthamstow, 7:11 courtesy Professor J. V. S. Megaw, 7:13 courtesy Surrey County Archaeological Unit, 7:24 courtesy The Society of Antiquaries of London and 9:21 courtesy Gordon House, Ornament Press. I am particularly grateful to Dr D. S. Neal for permission to use the complicated mosaic pattern 9:27. I also wish to acknowledge that several of his beautiful and accurate drawings have been the basis for illustrations in this book. To all these I extend my grateful thanks.

Selected sources

The arrangement by motif groups, each in a separate chapter, makes it impractical for the sources to be listed by chapters since the same sources often supply material for several motif groups. The most important of these are listed below. Specialised sources, used in the context of a single drawing or topic are quoted in *Notes on the illustrations*.

Akurgal, E., *Ancient Civilization and Ruins of Turkey*, Istanbul 1983.

Allchin, B. and Allchin, F.R., *The Rise of Civilisation in India and Pakistan*, Cambridge 1982.

Aldred, C., *Egyptian Art*, London 1980.

The Anatolian Civilizations, I–III, Council of Europe xviii European Art Exhibition. Turkish Ministry of Culture and Tourism, Istanbul 1983.

Aner, E. and Kersten, K., *Die Funde der älteren Bronzezeit des nordischen Kreises …*, Natinalmuseet, Copenhagen, Denmark.

Artamonov, M. (ed.), *The Dawn of Art*, State Hermitage Museum, Leningrad 1974.

Bain, G., *Celtic Art, The Methods of Construction*, London 1981. First published 1951.

Bain, I., *Celtic Knotwork*, London 1986.

Barnett, R.D., *A Catalogue of the Nimrud Ivories*, London 1957.

Barnett, R.D., 'Ancient Ivories in the Middle East and Adjacent Countries', *Qedem*, 14, Jerusalem 1982.

Barrett, D., *Sculptures from Amaravati in the British Museum*, London 1954.

Bénisti, M., *Le Médaillon Lotiforme, Dans la Sculpture Indienne du IIIe siècle avant J.-C. au VIIe siècle après J.-C.*, Paris 1952.

Betancourt, P.P., *The Aeolic Style of Architecture; a survey of its development in Palestine, the Halikarnassos Peninsula and Greece 1000–500 BC*, Princeton, New Jersey 1977.

Betancourt, P.P., *The History of Minoan Pottery*, Princeton, New Jersey 1985.

Black, J. and Green, A., *Gods, Demons and Symbols of Ancient Mesopotamia*, London 1992.

Blurton, T.R., *Hindu Art*, London 1992.

British Academy Corpus of Anglo-Saxon Stone Sculpture, general editor R.Cramp, London 1984.

Brögger, A.W., Falk, Hj., Shetelig, H., *Osebergfundet*, vol.iii, Kristiania 1920.

Bullough, D.A., *The Age of Charlemagne*, London 1980.

Burn, L., *The British Museum Book of Greek and Roman Art*, London 1991.

Campbell, S., *The Mosaics of Antioch*, Pontifical Institute of Medieval Studies, Toronto 1988.

The Celts, Exhibition Catalogue, Venice 1991.

Chin, L. and Mashman, V. (eds.), *Sarawak Cultural Legacy, a living tradition*, Sarawak 1991.

Clark, J.G.D., *Prehistoric Europe*, London 1952.

Christie, A.H., *Traditional Methods of Pattern Designing*, Oxford 1910. Reprinted as *Pattern Design*, New York 1969.

Cobbe, H. (ed.), *Cook's Voyages and Peoples of the Pacific*, London 1979.

Collon, D., *Catalogue of the Western Asiatic Seals in the British Museum – Cylinder Seals II, Akkadian, Post Akkadian, Ur III Periods*, London 1982.

Collon, D., *Catalogue of the Western Asiatic Seals in the British Museum – Cylinder Seals III, Isin/Larsa and Old Babylonian Periods*, London 1986.

Collon, D., 'The green jasper cylinder seal workshop in Buccellati', *Papers in Honour of Edith Porada*, Malibu 1986.

Collon, D., *First Impressions: Cylinder Seals in the Ancient Near East*, London 1987.

Cook, B.F., *Greek and Roman Art in the British Museum*, London 1976.

Cook, B.F. (ed.), *Cypriot Art in the British Museum*, London 1979.

Cook, B.F., *The Elgin Marbles*, London 1984.

Cooper, J.C., *An Illustrated Encyclopedia of Traditional Symbols*, London 1978.

Cotterell, A. (ed.), *The Penguin Encyclopedia of Ancient Civilizations*, Harmondsworth 1980.

Curtis, J., *Ancient Persia*, London 1989.

Day, Lewis F., *Nature and Ornament*, London 1908–9.

Dennys, R., *The Heraldic Imagination*, London 1975.

Eames, E., *Catalogue of Medieval Lead-Glazed Earthenware Tiles in the Department of Medieval and Later Antiquities, British Museum*, vol.i–ii. London 1980.

Eames, E., *English Medieval Tiles*, London 1985.

Edwards, I.E.S., *Tutankhamen, his Tomb and its Treasures*, London 1979.

Ellis, L., 'The Cucuteni – Tripolye Culture', *BAR*, International Series 217, 1984.

El-Said, I. and Parman, A., *Geometric Concepts in Islamic Art*, London 1976.

Errington, E. and Cribb, J. (eds.), *The*

Crossroads of Asia, Transformation in Image and Symbol, (Exhibition catalogue), Cambridge 1992.

Evans, Sir Arthur, *The Palace of Minos at Knossos*, vols. I–IV, London 1921–35.

Fitton, L.J., *Cycladic Art*, London 1989.

Fong, Wen (ed.), *Treasures from the Bronze Age of China*, An exhibition from the Peoples Republic of China, New York 1980.

Frozen Tombs, The Culture and Art of the Ancient Tribes of Siberia, British Museum exhibition Catalogue, London 1978.

Frutiger, A., *Signs and Symbols: Their Design and Meaning*, London 1989.

Fuglesang, S.H., 'Vikingetidens Kunst', *Norges Kunsthistorie*, Oslo 1981.

Furumark, A., *The Mycenaean Pottery. Analysis and Classification*, Stockholm 1941.

Gardiner, Sir Alan H., *Egyptian Grammar*, 3rd. ed., London 1957.

Geijer, A., *A History of Textile Art*, London 1979.

Glazier, R., *A Manual of Historic Ornament*, London 1948. First published 1899.

Gombrich, E.H., *The Sense of Order, A Study of the Psychology of Decorative Art*, 2nd ed. Oxford 1984.

Hamlin, A.D.F., *A History of Ornament*, London 1917.

Harle, J.C., *The Art and Architecture of the Indian Subcontinent*, The Pelican History of Art, Harmondsworth 1986.

Haseloff, G., *Der germanische Tierornamentik der Völkerwanderungzeit*, Berlin/New York 1981.

Hecht, A., *The Art of the Loom, Weaving, Spinning and Dying across the World*, London 1989.

Hepper, F.N., *Pharaoh's Flowers: The Botanical Treasures of Tutankhamun*, London 1990.

Herner, E., 'Spiral decoration in Early Bronze Age Scandinavia, a technical and qualitative analysis and study of production', *Bar -S552*, 1989.

Higgins, R., *Minoan and Mycenaean Art*, London 1967.

Higgins, R., *The Greek Bronze Age*, London 1970.

Higgins, R., *The Aegina Treasure, An archaeological mystery*, London 1979.

Hope, T., *Household Furniture and Interior Decoration*, London 1907.

Hubert, J. et al., *Europe in the Dark Ages*, London 1969.

James, T.G.H., *An Introduction to Ancient Egypt*, London 1979.

Jones, O., *The Grammar of Ornament*, London 1865.

Justema, W., *The Pleasure of Pattern*, New York, 1968.

Kantor, H., 'The Aegean and Orient in the second millennium', *Archaeological Institute of America* (Monograph no.1) 1947.

Karlsson, L., *Nordisk Form, om djurornamentik*, The Museum of National Antiquities, Stockholm, *Studies* 3, 1983.

Karo, G., *Die Schachtgräber von Mykenai*, München, 1930–33.

Kent, J.P.S. and Painter, K.S. (eds.), *Wealth of the Roman World AD 300–700*, British Museum exhibition catalogue, London 1977.

King, J.C.H., *Artificial Curiosities from the Northwest Coast of America*, London 1981.

Knox, R., *Amaravati, Buddhist Sculpture from the Great Stupa*, London 1992.

Kraft, J., 'The Goddess in the Labyrinth', *Religionsvetenskapliga Skrifter*, Åbo 1985.

Kruta, V., *The Celts of the West*, London 1985.

Lasko, P., *The Kingdom of the Franks, North-West Europe before Charlemagne*, London 1971.

László, G., *The Art of the Migration Period*, London 1974.

Lawrence, A.W., *Greek Architecture*, The Pelican History of Art, Harmondsworth 1957.

Leroi-Gourhan, A., *Préhistoire de l'art Occidental*, Paris 1971.

Lewis, P. and Darley, G., *Dictionary of Ornament*, Moffat and Newton Abbot 1990.

Longworth, I.H., *Prehistoric Britain*, London 1985.

Mack, J., *Emil Torday and the Art of the Congo 1900–1909*, London 1990.

Macnamara, Ellen, *The Etruscans*, London 1990.

Mallowan M.E.L. and Rose, J.C., *Prehistoric Assyria: The Excavations at Tell Arpachiyah*, 1935.

Mallowan M.E.L., *Nimrud and its Remains*, London 1966.

Mallowan, Sir Max, *The Nimrud Ivories*, London 1978.

Marks, R. and Payne, A., *British Heraldry from its origins to c.1800*. British Museum Exhibition Catalogue, London 1978.

Marshack, A., 'The Meander System: The analysis and recognition of iconographic units in Upper Palaeolithic compositions', *Form in Indigenous Art*. Canberra: Australian Institute of Aboriginal Studies, London 1977.

Marshack, A., 'Upper Palaeolithic Symbol Systems of the Russian Plain: Cognitive and Comparative Analysis', *Current Anthropology*, vol.20, no.2. 1979.

Marshall, F.H., *Catalogue of the Jewellery,*

Greek, Etruscan and Roman in the Department of Antiquities, British Museum, London 1911.

Marinatos, S., *Crete and Mycenae*, London 1960.

Mozsolics, A., *Bronze und Goldfunde des Karpatenbeckens*, Budapest 1973.

Matthew, W.H., *Mazes and Labyrinths*, London 1922.

Megaw, J.V.S., *Art of the European Iron Age*, New York 1970.

Megaw, J.V.S. and Megaw M.R., *Celtic Art, from its beginnings to the Book of Kells*, London 1989.

Meehan, A., *A Beginner's Manual*, London 1991.

Meehan, A., *Illuminated Letters*, London 1992.

Meehan, A., *Animal Patterns*, London 1992.

Mellaart, J., *Çatal Hüyük, A Neolithic Town in Anatolia*, New Aspects of Antiquity, London 1967.

Menghin, W. (ed.), *Germanen Hunnen und Awaren. Schätze der Völkerwanderungzeit* (Austellungskatalog des Germanischen Nationalmuseums), Nürnberg 1988.

Meyer, F. S., *Handbook of Ornament*, London 1894.

Mitchell. T.C. (ed.), *Captain Cook and the South Pacific*, British Museum Year book 3. London 1979.

Morphy, H. (ed.), *Animals in Art*, One world Archaeology, 7. London 1989.

Mountjoy, P.A., 'Mycenaean Decorated Pottery. A guide to identification', *Studies in Mediterranean Archaeology*, vol.LXXIII, Göteborg 1986.

Murray, P. and Murray L., *The Art of the Renaissance*, World of Art. London 1991.

Neal, D.S., *Roman Mosaics in Britain*, Britannia Monograph Series no.1, London 1981.

Nylén, E., *Bildstenar*, Visby 1978.

Osborne, H. (ed.), *The Oxford Companion to the Decorative Arts*, Oxford 1980.

Otto, B., *Geometrische Ornamente auf anatolischer Keramik: Symmetrien frühester Schmuckformer in Nahe Osten und in der Ägäis* (Keramikforschungen 1). Heidelberger Akademie der Wissenschaften für Antike Keramik. Mainz 1976.

Payne, A., *Medieval Beasts*, London 1990.

Peesch, R., *The Ornament in European Folk Art*, New York 1983.

Peck, W.H., *Drawings from Ancient Egypt*, London 1978.

The Phoenicians , Exhibition catalogue, Milan 1988.

Picton, J. and Mack, J., *African Textiles*,

London 1979.

Piggott, S., *Ancient Europe*, Edinburgh 1965.

Proctor, R.M., *The Principles of Pattern*, New York 1969.

Rawson, J., *Chinese Ornament; The Lotus and the Dragon*, London 1984.

Rawson, J., *Chinese Bronzes, Art and Ritual*, British Museum Exhibition Catalogue, London 1987.

Rawson, J. ed., *The British Museum Book of Chinese Art*, London 1992.

Renfrew, C., *The Emergence of Civilisation*, London 1972.

Robertson, D.S., *A Handbook of Greek and Roman Architecture*, Cambridge 1945.

Robertson, M., *Greek, Etruscan and Roman Vases in the Lady Lever Art Gallery, Port Sunlight*, Liverpool monographs in Archaeology and Oriental Studies, Liverpool 1987.

Rogers, J.M., *Islamic Art and Design 1500–1700*, British Museum Exhibition catalogue. London 1983.

Roesdahl, E., *Viking Age Denmark*, London 1982.

Rønne, P., 'Early Bronze Age spiral ornament – the technical background', *Journal of Danish Archaeology*, vol.8, 1989.

Roth, H., *Kunst der Völkerwanderungzeit*, Frankfurt am Main-Berlin-Wien 1979.

Rudenko, S.I., *Frozen Tombs of Siberia, The Pazyryk Burials of Iron-Age Horsemen*, London 1970.

Sandars, N.K., *Prehistoric Art in Europe*, The Pelican History of Art, 2nd.ed. Harmondsworth 1985

Schmidt, V., *Ny Carlsberg Glyptotek*, Copenhagen 1908.

Sheehy, J., *The Rediscovery of Ireland's Past: the Celtic Revival 1830–1930*, London 1980.

Sickman, L. and Soper, A., *The Art and Architecture of China*, The Pelican History of Art, Harmondsworth 1971.

Sieveking, A., *A Catalogue of Palaeolithic Art in the British Museum*, London 1987.

Smith, W.S., *The Art and Architecture of Ancient Egypt*, Harmondsworth 1958.

Speltz, A., *The Styles of Ornament*, London 1910. First published in German 1904.

Stead, I.M., *Celtic Art in Britain before the Roman Conquest*, London 1985.

Täckholm, V. and Drar, M., *Flora of Egypt*, vols. I–IV, Cairo 1941–1969.

Tait, H., *The Art of the Jeweller, A catalogue of the Hull Grundy Gift to the British Museum*, London 1984.

Tatton-Brown, V. (ed.), *Cyprus BC, 7000 Years of History*, London 1979.

Tatton-Brown, V., *Ancient Cyprus*, London 1987.

Teissier, B., *Ancient Near Eastern Cylinder Seals from the Marcopoli Collection*, Berkley 1984.

Thimme, J. (ed.), *Art and Culture in the Cyclades*, Karlsruhe 1977.

Tilbrook, A.J. and House, G., *The Designs of Archibald Knox for Liberty & Co.*, London 1976.

Trollop, E., 'Notices of Ancient and Medieval Labyrinths', *The Archaeological Journal*, vol.XV, London 1858.

Twohig, E.S., *The Megalithic Art of Western Europe*, Oxford 1981.

Vainker, S.J., *Chinese Pottery and Porcelain*, London 1991.

Vollbach, W.F., *Early Decorative Textiles*, London 1969.

Walberg, G., 'Kamares, A study of the character of Palatial Middle Minoan pottery', *Boreas, Uppsala Studies in Ancient Mediterranean and Near Eastern Studies*, 8. 1976.

Walberg, G., *Tradition and Innovation, Essays in Minoan Art*, Mainz 1986.

Walker, S., *Roman Art*, London 1991.

Washburn, D.K. and Crowe, D.W., *Symmetries of Culture*, Washington 1988.

Watson, W., *Style in the Arts of China*, New York 1974.

Watson, W., *Tang and Liao Ceramics*, New York 1984.

Weir, S. and Shahid, S., *Palestinian Embroideries*, London 1988.

Wersin, Wolfgang von, *Das Elementare Ornament und seine Gesetzlichkeit*, Ravensburg 1940.

Whitfield, R, and Farrer, A., *Caves of the Thousand Buddhas, Chinese Art from the Silk Route*, British Museum Exhibition catalogue, London 1990.

Williams, C.A.S., *Encyclopaedia of Chinese Symbolism and Art Motifs*, New York 1960.

Williams, D., *Greek Vases*, London 1985.

Wilson, D.M. and Klindt-Jensen, O., *Viking Art*, London 1966.

Wilson, D.M., *The Vikings and their Origins*, London 1970.

Wilson, D.M., *Anglo-Saxon Art*, London 1984.

Wilson, D.M., *The Bayeux Tapestry*, London 1985.

Wilson, E., *Early Medieval Designs*, London 1983.

Wilson, E., *North American Indian Designs*, London 1984.

Wilson, E., *Ancient Egyptian Designs*, London 1986.

Wilson, E., *Islamic Designs*, London 1988.

Wilson, E., *Roman Designs*, London 1999.

Youngs, S. (ed.), 'The Work of Angels' Masterpieces of Celtic Metalwork, 6th–9th cent. AD, British Museum exhibition catalogue, London 1989.

Zanker-von Meyer, D., 'Die Bauten von J.C. und Carl Jacobsen. Zur Bautätigkeit einer Industriellen familie in Dänemark', *Kunstwissenschaftliche Studien*, Bd.52, Berlin 1982.

Zarnecki, G. et al., (ed.), *English Romanesque Art 1066–1200*, Exhibition catalogue, London 1984.

Zwalf, W. (ed.), *Buddhism; Art and Faith*, British Museum Exhibition catalogue, London 1985.

Index